THEATRE IN MARKET ECONOMIES

Theatre in Market Economies explores the complex relationship between theatre and the market economy since the 1990s. Bringing together research from the arts and social sciences, the book proposes that theatre has increasingly taken up the mission of the 'mixed economy' by seeking to combine economic efficiency with social security while promoting liberal democracy. McKinnie situates this analysis within a wider context, in which the welfare state's tools have been used to regulate, ever more closely, the lives of citizens rather than the operations of markets. In the process, the book invites us to think in new ways about long-standing economic and political problems in and through the theatre: the nature of industry, productivity, citizenship, security, and economic confidence. *Theatre in Market Economies* depicts a theatre that is not only a familiar cultural institution but is, in unexpected and often ambiguous ways, an exemplary political-economic one as well.

MICHAEL MCKINNIE is Reader in Theatre at Queen Mary University of London. He is the author of *City Stages: Theatre and Urban Space in a Global City*, which was awarded the Ann Saddlemyer Award by the Canadian Association for Theatre Research, and the editor of *Space and the Geographies of Theatre*. His research is interdisciplinary, focusing primarily on the intersection between theatre, political economy, and urban development.

THEATRE AND PERFORMANCE THEORY

SERIES EDITOR

Tracy C. Davis *Northwestern University*

Each volume in the Theatre and Performance Theory series introduces a key issue about theatre's role in culture. Specially written for students and a wide readership, each book uses case studies to guide readers into today's pressing debates in theatre and performance studies. Topics include contemporary theatrical practices; historiography; interdisciplinary approaches to making theatre; and the choices and consequences of how theatre is studied; among other areas of investigation.

BOOKS IN THE SERIES

JACKY BRATTON, *New Readings in Theatre History*

TRACY C. DAVIS AND THOMAS POSTLEWAIT (EDS.), *Theatricality*

SHANNON JACKSON, *Professing Performance: Theatre in the Academy from Philology to Performativity*

RIC KNOWLES, *Reading the Material Theatre*

NICHOLAS RIDOUT, *Stage Fright, Animals, and Other Theatrical Problems*

D. SOYINI MADISON, *Acts of Activism: Human Rights as Radical Performance*

DEREK MILLER, *Copyright and the Value of Performance, 1770–1911*

PAUL RAE, *Real Theatre: Essays in Experience*

MICHAEL MCKINNIE, *Theatre in Market Economies*

THEATRE IN MARKET ECONOMIES

MICHAEL MCKINNIE
Queen Mary University of London

Shaftesbury Road, Cambridge CB2 8EA, United Kingdom

One Liberty Plaza, 20th Floor, New York, NY 10006, USA

477 Williamstown Road, Port Melbourne, VIC 3207, Australia

314–321, 3rd Floor, Plot 3, Splendor Forum, Jasola District Centre, New Delhi – 110025, India

103 Penang Road, #05–06/07, Visioncrest Commercial, Singapore 238467

Cambridge University Press is part of Cambridge University Press & Assessment, a department of the University of Cambridge.

We share the University's mission to contribute to society through the pursuit of education, learning and research at the highest international levels of excellence.

www.cambridge.org
Information on this title: www.cambridge.org/9781009346429

DOI: 10.1017/9780511722257

First published 2021
First paperback edition 2023

A catalogue record for this publication is available from the British Library

Library of Congress Cataloging-in-Publication data
NAMES: McKinnie, Michael, author.
TITLE: Theatre in market economies / Michael McKinnie.
DESCRIPTION: Cambridge ; New York : Cambridge University Press, 2021. | Series: Theatre and performance theory | Includes bibliographical references and index
IDENTIFIERS: LCCN 2020039520 (print) | LCCN 2020039521 (ebook) | ISBN 9781107000391 (hardback) | ISBN 9780511722257 (ebook)
SUBJECTS: LCSH: Capitalism and theater. | Theater – Political aspects – Great Britain – History – 20th century. | Theater – Political aspects – Canada – History – 20th century. | Theater – Political aspects – United States – History – 20th century. | Theater and society – Great Britain – History – 20th century. | Theater and society – Canada – History – 20th century. | Theater and society – United States – History – 20th century.
CLASSIFICATION: LCC PN2041.E27 M35 2021 (print) | LCC PN2041.E27 (ebook) | DDC 792–dc23
LC record available at https://lccn.loc.gov/2020039520
LC ebook record available at https://lccn.loc.gov/2020039521

ISBN 978-1-107-00039-1 Hardback
ISBN 978-1-009-34642-9 Paperback

For Mum and Dad

Contents

Figures

Acknowledgements

I am enormously grateful to all those who have played a part in creating this book. There are too many to mention here, and my apologies are extended to those I have not named but should have. Ruth Fletcher has lived with this book as long as I have, and for that, she has my greatest appreciation and sympathy. Thanks also to Tracy Davis for asking me to write this book in the first place and then for being – as always – such a perceptive and helpful reader when I (finally) did. My colleagues in Drama at Queen Mary University of London continue to be amazingly supportive, especially at a time when universities in the United Kingdom – and especially arts disciplines – have been under sustained attack, from without and within. I would particularly like to thank Shane Boyle, Bridget Escolme, Jen Harvie, Caoimhe McAvinchey, Aoife Monks, Nick Ridout, Catherine Silverstone, and Martin Welton for their intellectual engagement and general encouragement over the life of the project. Some of the ideas contained in this book were first presented at QUORUM, Drama's research seminar series; thank you to the graduate students who were organising it at the time. I would also like to thank my students for challenging me to think about issues in different ways than I otherwise might have (especially my former PhD students – particularly Charlotte Bell, Tim Edkins, Valeria Graziano, Sarah Grochala, Elyssa Livergant, and Philip Watkinson).

This book has also benefited from the support, in many different ways, of colleagues in the wider academic world. I will not try to name them all, but some bear special mention: Peter Dickinson, Erika Fischer-Lichte, Kirsty Johnson, Stephen Johnson, Ric Knowles, Hélène Lecossois, Debbie Lisle, Louise Owen, Mark Phelan, Lionel Pilkington, Kim Solga, Joanne Tompkins, Benjamin Wihstutz, and Keren Zaointz. I am also grateful to the Social Sciences and Humanities Research Council of Canada for supporting the dissemination of some of this work as it developed, as well as to the American Society for Theatre Research, the Arts and

Culture after Mega-Events conference at Simon Fraser University, the European Society for the Study of English, the Irish Society for Theatre Research, the Institut für Theaterwissenschaft at the Free University of Berlin, the Interdisciplinary Program in Theatre and Drama at Northwestern University, and the Stewart Parker conference at Queen's University Belfast.

Certain individuals generously shared their expertise at key moments. Rose Whyman helpfully clarified some issues related to Stanislavsky for me. Martin Young drew my attention to useful historical material of which I was unaware. Loren O'Dair gave me an actor's perspective on some of the production practices I was thinking about, and Fiona Bardsley gave me a stage manager's perspective – both of which were invaluable. Jim Arnold was an incredible resource, and although I did not end up writing directly about some of the things we discussed, his knowledge about theatre infrastructure undoubtedly shaped my thinking throughout this book.

Chapter 2 develops ideas first published in Michael McKinnie, 'Rethinking Site-Specificity: Monopoly, Urban Space, and the Cultural Economics of Site-Specific Performance', in Anna Birch and Joanne Tompkins, eds., *Performing Site-Specific Theatre: Politics, Place, Practice* (Palgrave Macmillan, 2012); and Michael McKinnie, 'Performing Like a City: London's South Bank and the Cultural Politics of Urban Governance', in Erika Fischer-Lichte and Benjamin Wihstutz, eds., *Performance and the Politics of Space: Theatre and Topology* (Routledge, 2013). Chapter 5 builds on work originally published in Michael McKinnie, 'Olympian Performance: The Cultural Economics of the Opening Ceremony of London 2012', in Peter Dickinson, Kirsty Johnson, and Keren Zaiontz, eds., *Public: Mega-Event Cities*, 53 (Spring 2016). I am grateful to the publishers for permission to reproduce portions of that material here.

Finally, my deepest gratitude goes to my family, immediate and extended. You know who you are, and I am indebted to all of you.

INTRODUCTION

Show Business

> [T]he day is not far off when the economic problem will take the back seat where it belongs, and . . . the arena of the heart and head will be occupied, or reoccupied, by our real problems – the problems of life and of human relations, of creation and behaviour and religion.
>
> John Maynard Keynes, 'Preface', *Essays in Persuasion* (1931)[1]

Keynes was wrong. Nearly a century later, the 'economic problem' is no closer to being put in its proper place. If anything, it now seems more ubiquitous and more intractable, especially as financialisation has become an increasingly common – but often fiendishly difficult to understand – feature of everyday life for people around the globe. The real problem *is* the economic problem, is it not? Keynes's optimism about the future, and the role of economics within it, now seems almost wilfully naive. And the idea that life's 'real problems' might lie in the cultural and spiritual realms almost borders on fantasy.

It is no accident that when the newly formed Arts Council of Great Britain issued its first annual report soon after the great economist's death in 1946, it reiterated the words of Keynes, its inaugural Chairman, that 'the economic problem' would soon be overtaken by the 'real problems' that were within the Arts Council's domain. 'That was Lord Keynes faith', it proclaimed. 'The Arts Council will endeavour to uphold it.'[2] This formulation – the economy in its place over there, culture in its place over here – is now a very familiar one. For those of us with an interest in theatre today, the idea that the economic problem might be 'solved' so that we can get on with the more creative pursuits that preoccupy us (our 'real problems') can be tremendously appealing, especially in an age when economism rules even more supreme than it did in Keynes's time. (We live in a historical moment, after all, when Very Serious People not only propound economically risible notions like 'expansionary fiscal contraction'; they put them into effect, with devastating consequences.[3]) But this also suggests that the economy and the arts can somehow be disentangled, and that proposition is no more tenable today than it was in 1946, at the birth of the Arts Council, or in 1931, when Keynes was writing during the depths of the Great Depression. Indeed, the economic problem not only remains an acute one; it is an especially real problem in and for the theatre.

It is not only an economic problem, though; it is a political one too. By 'problem' I do not mean a kind of obstacle or malady. Instead, I mean that the question of theatre's relationship to market economies, and to the political institutions that help sustain social processes of marketisation, continue to be worked through in all kinds of places, and in all manner of ways. They are problems that, as I will show, arise insistently but often obliquely, more through the infrastructures of performance than, say, as the subject matter of a given production or play (though they can arise here too, just not as straightforwardly as one might expect). Frequently, they are being worked through at the level of theatrical production. At other times, they emerge through the social form of individual performances. They are regularly spatial concerns, and usually institutional ones as well. The distinctive political economy of theatre itself is a problem, as is theatre's relationship with the market and the state more broadly. While these problems arise in distinctive ways at different moments, they nonetheless prompt questions that go well beyond the particular circumstances underlying them.

This book explores the relationship between theatre and the market economy during roughly the past two decades in the United Kingdom, Ireland, Canada, and the United States. I argue that, when seen together, these cases reveal a theatre that is increasingly taking up the mission that once brought together social democracy and reformist liberalism, and that found its clearest expression in the idea, and rather more complicated practice, of the 'mixed economy': to combine economic efficiency with social security, while promoting liberal democracy. Intriguingly, theatre's assumption of this mantle has happened during much the same time as the purchase of social democracy and the centre-left have declined within electoral politics (and political thought generally) and the tools of the welfare state have been used to regulate ever more closely the lives of citizens rather than the operations of markets. But the theatres I examine demonstrate that this grand bargain remains deeply attractive, even when – perhaps especially when – it has been repeatedly undermined in society at large (sometimes by persistent attack from its antagonists, but just as much by contradictions embedded deeply within it). These theatres insist, in different ways, that the mixed economy remains viable. We just have to go to the theatre to see it at work.

In order to stake this claim, though, theatre has to confront many of the same problems that have preoccupied a significant strand of political economy since the early twentieth century. And it has to deal with the fact that these problems take on a different inflection during a time of growing precarity, recurring 'wars on terror', and increasing concentrations of wealth. How can production be organised efficiently? How can productivity be improved? How can social citizenship be realised? How can these citizens feel secure? How can a better political and economic future for society as a whole be achieved? The cases I examine suggest that theatre, as both social institution and artistic discipline, is taking up these questions from a somewhat different position than the one it occupied through much of the latter half of the twentieth century (at least in those theatre cultures I discuss). Rather than being a relatively minor, if often high-status, institutional beneficiary of the welfare state, these theatres are actually grappling with enduring political-economic problems – sometimes obliquely but nonetheless insistently – in times and places when the welfare state is often being turned to less high-minded ends than it once was. At times, they even *do* a kind of political economy themselves, whether they are aware of it or not. Taken together, they imply a theatre that is less the subject of political economy, and more its interlocutor.

Being theatres, though, they also *make a show* of doing these things. At first glance, a theatrical political economy could appear a bit of a dog-riding-a-bicycle trick: eye-catching enough, but at base a ridiculous spectacle. But I do not think it is, for two reasons. First, these theatres often engage plausibly with political-economic problems because theatre – and this applies as much to not-for-profit as commercial theatres – has often had a more intimate and extensive relationship with the market, as well as the political institutions sustaining processes of marketisation, than might sometimes appear to be the case. Second, because showing matters. Cultural historian Jean-Christophe Agnew argues that in the early modern period, theatre gave 'practical and figurative form' to 'a social abstraction – commodity exchange – that was lived rather than thought'.[4] Much of this logic still holds true today. Now, commodity exchange may be ubiquitous, but widespread financialisation has arguably only widened the gap that Agnew identifies between the lived experience of marketisation and its conception – the effects of financialisation are all around us, but it can be awfully difficult to discern exactly how it all works. In this context theatre's ability – mimetic, institutional, and social – to give 'practical and figurative form' to both financialisation *and* political-economic aspirations that persist in its wake, is enormously attractive.

The period that this book spans – the late 1990s until the present day – is a key transitional phase in political economy in Europe and North America. It includes the ascendancy, and then unravelling, of the centre-left 'Third Way' and the subsequent emergence, and then entrenchment, of the age of austerity (with the 2008 financial crisis as the linchpin connecting them). I will discuss how the distinctive political and economic features of this period pertain to individual theatrical cases in subsequent chapters. But some larger trends are worth highlighting here. It is easy to assume that the two parts of this period are opposed to each other, where austerity is an almost inevitable backlash against the fiscal profligacy of the Third Way (this is how it has often been presented in the media in the United Kingdom, and it has been the consistent line of the Conservative – and Conservative-led – governments elected in the UK since the financial crisis). But a lot of the groundwork for austerity was laid during the years leading up to the financial crisis, and many of these features span the entire period.

This is a time during which a long-term decline in economic productivity growth in many countries became chronic, and this deterioration was often accelerated by increasing financialisation. While the effects of financialisation were felt most acutely in places that were especially reliant on the financial sector, such as London and the UK, its impact can be seen through much of the Global North in the widespread dependence on personal debt and low-cost imports – rather than improved productivity, competition, or 'innovation' – to fuel economic growth. Alongside this came an increasing reliance on assets, especially on property and stocks, as a source of wealth. When the US subprime mortgage bubble burst in 2007, it demonstrated the extent to which the real estate market, and the easy access to credit on which it relied, had become central to American wealth creation. But it also illustrated the interdependence and fragility of the global banking system, as the subprime contagion spread through many of the world's economies (some of which, such as Ireland, already had their own localised property bubbles – as one Irish economist ruefully observed after that country's economic crash, 'We were going to get rich building houses for each other').[5]

These developments were not exactly surprising, given that stagnant wages in many countries (both in terms of salaries and pensions, which are simply deferred wages) encouraged people to become speculators in order to secure their current and future well-being. States, at all levels of government, became more and more dependent on the proceeds of these developments; for example, an already-affluent city such as Toronto, which experienced one of the world's largest property booms during the 2000s, became worryingly reliant on highly volatile revenues from a real estate levy to fund its core operating budget. 'Progressive' and conservative governments alike extended favourable tax treatment to corporations and to unearned income, such as capital gains (which were frequently taxed at a lower rate than wage income). A resistance to regulating the financial sector – initially from a Labour government in the UK and a Democratic administration in the US – persisted even after the financial crisis. In 2012, Boris Johnson, then Mayor of London, decried the spectre of an 'endless orgy of stable door banging and excessive regulation on the financial services sector', even after a money-laundering scandal had been revealed at London-based HSBC bank.[6]

This is also, of course, the period during which the arts became the 'creative industries'. It is easy to sneer at the rickety empiricism and tactical opportunism of creative industries thinking. In many ways sneering is entirely justified – if financialisation is late capitalism's tragic industrial strategy, the creative industries are its farce. It is hard not to be cynical in the face of inane proclamations about the creative industries such as this one issued by the UK's Department of Digital, Culture, Media, and Sport in 2018:

> These are all part of the Government's modern Industrial Strategy, and its the sector deal [*sic*] which will drive the development of the most potentially revolutionary, cutting-edge technologies, and accelerating their adoption in real-world, industrial environments in order to realise their benefits for business, consumers and wider society.[7]

It is also difficult to escape the possibility that theatre – as a key player in the creative industries – has helped exacerbate the defects of an economy that speculates rather than produces actual things. In *Fantasy Island*, economic journalists Larry Elliott and Dan Atkinson argue that in the UK the 'creative economy' provided cover for the sorts of speculation that would, a year after their book was published, bring about the financial crisis of 2008:

> Some explanation has to be provided for Britain's increasingly lopsided economy, dominated as it is by those not-so-heavenly twins – the City of London and the housing market. And that explanation is that the UK's future lies not – as might seem apparent at first glance – in the drinking factories, the estate agencies and the clothing chains that make up Britain's monochrome identikit

> high streets, but in the knowledge economy. Even more laughable, some cling to the idea that the way ahead is the even-more nebulous 'creative economy'. This fantasy, a particular favourite of ours, is that while Britain may no longer carry the overt industrial clout it once did in the days when it was the workshop of the world, it can still be the world's creative hub (copyright T. Blair).[8]

Whereas other countries actually manufacture things, in Britain 'we count the money and we do the bullshit'.[9] And, just to be clear, 'Bullshit Britain reaches its apotheosis in the lionisation of the cultural industries'.[10]

Given the huge volume of guff that has been spouted about the creative industries during recent decades, such a bracing take is refreshing, even if its authors exaggerate for effect. Elliott and Atkinson are not wrong, either, about the extent to which finance and culture have become entwined in Britain since the 1990s. But the following chapters suggest that the relationship between culture, politics, and economics during this period is more complicated than they claim, and the position of theatre within this constellation is more ambiguous and ambivalent than we might expect.

Each of the cases I examine begins to pick apart threads of an older cultural economic script that became plausible the latter half of the twentieth century, as many cultural economies began to rely more on public, rather than private, capital to produce their goods and services, and the relation between their theatre industries and market economies frequently became more refracted. That story goes something like this: theatre is a declining industry; it is inefficient; and its benefits are largely intangible or, perhaps, lie primarily in the cultivation of old-fashioned public and private virtues. But if the following cases illustrate the limitations of this story, they also defy more recent, creative industries-led claims of a cutting-edge role for culture in the political and economic life of market society. The theatre that these cases collectively delineate is neither archaic nor avant-garde (and neither nostalgic nor utopian, for that matter). Instead, these theatres propose something more ambiguous: that they can capitalise upon the processes of marketisation, while resolving (or at least managing) the social antagonisms that marketisation leaves in its wake. Whether this proposition is ultimately viable – or even desirable – is very much open to question. But these theatres make their case very persuasively nonetheless.

Theatre, Polity, Economy

A recurring concern throughout this book is the evolving nature of theatre's relationship with political economy. As I will show, concerns that have historically been the remit of political economy – broadly speaking, the relationship between capital, labour, and the state – frequently arise within and in relation to theatre and performance. They are also often issues of economic geography, both in terms of theatre's own spatial economies and in terms of the broader economic environments in which theatre is a cultural economic agent. These do not always arise in discrete regions of the theatrical enterprise, or in familiar locations where our critical predispositions might lead us to look for them (i.e., they are not always best seen onstage). They arise, instead, throughout the entire domain of performance.

Theatre has been caught up with political economy, and political economy with theatre, for a very long time. But one of the effects of marketisation in Euro-American societies over at least the past two centuries is to make political economy and art appear to be alien domains to each other, or, at the very least, make it seem plausible that encounters between them could be quarantined in isolated parts of the artistic or theatrical enterprise (say, within fields such as arts policy or theatre management). As Agnew observes:

> Far from contradicting the claims of political economy, the Victorian champions of Civilization merely consented to operate outside its dominion. Aestheticism and economism effectively cartelized the social world by dividing cultural exchange and market exchange into separate disciplinary jurisdictions. As a consequence, the juncture of these two aspects of life vanished from view, and the deep and unacceptable division *within* market culture reemerged as the deep but eminently acceptable division *between* the market and culture.[11]

This 'cartelization' of the social world has always been precarious, and it begins to dissolve as soon as one asks how a given performance has come to exist in the first place. But its persuasiveness has never depended on its veracity. Instead, its power lay more in its ability to induce, as Agnew puts it, a 'discrete and retrograde amnesia [that] appears to repeat itself each time experience rediscovers and relives the antagonism of market relations in a form that ideology has yet to resolve'.[12]

The cases that follow all negotiate this unsettled terrain, in which performance holds out the possibility that it might theatrically manage the antagonisms of market relations in ways that are not possible outside the theatre, whether through its working processes and practises, its social and spatial forms, its events, or its institutions. But at the same time, this theatrical management happens from deep within market society, and always in relation to the political institutions that sustain the process of marketisation. And it does not defuse the market's power – instead, it recasts the market (and theatre's relation to it) in different, and differently productive, forms.

At this point, however, it is worth taking a step back to clarify what I mean by 'the market', 'marketisation', and 'market society'. Although I often use 'the market' in the singular, in practice capitalist economies are constituted through multiple markets, and the process of marketisation unfolds unevenly across time and space. But 'the market' and 'marketisation' are useful theoretical constructs, so it is worth elaborating upon how I deploy them in the rest of this book. I extend the long tradition in political economy – one that includes, from different vantage points, Keynes, Karl Polanyi, and Karl Marx – of resisting the abstraction of 'the economy' from other social spheres and institutions. Political theorist Ellen Meiksins Wood rightly stresses the need to avoid 'the rigid conceptual separation of the "economic" and the "political" which has served capitalist ideology so well ever since the classical economists discovered the "economy" in the abstract and began emptying capitalism of its social and political content'.[13] Similarly, Judith Butler argues that 'one of the achievements of capitalism was the analytic distinction between the domain of the social and the domain of the economic. "Disembedding" economic structures from their social and historical conditions and conventions is precisely the condition of economic formalism'.[14] This 'separation' and 'disembedding' risk turning the economy into a kind of fetish, endowing it with mystical powers (which can only be interpreted by its high priests, professional economists) and subordinating other forms of human relations to its indifferent calculus.

Abstracting the economy from other social spheres also elides the fact that the market is but one social institution among many others. Polanyi's *The Great Transformation* (1944) is the most sustained elaboration of this institutionalist idea (though, ironically, he rarely uses the term 'embedded' in this work).[15] For Polanyi, the market is an evolving social institution rather than, as Agnew sceptically characterises it, a 'timeless, natural arrangement for human needs'.[16] A key ideal of marketisation, though, is to make it seem as if the latter were the case. The market, which was once a distinctive sphere – a place, even – within the economy (and both within society) subsumes the whole economy and ultimately society itself; instead of speaking of 'market and society', or 'society with markets', it is possible – and often more accurate – to speak of 'market society'. In perhaps the best-known passage of *The Great Transformation*, Polanyi argues:

> [T]he control of the economic system by the market is of overwhelming importance to the whole organization of society: it means no less than the running of society as an adjunct to the market. Instead of economy being embedded in social relations, social relations are embedded in the economic system. The vital importance of the economic factor to the existence of society precludes any other result. For once the economic system is organized in separate institutions, based on specific motives and conferring a special status, society must be shaped in such a manner as to allow that system to function according to its own laws. This is the meaning of the familiar assertion that a market economy can function only in a market society.[17]

If marketisation has unfolded in ways that Polanyi could not have imagined in 1944, the political-economic logic he delineates remains credible. For Polanyi, the market is not something that simply exists; it has to be made and remade, through a combination of long-term evolution and off-the-cuff improvisation. The market is also an inherently unstable entity, so it requires constant attention from other institutions in order to sustain it. Two recent economic episodes make this fact startlingly clear: the financial crisis of 2008 and the COVID-19 pandemic of 2020. Without massive state intervention, global financial markets would almost certainly have collapsed in 2008, and entire economies would likely have failed in 2020.[18]

Thus the market cannot marketise on its own. It must be embedded with other social institutions (especially, for Polanyi, the state and the law) in order for marketisation to proceed. But what if we put theatre, as an enduring cultural institution that has historically been caught up with larger processes of economic development, into the mix as well? To do this is not to claim a privileged role for theatre within marketisation or to exaggerate theatre's economic importance. It is simply to prompt deeper reflection on the distinctive role of theatre within market societies, especially when – as with all of the cases that follow – theatre confronts the vicissitudes of marketisation but is no longer (wholly or predominantly) marketised itself. This somewhat refracted relationship is a recurring concern of this book, and it is a relationship underpinned by the dominant model of theatre financing and governance that evolved over the twentieth century (a model that would have seemed eccentric in, say, the robustly capitalist theatres of Britain or the United States in the nineteenth century). All of the theatre industries I explore are supported by some combination of public subsidy, distinctive legal status, special tax provisions, and more. This is most obviously the case for not-for-profit theatre but applies to some extent to commercial theatre as well (for example, there are many private-public arrangements that underwrite the construction and/or operation of performance venues in the US and the UK). To greater and lesser degrees, these theatre industries are also split into a not-for-profit, 'artistic', sector, and a commercial, market-driven sector, with the consequence that the relationship between theatre and the market can appear, misleadingly, to be more contained than it otherwise might. Ironically, this bifurcation occurred after the historical transition to market societies (where markets – plural – cease to be elements within society and the singular, abstracted market emerges as the universal organising logic of society itself) was largely complete.[19] But it implied that theatre could, to some extent, sidestep broader marketisation; or, at the very least, a marketised theatre could be hived off into a commercial sector that, whatever its economic merits, would usually be seen as artistically inferior to a not-for-profit or state-sponsored sector. The chapters that follow, however, show that the relationship between the state, the market, and the theatre is more fluid than this 'cartelization' implies.

At the same time, I want to resist seeing theatrical phenomena as economic only when they take monetary form, such as box office income, wages, grants, philanthropic donations, and so on. The money economy is only one part of the larger economy, and it is only one part of the theatre economy too. The economic concerns that I discuss in the following chapters are as much relational – social, spatial, and theatrical – as they are pecuniary.

In the past, I have often thought about how broader economic forces impinge upon theatre (for example, how performance has been caught up with urban development).[20] I have tended to figure the economy's relationship to theatre as mostly an exogenous one, where theatre negotiates economic forces that are largely external to itself, even if it makes and remakes these forces in its own distinctive ways. As this book demonstrates, I still think this approach can yield significant insights. It is also important, though, to attend to economic practices that arise endogenously, within theatre itself. But how do we know if the phone call is coming from outside or inside the house? Two relatively recent examples that illustrate this location problem (as we might call it) are Jonathan Burston and Dan Rebellato's analyses of what Burston first termed 'McTheatre'.[21] Both are highly critical of forms of theatrical production whose goal is not to create original performances but rather to replicate a standardised product in any number of places around the globe (so that *Miss Saigon*, say, will largely be the same show whether it is performed in London, New York, Toronto, Sydney, Singapore, or anywhere else). The McTheatre trope makes a lot of sense, because the 'Mc' prefix connotes standardisation to a greater extent than possibly any other form of economic shorthand in popular use today. It also serves a useful counterintuitive purpose when making arguments about theatre – where such standardisation is often imagined either not to apply or not to be desirable – and it draws attention to the fact that theatre work can be just as boring and routine as any other form of work. Burston's characterisation of megamusicals as 'Fordist' and Rebellato's discussion of the parallels between early twentieth century time-and-motion studies of factory work and the production practices of megamusicals are considered and thought-provoking. But the semblances they identify appear not necessarily because theatre has taken up the production practices of industrial capital but because its own working practices were already industrial (and this applies to greater and lesser degrees in both commercial and not-for-profit theatre sectors). Theatre did not have to turn to Henry Ford or Frederick Taylor to work out how to manage labour, time, and motion in routine ways. It had already worked out how to do that very well on its own, long before the birth of the assembly line.

Readers may note as well that I do not examine any plays or performances that directly address political economy, or even just economics, in this book. There are a few reasons for this absence. As I discuss later, it is important to resist the presumption that the best place to see theatre encountering political economy is onstage; sometimes it is, but a lot of times it is not. Even when focusing our attention on the stage makes sense, 'economics plays' (for lack of a better term) do not necessarily reveal much about the types of theatrical relations and forms of economic management that concern me here. As someone who lives and works in London, I have become pretty familiar with the significant number of economics plays produced here in recent years. The growth in this genre is hardly surprising given the city's prominent position within international financial markets. (It also probably has something to do with the fact that mainstream English theatre has tended to see itself, somewhat presumptuously, as possessing special insights into 'the state of the nation'.[22]) Some of these performances have undoubtedly found inventive ways to represent crises in contemporary capitalism theatrically; Jude Christian's terrific English-language staging of German playwright Falk Richter's *Trust* at the Gate Theatre in 2018 was, for me, the most theatrically pleasurable and intellectually stimulating example of these. But just as often, economics plays attempt to avoid theatre's economic problems rather than engage them. By this I mean that they can sometimes treat the economy (or political economy) as something that is external to theatre rather than something in which theatre is deeply imbricated; disavowal becomes a precondition of mimesis. This abjuration is perhaps starkest in pieces that adopt an explanatory mode, such as David Hare's *The Power of Yes: A Dramatist Seeks to Understand the Financial Crisis* (2009). The play's explication of the 2008 crash depends on contrasting an ostensibly disordered and amoral political economy with an eminently sensible and incorruptible theatre. In order for such a play to work, theatre and the market must be constructed, erroneously, as 'worlds apart' (to use Agnew's phrase).

In what follows, I also periodically characterise the performances that theatre creates as economic 'products'. Strictly speaking, when I use this term I am referring to the *goods and services* that theatre produces, and which audiences (broadly defined – these need not be limited to the spectators of an individual show) consume at a price. The conventional distinction between goods and services is that a good is tangible (because it takes physical form) whereas a service is intangible (often because it is provided by a person). Theatre arguably produces more services than goods, and theatre industries are usually categorised as service industries within the standard tri-partite model of industrial classification (in which natural resource extraction is primary industry, manufacturing is secondary, and services are tertiary). But the goods versus services distinction is more of a continuum than a binary, and it is common that a product will be comprised of both goods and services; in the theatre, for example, a 'show' might feature services (an actor's performance) and goods (the programme, the published script on sale in the lobby, and so on). The goods and services that theatre produces, and the social value given to them, can also be conceived more expansively than the market often suggests. The term 'product' is expansive enough to encompass both theatrical goods and services, but I want to retrieve the term from a narrowly marketised inflection as well.

My approach to all of these issues is broadly materialist but, as my invocation of Keynes illustrates (and, later, my use of Michel Foucault will show), it is ecumenically so. I hope to avoid the somewhat bleak version of materialism that Jen Harvie warns against in *Theatre and the City*, which, she argues, 'can be almost totalising in its negativity or, even cynicism'.[23] Instead, I am inclined towards the more dialectical and geographically situated materialism described by Harvey:

> There is much to be learned from aesthetic theory about how different forms of spatialization inhibit or facilitate processes of social change. Conversely, there is much to be learned from social theory concerning the

> flux and change with which aesthetic theory has to cope. By playing these two currents of thought off against each other, we can, perhaps, better understand the ways in which political-economic change informs cultural practices.[24]

My goal, then, is to attend – as systematically as possible – to the extensive and often fiercely complicated ways that theatre is embedded with the market economy in particular times and places. Doing this means thinking about theatre through political economy, economic geography, social theory, and more – theatre and performance studies get us some of the way, but they are not enough on their own.

Theatrical Roles

Taken together, the theatrical cases I examine play at least three important roles vis-à-vis markets and marketisation. To adapt a phrase from anthropologists Federico Neiburg and Jane I. Guyer, they *enact the real economy* in economic contexts that have become increasingly dominated by finance capital and rentier forms of economic activity.[25] They are also distinctively theatrical forms of what David Harvey calls a *spatial fix*, and, in the process, they ameliorate long-standing productivity problems within live performance itself and within the broader economy of which theatre is a part (though this remediation may only be temporary). And they function as what I will call *localisation machines*: apparatuses that render otherwise intangible or remote political and economic relations concrete and proximate through their social and spatial forms.

I will take these roles in turn. The proposition that theatre enacts the 'real economy' may seem counterintuitive. What is theatre if not a paradigmatic 'creative' industry? Or at least a boutique enterprise that prospers under financialised capitalism? How can theatre – a medium shot through with immateriality – be an instance of the 'real' economy, in which workers produce actual, concrete things? (The Latin root of 'real', after all, is *res,* or 'thing'.) While the concept of the real economy has evolved over time certain qualities have tended to persist, and these are as apparent in contemporary theatre enterprises as they are in the more 'industrial' sectors from which 'creative' industries are often distinguished: economic activity that can be observed, measured, and administered; the systematic production of goods and services through the coordination of capital and labour; and the creation of value that can simultaneously be quantified and socially experienced. The fact that theatre's immateriality has historically attracted attention does not diminish the fact that a significant amount of theatrical activity is resolutely material, and theatre's social, political, and economic value depend on this materiality. To the extent that some characteristics of the real economy might seem problematic for theatre – such as its reliance on a calculus of productivity rooted in a labour theory of value – these can often be overcome by looking for theatrical value elsewhere. And some theatrical qualities usually considered malign within market economies – for example, a tendency towards monopoly – can, as I will show, become benefits rather than drawbacks in certain circumstances.

The cases that follow also illustrate the limitations of 'creative industries' discourse in capturing the 'real' economic qualities of contemporary theatre. Creative industries discourse became pervasive in artistic, political, and academic spheres from the 1990s on, as arts advocates began to recast the value of artistic activity in more market-friendly terms (in the UK, for example, creative industries thinking dominated New Labour cultural policy, but its influence can be seen around the world). Although it has drawbacks of its own, the generic creative industry trope begins to break down when one tries to apply it to the specific industries, like theatre, that it supposedly encompasses: it overplays the pervasiveness and frequency of innovation within theatre production; it misattributes and misrepresents theatre's industrial character; it elides the divisions and hierarchies of labour through which theatre production is commonly organised; and it often deploys a crude and empirically slight economism (which, owing to its suspect metrics and whiff of technocracy, ultimately ends up reanimating long-standing academic and practitioner anxieties about theatre and economics in ways that are critically unhelpful and politically questionable over the longer term). The creative industry hermeneutic both conscripts and subordinates live performance within its corporatist logic, and in the process elides some of the important economic work that theatre is actually doing.

Quantitatively, the creative industries model often locates the monetary value of creative industries in their aggregated contribution to the economy as a whole. This results in now-familiar proclamations along the lines of 'the creative industries contribute *x* dollars/euro/pounds/rubles/real/renminbi/etc. and *y* percent of GDP [Gross Domestic Product] to the economy of *z*'.[26] Because creative industries discourse seeks both to describe and instantiate the 'new economy' paradigm that the creative industries themselves ostensibly exemplify best, it is imperative that the values of *x* and *y* be as large as possible (something that can be assisted by delimiting the geographical boundaries of *z* according to whatever configuration produces the optimal amounts). But in most economies 'high' art forms such as theatre, classical music, dance, and fine art, even when taken together, comprise a fairly modest economic output in relation to many other sectors of the economy, and therefore seem less deserving of the special attention that creative industries proponents seek. That their output tends to be highly concentrated in a relatively small number of urban centres, or zones within those centres, also makes advocacy on their behalf more complicated than might otherwise be the case – as proponents of the arts know, politicians are often wary of increasing public subsidy for the arts if the benefits of that subsidy are seen to flow largely to culturally dominant metropoles, or particular neighbourhoods within them.

The creative industries hermeneutic seeks to address these problems, at least in part, by blurring the distinction between those expressive media that create commodities that circulate independently of their point of production and those that do not, in order to create a larger industrial sector and make the aggregate output (and employment) of that sector appear much greater. Thus the creative industries include not only theatre and other historically related art forms but also sectors such as digital media, advertising, and software design. Expanding the industrial category in this way may have some tactical benefits to proponents of theatre (for example) when they can 'piggyback' their advocacy on the output of a cohort of affiliated industries that now looks more substantial than it did previously. But doing this also betrays theatre's own subordination within that newly expanded industrial field – for politicians and academics alike, it has been the so-called 'cutting edge', and more determinedly market-driven, elements of the creative industries that have tended to attract the most attention.

Prefacing 'industry' with 'creative' creates qualitative and political problems as well. However difficult it is to define as an industrial characteristic, and however questionable it is to ascribe it to a discrete cluster of producers, creativity in general is hard to argue against; how can inventiveness and imagination be bad, especially when one's own industry seems to be able to claim special purchase on them? Jamie Peck, though, argues that creative industries and creative cities discourses help 'commodify the arts and cultural resources, even social tolerance itself, suturing them as putative economic assets to evolving regimes of urban competition'.[27] The rhetoric of creativity also often involves a semantic sleight-of-hand that romanticises many features of contemporary creative industries (through such language as 'flexibility' and 'innovation') while, in the process, eliding the extent to which they depend on widespread exploitation of their workforces. As Angela McRobbie points out, contemporary creative industries like theatre not only often involve low incomes, unwaged labour, short-term contracts, and recurring periods of unemployment, they depend on them. To those who work in these industries, creativity frequently denotes systemic precarity.[28] The term also overplays the extent to which 'creativity' is what makes theatre productive as an industry. Instead, the complex interplay of systems, spaces, relations, infrastructures, and institutions defines theatre's economic efficacy as much as creativity does.

The theatrical real economy, then, shares a number of features with other sectors in the real economy. It is part of the real economy, not a 'creative' bolt-on: it manufactures products of monetary and experiential value; it is productive, sometimes in novel ways; it creates new types of dividends; and it institutionally helps manage the upheavals of marketisation. That this theatrical real economy stands in opposition to an 'unreal' economy based on finance and rent-seeking is a major part of its appeal.

I should clarify what I mean by 'rent-seeking' here. Rent-seeking refers to types of unproductive economic activities in which incomes are derived not through investments in the production of goods and services but instead from monopoly control of assets, such as in property speculation, natural resource extraction, 'big tech', and some of the more exotic features of the global financial system. In the real economy there is a tangible and often reassuring relationship between investment, production, and consumption, even if – in reality – this relationship often depends on economic exploitation and the reassurance it offers is double-edged. (As the administration of US President Donald Trump has highlighted, it is all too easy for invocations of the real economy to trade on a racist and patriarchal nostalgia for the White male manufacturing worker.) But financial and rentier economies threaten to detach capital from production, and production from goods and even services (let alone production from profits). Productivity – that fixation of modern economics – risks vanishing entirely. All of this has been accelerated by numerous governments giving preferential tax treatment to unearned rather than earned income in recent decades; taxation of capital gains and inherited wealth is significantly lower than the taxation of wages in the economies I discuss. (This preferential treatment gives rise to scenarios like the well-known one where the American billionaire investor Warren Buffet's effective tax rate is lower than his secretary's, since his income is largely derived from investments while hers is derived from wages.) Set against this backdrop, the theatrical real economy starts to become unusually attractive, especially since it offers distinctive, sometimes unexpected, ways to redress the economic opacity and social turbulence that marketisation generally, and the unreal economy especially, entails.

Another role that theatre plays is as spatial fix, particularly as a remedy for productivity problems within live performance itself, and within the broader economy of which theatre is a part. In Harvey's formulation, a spatial fix (or spatio-temporal fix) entails the geographical reorganisation of production in order to stave off some of capitalism's intrinsic economic contradictions.[29] As Bob Jessop characterises it:

> A spatio-temporal fix resolves, partially and provisionally at best, the contradictions and dilemmas inherent in capitalism by establishing spatial and temporal boundaries within which a relatively durable pattern of 'structured coherence' can be secured and by shifting certain costs of securing this coherence beyond these spatial and temporal boundaries. This sort of spatio-temporal fix displaces and defers contradictions both within a given economic space and/or political territory and beyond it.[30]

A familiar spatial fix occurs when a manufacturer relocates production to a lower-wage jurisdiction in order to seek a cost advantage over its competitors. Another happens when industries relocate from city cores to suburban or ex-urban locations, as was common in North America after the Second World War (a migration assisted by large-scale, publicly financed road-building programmes). But a spatial fix can also be theatrical, where, for example, a performance district or site displaces and defers market tensions, albeit in particular ways and sometimes only for a short time.

Spatial fixes attempt to manage contradictions and crisis tendencies inherent in accumulation and, as Chapter 2 illustrates, these arise especially forcefully in the theatre in relation to what economists William J. Baumol and William G. Bowen famously referred to as the 'cost disease': the difficulty of live performance to achieve productivity gains at the same rate as the wider economy, due to high fixed costs that result from the inseparability of its workers from the products they create.[31] In Marx's theory of accumulation, production depends on the continual reinvestment of surplus value, and on the reproduction of the conditions that make this process possible. Marx argues that commodities, once created, 'must then be thrown back into the sphere of circulation. They must be sold, their value must be realized in money, this money must be transformed once again into capital, and so on, again and again'.[32] What matters is not that the production process stays the same – indeed, it will always change – but that it keeps going. There is always a risk, though, that capital will not find an outlet, resulting in 'overaccumulation' (e.g., when capital already floods a market, then new investment risks devaluation, or there may be labour, political, technological, or resource constraints that hamper the circulation of capital).[33] When overaccumulation happens, as it periodically will, an economic tremor ensues. If this tremor is large enough, something like a slowdown or a recession may occur. Worse, a full-blown economic crisis may result, such as the Great Depression of the 1930s or, in a different way, the near-meltdown of 2008.[34]

For Harvey, staving off the persistent threat of overaccumulation involves geographically reconfiguring and expanding capital's domain, most commonly through seeking out new markets for labour and commodities (the most recent iteration of this dynamic has come to be known, somewhat imprecisely, as globalisation). Different forms of spatial fix may result: a company may relocate production from, say, the United States to Mexico in order to lower its labour costs; or it may try to sell its goods to different markets, as natural resource-rich countries such as Australia and Canada did to the BRICs (Brazil, Russia, India, and China) following the events of 2008 (with the consequence that they avoided the worst of the economic fallout of the financial crisis). Spatial fixes may also involve much more localised activities, such as urban redevelopment within a city, which is often predicated on integrating an area more fully into that city's economy.

To be sure, there are hermeneutic limits to the spatial fix. Jessop argues that Harvey underplays its political dimensions, with the consequence that its explanatory force is more ad hoc than it might otherwise be. He contends that although the spatial fix usefully avoids a '"soft" economic and political sociology' of capital, it does not account for 'capitalism's extra-economic dimensions at the same high levels of abstraction and to the same extent as its economic dimensions nor [show] convincingly how they belong to the essential "internal relations" of capitalist societies'.[35] (Not unlike Polanyi, Jessop's main concern is with law and the state, which he argues need to be incorporated into any theory of the spatial fix.)[36] Jessop makes an important point: economic and 'extra-economic' dimensions are inseparable from accumulation, and so politics must be seen not as an adjunct to the market (or its handmaiden) but as integral to its operations.

The same could be said of culture. Indeed, some political economists, Jessop among them, have attempted in recent years to elaborate a 'cultural political economy' that seeks to expand the field's traditional focus on the state-capital-labour nexus and integrate social and ideological concerns into its analyses (though they largely mean 'cultural' in a social scientific, rather than artistic, sense).[37] Migrating the spatial fix to theatre, however, requires a certain level of care. Doing so could result in the vulgar economism that Jessop warns against, where the operations of theatre become either naively mimetic of accumulation or only worth considering when they take their most superficially capitalist forms (such as the commercial theatre). It could also frame theatre's relationship to the broader economy as narrowly and crudely ideological, where theatre performs a superstructural function useful to the reproduction of market relations but where its own political-economic character is elided (or, concomitantly, where its characteristics are seen as so peculiar to live performance industries that they can reveal little about broader political-economic processes and relations, and the position of theatre within them).

The following chapters suggest, however, that theatrical spatial fixes are not only possible but are at times unusually effective. Theatrical spatial fixes encompass both short-term and long-term investments in the built environment and each can be successful and complement the other. The theatrical geography of contemporary London, for example, is very clearly produced through both short-term and long-term spatial fixes. On the one hand, these fixes involve investments in theatre's own infrastructural capacity. Since the late 1990s, there has been a significant investment in cultural venues while, at the same time, a huge increase in theatre-making outside of conventional performance spaces – one does not supplant or undermine the other. Quite the opposite, in fact: that a healthy number of theatre companies have produced work in both types of performance spaces suggests that they can successfully capitalise upon either. On the other hand, these investments increase theatre's productivity in relation to the wider economy by putting (or at least appearing to put) parts of the built environment into (or back into) circulation within London's urban economy. They help integrate these places into broader networks of production, consumption, and governance, and, in the process, hold out the possibility of economic circulation without friction.

All of this demonstrates that theatre negotiates (and operates in) markets that span cities, regions, countries, and even the globe. But its ability to do so frequently hinges on theatre functioning as a kind of localisation machine. By this, I mean that it makes broader political and economic relations sensible and manageable at close proximity, even if this localisation may at times be as much promissory as actual, and even if it sometimes occludes the inequalities that these relations involve. One effect of this localisation is to make theatrical, political, and economic relations commensurate with – if not the same as – each other in a tightly bounded time and place. The result is often reassuring, if not always entirely convincing.

This is a very different – and more explicitly processual and historical – sense of 'the local' than the vernacular one of an already-existing place defined in contradistinction from other, larger geopolitical domains. It also complicates some of the more positivist connotations of the local that its conjunction with theatre might unwittingly invoke: as the locus of resistance to markets and states, and to larger forces of accumulation (if that most local of recent theatrical trends – 'site-specific' performance – has revealed anything it is that local theatre is just as likely to depend on global capital, especially in the form of property development, as it is to resist it); or as the 'nice' counterpart to 'nasty' phenomena like nationalism or globalisation (as I will show in Chapter 4, recasting the local as the civic – theatrical or otherwise – does not retrieve it from larger geopolitical or geoeconomic networks either).

Localisation is not a straightforward or predictable process, though, and it is as likely to be refractive as reflective. It can also occur by different theatrical means, including managerially, formalistically, operationally, and institutionally. So, for example, the blocking annotation that I explore in Chapter 1 can be seen as a form of spatial management within theatrical production. It is simultaneously a way to codify and discipline theatrical labour within the confines of the single rehearsal room and, through its notational abstraction of the work from the worker, a way to extend theatrical labour power over time and space (potentially around the globe). It is a highly efficient theatrical, political, and economic code, one which potentially encompasses the most 'local' forms of theatrical production (tracking, microcosmically, a particular actor's movements across a specific stage) and the most 'global' forms of theatrical production (guiding, macrocosmically, an abstract performer's movements across a hypothetical stage somewhere else).

We can see a similar economic logic playing out in different but related ways through theatre's spatial forms. If we think of the places of performance as theatrical fixed capital rather than, say, in terms of their architectonic, semiotic, or phenomenological qualities, then how this formalistic localisation works begins to become clearer. Fixed capital commonly refers to the physical infrastructure necessary for production to happen, but which is not, itself, used up within a production cycle or sold at the end of it in the manner of a commodity. Most commonly, it takes the form of assets such as transport links, equipment, and buildings. Unlike circulating capital, such as operating expenses, fixed capital is both tangible and durable: it has material form; it has a considerably longer lifespan than any individual good it helps produce; and it transfers its value slowly, over multiple production cycles. While fixed capital may take any number of forms, depending on the requirements of the production process and the products being produced, it is frequently spatial in character, in at least two senses: it often involves an investment of capital in place and the spatialisation of capital as place. Its distinctive temporality is also notable, as infrastructure created through the investment of fixed capital may have a considerable lifespan, usually because the cost of creating it in the first place is substantial and its value is realised slowly. Constructing a factory, for example, often involves considerable expense; it may take many years to recuperate the cost of that initial investment; and the building constructed may persist long after its initial productive use has ceased (which raises complex questions about whether and how it might be used productively in other ways).

That theatrical production has historically involved investments of (relatively) immobile fixed capital is not in question – the construction of theatre venues over millennia, around the world, is clear evidence of that. And as theatre is an activity that often involves highly specialist infrastructure, this investment can be substantial. Alternative deployments of fixed capital such as temporary venues or site-specific performance do not necessarily escape this economic logic, since they frequently involve extending the life of fixed assets by taking otherwise unproductive sites into production (and, as I will show in Chapter 2, the process of doing this has become inextricable from property relations that go well beyond a single address).

Although its name might seem to imply otherwise, fixed capital always contains mobile and immobile elements – an airplane is mobile fixed capital, but an airport is immobile fixed capital – and its ability to generate value depends on the interplay between them, potentially across multiple scales. This does not mean that theatre's creators and spectators have always been comfortable with how this dialectic has played out in the context of performance. On the one hand, theatre-building, and theatre buildings themselves, have been a significant preoccupation of theatrical modernity in Euro-American theatres (whether in terms of their productive capacity, their qualitative features, or their broader social and economic value). On the other hand, there has been a recurring desire to escape the confines of this infrastructure, to reject the built forms of the institutional theatre in favour of an ostensibly more plastic spatiality.[38] The international adoption of a brutalist architectural vernacular in the design of many theatre buildings following the Second World War arguably intensified these longings, since this sometimes-imposing style could seem to be especially constraining, and monumental theatres could be especially 'brutal' interventions in the urban landscape. It is no accident that when Marvin Carlson criticised the imperiousness of post-war monumental theatres in *Places of Performance* (1989), the first major English-language study of theatre architecture, two of London's modernist masterpieces – the National Theatre and the Barbican Centre – featured in his analysis.[39] But the seemingly contradictory aspirations to build a 'home' for theatre and to take theatre 'out into the world' delineate a spatial dialectic that not only characterises theatrical modernity but helps constitute it. This dialectic is as much an economic as a creative one, a productive rechannelling of theatre's otherwise ambivalent relationship with fixed capital, through different built forms and scales, and to different effect depending on the time and place.

In other instances, theatre's ability to localise political and economic relations plays out most clearly institutionally. This is partly because of theatre's position as an almost paradigmatically civil institution. But here I mean civil institution in an embedded, political-economic sense rather than, say, as an institution that is equidistant from politics and economics, and especially the state and the market. My thinking here is informed by Michel Foucault's lectures on biopolitics, which I discuss in Chapter 4. For Foucault, civil society is a way to address a particular problem that arises from marketisation (though the use of 'marketisation' here is my own): how to govern social subjects who are defined first and foremost as economic agents, and whose economic self-interest – which is necessary for Adam Smith's 'hidden hand' of the market to function – threatens to undo the social bonds that make political-economic governance possible in the first place. This problem becomes increasingly acute the deeper marketisation extends and the more pervasive markets become.

Foucault suggests that civil society has a geographical dimension, in that it localises social bonds that would otherwise disperse through marketisation, but it is difficult to discern how this might actually play out in practice (this is Foucault, after all). Theatre can sometimes fulfil this function especially well, though: by providing social and spatial infrastructures in which macro-level political and economic relations might be refigured (without necessarily being repudiated) at close proximity; and by offering theatrical hypotheses of what it might mean to be embedded in political-economic relations without being subsumed by them. In effect, theatre institutionally models ways of negotiating markets without feeling marketised.

All of this depends on thinking about theatre's institutional efficacy – its 'civic promise', to coin a phrase – somewhat differently than we otherwise might. Those of us with an investment in theatre often see its social value as residing, at least partly, in its ability to forge temporary communities of otherwise disparate groups of people by bringing them together in the same time and place and focusing their attention on a common object. But what if we think of this theatrical gathering as an assembly of political and economic agents as much as a social community? Here theatre becomes an exemplary space of political-economic governance, and an institution that culturally unites political and economic forces in a way that the state or the market (or the state and the market, together) sometimes struggle to do.

Theatre's Mixed Economies

On the face of it, the cases I examine might seem to be a rather idiosyncratic bunch. They undoubtedly reflect my own personal and professional histories. But the chapters that follow address, in turn, that series of political-economic questions that theatre necessarily confronts as it takes up the mantle of the mixed economy: How can production be organised efficiently? How can productivity be improved? How can social citizenship be realised? How can these citizens feel secure? How can a better political and economic future for society as a whole be achieved? These chapters demonstrate that what might start out as fairly microcosmic economic questions about theatre's everyday production practices quickly begin to expand into much larger – and more emphatically political – questions about the relationship between theatres, markets, and states since the 1990s. Along the way, they reveal a theatre that is neither heroically resistant nor bluntly instrumental – it is a much more complicated picture than that. And the totality of its operations cannot be glimpsed through a single case or place. Instead, a larger portrait emerges only cumulatively, through the adoption of a series of different vantage points and at different scales (whether local, regional, national, or international).

I begin Chapter 1, appropriately enough, with a night at the theatre. This chapter was prompted by seeing the Old Vic Theatre production of Michael Frayn's *Noises Off* in the West End in London in 2012. As those familiar with this oft-produced play will recall, *Noises Off* depicts a theatre company touring a tired production of a fictional farce through the regions of England. The play concludes with the complete breakdown of a performance, as company members fall out with each other, forget their lines, and crash into the scenery (among other things). I have always liked *Noises Off.* It is meticulously constructed and requires an enormous amount of acting and staging skill to realise successfully. It is also a play that asks challenging questions about theatre as an industry: about its reliance on systems and replicability as much as creativity and ephemerality in its production processes; about the complex materiality of theatrical work; about its labour hierarchies and pervasive managerialism; and about its remarkable ability (by portraying, in this rare instance, an atypical failure) to reproduce theatrical labour power over time and space, again and again, very efficiently. These qualities become especially notable in a political and cultural economy where they are increasingly seen as old fashioned, and where the notion that they could be exemplified is in the theatre seems almost perverse. *Noises Off,* in London in 2012, demonstrated exactly the opposite of what it depicts: that theatre is often driven by the imperative to produce, and that it is remarkably industrious, just not in ways we might expect or necessarily value.

In doing this, *Noises Off* also illustrates the importance of one of the most quotidian, almost taken-for-granted elements of theatrical production: blocking. For me, blocking is interesting because it involves the spatial coordination of theatrical labour vis-à-vis stage technologies and audiences, and it results in highly detailed forms of notation that describe both an actually existing production here and now, and possible future ones, elsewhere, in the future. Some of theatre's most extensive and intensive spatial management occurs through blocking, and it is through blocking that we can see the nexus of labour relations on which much theatrical production today has come to depend. As I will also discuss, in relation to the National Theatre's 2000 production of *Noises Off* (which transferred to the West End and then to Broadway) and its 2011 production of Nick Dear's *Frankenstein* (in which the two main actors swapped the lead roles from performance to performance), blocking also highlights the extent to which theatre relies on standardisation and abstraction in order to be efficient, historically in advance of some paradigmatically 'industrial' forms of mass production, such as the assembly line. Blocking demonstrates theatre's ability to abstract and reproduce theatrical labour power efficiently over time and space as well (sometimes with all the potential to increase income that this entails). In short, blocking tells us a lot about the economic geography of theatrical production and just how industrious theatre can be.

In the next chapter, my focus shifts from production to productivity. The story of live performance's productivity has commonly been told as one of chronic failure. Indeed, figuring out why this failure occurs, and what might be done about it, has been one of the main preoccupations of cultural economics since it emerged as an academic field in the 1960s. The problem of the 'productivity gap' (to adopt a widely used term in economics) has also resurfaced in recent theatre scholarship as a way to help understand why theatre industries might have appeared out of step with the political-economic revolutions that occurred in many market economies during the 1970s and 1980s.[40] But concern about the productivity of live performance goes back to at least the eighteenth century and appears in some of the foundational thinking of political economy writ large. It is not just Baumol and Bowen who were preoccupied with live performance's ostensible lack of productivity, it was Adam Smith too.

My reading of theatrical productivity starts from a different place than others and, as a consequence, arrives at a different destination. Those thinking about theatrical productivity have predominantly focused on theatre's labour process when measuring it. There is nothing inherently wrong with this; measuring the ratio of labour inputs to outputs produced is a legitimate way to determine how economically efficient an enterprise (or industry or country) is at any given moment. Indeed, when one measures theatre's productivity in this manner, some knotty problems quickly emerge: theatre spends an awful lot of time and effort creating products that are evanescent rather than durable; in many countries, it depends on public subsidy rather than the box office to cover its costs; and it expends broadly similar amounts of time and effort making its products as it did centuries ago (unlike many other industries, whose reductions in production costs seem radical by comparison). And conventional ways of measuring theatrical productivity tend to assume that the production cycle of the theatrical good is completed onstage, rather than in some other part of the theatrical enterprise. But this is not the only way to measure theatrical productivity. Instead of focusing on theatre's labour process, and highlighting what happens onstage, what if we pay more attention to forms of productivity generated by other parts of its infrastructure?

It is by way of answering this question that I turn to London's South Bank. The South Bank is best known today for the collection of monumental arts venues that stretch along the southern reach of the River Thames, including, perhaps most notably, the National Theatre. These venues were constructed over three decades following the Second World War and, by the 1980s, had come to symbolise a type of welfare state political economy that was increasingly seen as anachronistic as the UK moved towards a more service-driven, and especially financialised, economy. Later, they also seemed at odds with the type of rough-and-ready, often temporary, performance venues that were springing up across the city, a good example of which emerged several few hundred metres from the National Theatre: the Waterloo tunnels, which were carved out of disused railway storage under Waterloo Station (a part of these were later renamed The Vaults after being taken over by a different producer). In Chapter 2, I argue that the National Theatre and the Waterloo tunnels are in fact two sides of the same coin, in that they spatially and socially model complementary forms of urban productivity that are tremendously appealing in London today. In a time when finance capital is preeminent and almost confoundingly liquid, the South Bank is reassuringly concrete, literally and figuratively. It also holds out the possibility of feeling productive when that experience is less and less available within London's increasingly service-based economy.

If a recurring critical gambit of this book is to refigure our understanding of contemporary theatre's own economic character, another is to resist an unduly narrow or excessively pessimistic economism, through theatre. Chapter 3, which explores the relationship between theatre and the (only partly realised) 'peace dividend' in Northern Ireland since the passage of the Good Friday Agreement in 1998, illustrates why the latter approach can be useful. The concept of a dividend is not difficult to grasp: it is a return that exceeds the capital originally invested. But a 'peace dividend' is a trickier thing to pull off, since it involves not only the cessation of conflict but the marketisation of civil comity, with newly established political institutions making Northern Ireland as safe for private capital as for its residents. Although a significant reduction in armed conflict has occurred since the Good Friday Agreement, the political institutions the Agreement established have nonetheless proved chronically dysfunctional during the two decades following their creation. And if the peace process has undoubtedly resulted in some economic growth during this time, especially in the early 2000s, private investment has also been sporadic, concentrated in low-wage service industries, and unevenly distributed across the North's six counties (a fact that growth in high-profile sectors such as film and television production sometimes occludes). While those living in Northern Ireland generally welcome the radical diminution in armed conflict that has accompanied the peace process, they are often, rightly, circumspect about the extent to which the much-touted peace dividend has been achieved, politically and economically.

But if we think about the peace dividend in theatrical instead of marketised terms glimpses of it might begin to emerge, without (and this key) abandoning the economic valences that made the formulation so attractive in the first place. Looking back at more than twenty years of post-Agreement theatre in Northern Ireland one production stands out in this regard: Tinderbox Theatre's production of Stewart Parker's *Northern Star* in 1998, in the First Presbyterian Church in the centre of Belfast. *Northern Star* is set during the failed uprising for Irish independence in 1798, which was led by the Belfast-based United Irishmen. The time and place of the Tinderbox production was propitious: immediately post-Agreement, thirty years after the first civil rights marches in Derry, in the rebellion's bicentenary year, and in the church where many of the rebellion's leaders likely worshipped. When actor Conleth Hill, playing United Irishman Henry Joy McCracken, directly addressed the theatre audience as 'citizens of Belfast', the production temporarily conjoined politics with economics more effectively than the state or private capital had, and possibly has, since the Agreement. It did this by proclaiming theatre to be an exemplary civil institution in Northern Ireland, and its spectators to be the consummate social citizens that many in the post-Agreement period desired but struggled to bring into being. For a brief but very persuasive moment, the Tinderbox *Northern Star* suggested that the greatest dividend of peace was to be a bourgeois theatre spectator in the First Presbyterian Church.

One of the attractions of the Tinderbox *Northern Star* was that it gave material form to political-economic aspirations that were popularly espoused but at best embryonically present in society at large. It also intervened at a historical moment when the state was actively seeking to reduce its security presence. Chapter 4, in contrast, examines theatre's institutional appeal in relation to a mature market that has evolved to operate at a geopolitical and geoeconomic scale. It is also a market that increasingly depends on highly visible and disciplinary forms of securitisation. My case study here is the Haskell Free Library and Opera House, a public library and theatre which straddles the border between Canada and the United States: the northern part of the building lies in Stanstead, Quebec, and the southern part in Derby Line, Vermont. Until fairly recently, residents of the neighbouring towns tended to treat the border not so much as an international frontier but more as an unremarkable feature of local life. This changed decidedly after the 9/11 bombings in the US in 2001. Following these events, the American government aggressively pursued a series of political and economic securitisation programmes, many of which were subsequently emulated by the Canadian government.

Now, the Haskell is the only place on the Canada-US border that can be crossed without state sanction (though this crossing depends on some fairly intensive border management inside and outside the building). An institution that has often attracted attention because it seemed a quirky vestige of a gentler age gained new and distinctive social import with this latest push for securitisation.

In this chapter, I argue that the Haskell's appeal – as a local cultural institution that promises to manage the antagonisms which securisation entails – is an effect of marketisation rather than a rejoinder to it. And as the history of the Haskell and the US-Canada border shows, this has been the case to some degree or other since its construction at the turn of the twentieth century. At the same time, though, the Haskell performs a distinctive role within the current political-economic scene: it localises forms of social exchange at a time when these have grown progressively more abstract and disciplinary, and it refigures them in forms that seem proximate, comprehensible, and manageable. Agnew argues that over the *longue durée* of global economic history the market's historical meaning has shifted 'from a place to a process to a principle to a power'.[41] One key consequence of this trajectory is 'a gradual displacement of concreteness in the governing concept of commodity exchange'.[42] The market appears to be everywhere and nowhere, yet its effects on everyday life remain insistently material. In this context, the Haskell holds out the possibility of sidestepping the historical logic of marketisation by re-socialising security, even if its potential to do so depends on its position within that very process. Although its civic efficacy is secured through marketisation the Haskell does something that marketisation – in its securitised variant – does not: provide a concrete place in which intimate yet public forms of social exchange can occur. Such a place becomes especially important when the market and the state increasingly appropriate exchange to themselves, rendering it immaterial and punitive at the same time.

Chapter 5 examines theatre's role in a time of austerity. After the financial crisis in 2008, there was much talk of the return of Keynesian economics, as governments in many countries intervened to save the global banking system from collapse. But this turned out to be a narrowly conceived and short-lived version of Keynesianism. It was largely confined to states playing their historical role as the guarantors of markets in the last instance, by taking responsibility for huge amounts of bad debt incurred by the banks, whether by transferring it to their own balance sheets or squeezing other countries – most notably Greece – on behalf of their own financial institutions. Fiscal stimulus tended to be minimal and was often quickly followed by severe constraints on public spending. As economist Joseph Stiglitz put it, 'Yes, we were all Keynesians – but all too briefly. Fiscal stimulus was replaced by austerity, with predictable – and predicted – adverse effects on economic performance.'[43]

The UK has undoubtedly been one of the poster children of austerity. By the time of the crisis, London had arguably become the world's capital of global finance, and British politicians – progressive and conservative alike – had spent a great deal of time and energy cultivating the City of London (as London's financial sector is often called). At its height in 2009, the financial sector contributed 9.2 per cent of the UK's economic output; by comparison, in 1992, at the time of the UK's last major recession, it was 5.5 per cent (unsurprisingly, it declined again after the crash to just under 7 per cent by 2018, though given that the real estate market was picking up a substantial part of the slack the picture remained complicated).[44] In London, though, financial services remained a much larger part of the city's economy and by 2017 still represented 15 per cent of its output.[45]

By international standards, the UK's financial sector is large but not exceptionally so. The UK is among a group of countries – including Australia, Switzerland, the United States, Canada, Ireland, and the Netherlands – whose financial sectors contribute from 7 per cent to 9 per cent of their total economic output.[46] What distinguishes the UK is the amount of political clout the financial sector gained during the 1990s and 2000s, the comparatively light state regulation that followed from this, and the central position it had in the global banking system. Together, these features meant that when the crunch came UK banks were holding a lot of bad debt. What also distinguishes the UK is its long-term political commitment to austerity economics. After the Labour government had stabilised the banks in the immediate aftermath of the crisis, the Conservative-Liberal Democrat government elected in 2010 cut billions from public spending at a time when economic growth was only just starting to recover. This approach continued, to greater and lesser degrees, through the entire decade that followed. Successive governments also remained committed to the financial sector and the property market as engines of the country's economic growth.

In Chapter 5, I turn to a moment at the height of austerity where theatre, rather than the state, sought to instil economic confidence: *Isles of Wonder*, the theatrical performance at the heart of the opening ceremony of the 2012 Olympic Games in London, which remains possibly the most-watched live theatrical performance in UK history. In the social psychology of market economies, confidence is hugely important – it is what encourages economic investment when political and economic conditions are uncertain. In Keynesian economics, public investment in infrastructure is especially important when confidence is shaky, since it creates assets that testify to a better economic future and, ideally, it improves the productivity of the economy as a whole. But the London Olympics were in many ways a travesty of this Keynesianism: although they involved significant public investment at a difficult economic time, many of the assets produced were handed over to private interests at cut-rate prices. *Isles of Wonder*, though, showed how theatre might successfully – if uneasily and perhaps only temporarily – combine Keynesian with austerity economics and, in the process, make the Olympics' infrastructure seem more productive. Its enormous popular appeal lay not only in its artistic creativity but in its political-economic ingenuity as well.

Conclusion

When Keynes, in the proclamation I quoted at the outset of this introduction, talked about putting the economy in the backseat he was not simply inverting the now-familiar hierarchy of economics over culture, or positing them as domains wholly alien to each other. Instead, he was suggesting – admittedly obliquely – that putting the problem into perspective required re-embedding the economy in social relations in their broadest sense, where the market was simply one institution among many (and, having done this, we could devote more attention to other, equally important, things, like theatre).

At the same time, it is worth re-embedding theatre in political and economic relations (also in their broadest senses). This book suggests that theatre is better at managing the problems that arise from this than we might, at first, think. There's a difference, though, between managing problems and solving them (or, in Keynes's words, moving beyond them). However effectively theatre manages these challenges, there will inevitably be moments of ungovernability or unanticipated consequences along the way: the same production techniques that liberate theatrical labour are also the ones that discipline it; theatrical productivity may come at the expense of semantic efficacy; theatre provides living, breathing hypotheses of alternative political-economic relations, but these may only be tenable in the theatre; the proposition that theatre might be a way to deal with marketisation is only plausible because of theatre's position deep within it; and theatre's ability to resolve political-economic antagonisms may be exciting, but it may be a poor model for social action in society at large. The cases I explore delineate a theatre that is in many ways an exemplary political-economic institution as well as a cultural one, often with its participants as ideal political and economic subjects. How we might feel about this, though, is very much open to question.

CHAPTER I

Industry

SELSDON: What's he saying?
FLAVIA: He's saying, he's saying – just get through it for doors and sardines! Yes? That's what it's all about! Doors and sardines! (*To* Lloyd.) Yes?
LLOYD (*helplessly*): Doors and sardines!
OTHERS: Doors and sardines!

> *They all try to put this into practice.* Philip *picks up the sardines and runs around trying to find some application for them. The others open various doors, fetch further plates of sardines, and run helplessly around with them.* Lloyd *stands helplessly watching the chaos he has created swirl around him.*
>
> Michael Frayn, *Noises Off*, Act 3[1]

In Michael Frayn's oft-revived three-act comedy *Noises Off*, a troupe of actors attempts to mount a provincial English touring production of a fictional farce, ironically titled *Nothing On*. In Act 1, during a dress rehearsal in the southwestern seaside town of Weston-Super-Mare, the unprepared company struggles to get ready for opening night. Act 2 takes place one month later, in Ashton-Under-Lyne, near Manchester in the northwest. With relationships between them fraying, the actors deliver a shambolic matinee performance, which the audience views from the perspective of backstage. Finally, in Act 3, the company arrives in Stockton-on-Tees, in northeast England, after a ten-week run. By this point, the show is in crisis: there is open warfare among members of the cast, the toll of touring has proven too great, and it is unclear that a performance will even be possible that night. After the opening curtain fails to rise, Tim, the Stage Manager, steps forward to address the audience, with the costume of the Burglar he is supposed to play later in the performance clearly visible under his dinner jacket. 'Good evening ladies and gentlemen', he begins wearily. 'Welcome to the Old Fishmarket Theatre, Lowestoft, or rather the Municipal Theatre, Stockton-on-Tees, for this evening's performance of *Nothing On*. We apologise for the slight delay in starting tonight, which is due to circumstances . . . '.[2] What follows is the complete disintegration of the ensuing performance, which culminates in the final curtain jamming and, with the actors trying to drag it down, detaching completely and falling 'on top of them all, leaving a floundering mass of bodies on the stage'.[3] The end.

Noises Off is about theatrical failure, of course, and many of its pleasures derive from the inability of its characters to fulfil the basic conventions of an effective performance. They stumble through their lines, they fall over the furniture, and they mistime entrances and mislay props with comical regularity. These failures would be bad enough in any theatrical performance but are even worse in a farce, which, perhaps more than any genre, depends on actors completing precisely choreographed stage actions with metronomic consistency, show after show. When the actors of *Nothing On* run 'helplessly' around the stage, plates of sardines in hand, trying desperately to 'find an application for them', or 'open various doors' in the vain hope that at least one will be correct, it signals not only a comically terrible performance but the complete breakdown of theatrical production itself (Figure 1.1). In the end, *Noises Off* suggests, theatre comes down to sardines

Figure 1.1 Celia Imrie with a plate of sardines, *Noises Off*, Novello Theatre, London, 2012 (Getty Images)

and doors – knowing what to do with them and doing so correctly, repeatedly, in different times and places.

An obvious irony of *Noises Off*, of course, is that its representation of theatrical failure demands enormous skill and discipline from those who stage it – the successful representation of failure depends on a smoothly operating mode of theatrical production. When the actors in *Nothing On* are reduced to shouting, 'Doors and sardines!', they also highlight not only the centrality of scenery and props to theatre but, more importantly, the spatial management that underpins their use and how debilitating, when taken to an extreme, the inability to execute it can be. When an actor does not enter on time, cross the stage to the right spot, or put a prop in the correct place, theatrical production can break down entirely. But theatrical failure in this sense is so vicariously appealing because it is relatively uncommon. In showing the failure of theatrical production, *Noises Off* draws attention to how often theatrical production succeeds.

This chapter is not really about *Noises Off*. Or, rather, it is only partly about *Noises Off*, in that it was seeing a performance of the play in London in 2012 that prompted me to think about a fundamental problem of making theatre: how to produce a performance – in the general sense of manufacturing a product rather than in the specialist sense of financing a show – and then reproduce it over time and space. There are any number of ways to think about this problem. But it is undoubtedly one of economic geography and one of management, in that theatre, whether undertaken for profit or not, has developed highly effective ways of spatially mobilising resources in order to produce goods and services (live performances) for consumers (audiences). And it is very adept at doing this over and over again, show after show.

Although *Noises Off* has always been popular in both professional and amateur repertoires, it is notable that there have been multiple high-profile productions of the play, in well-known subsidised and West End theatres, in London during roughly the past fifteen years. These have often involved extended runs and commercial transfers (in some cases to Broadway as well as the West End), all by different companies or producers. I cannot think of another play with a similar production record during this time. This could just be coincidence, but it is also fair to suggest that the play's theatrical mechanics – which are central to its appeal – began to take on a different inflection during a time when the workings of London's wider economy grew increasingly opaque (even if the effects of their operations were not). Part of the appeal of *Noises Off* now is that it allows audiences to identify a clear relationship between economic cause and effect – between the mechanics of the production process and malfunction – in a way that has become more difficult to achieve in the wider economy.

It also throws into stark relief how intensively and extensively theatre spatially manages its labour-vis-à-vis other forms of stage technology. *Noises Off* highlights, as well, the importance of systems and replication within this process, so that a performance can be reproduced over time and space. And it draws attention to the fact that such practices and processes happen at the microcosmic level of theatrical production (ironically by putting them on full display, under the glare of stage lights).

Noises Off shows that one form of spatial management is key to this process: blocking. Put simply, *blocking* refers to the spatial organisation of theatrical labour in relation to stage technologies (e.g., props like sardines, scenography like doors, lighting, costumes, and so on) and spectators (predominantly, though not exclusively, in relation to their visual and aural registers). It may refer simultaneously to the movement of actors onstage and, just as importantly, the notation of that movement (which may take various forms, such as the graphic and textual mark-up within a stage manager's prompt book or stage directions in a published script). As Ric Knowles observes, blocking is an important element in creating meaning in theatre:

> Proximity or distance and the movement through space are central to meaning-making in the theatre, as are the vertical and horizontal axes of the spaces of performance and reception, the arrangement of actors and audiences into groups, the arrangement of the auditorium, the stage, and the performers in ways that direct the audience's gaze. 'Blocking' in the theatre (the arrangement and movement of actors in space) is used to produce tension, reveal relationships of power, relative status, distance, or intimacy as actors group themselves together, stand apart, invade on another's personal space, or organise themselves in dynamic or static, comfortable or tense relationships to one another, the set, and the furnishings.[4]

The importance of blocking within many theatrical production processes is demonstrated by the amount of time and attention devoted to it during rehearsal, the care and oversight given to it during the course of a run, and the extent to which it is the concern of multiple participants in the endeavour. While the division of labour in modern theatre usually involves the separation of tasks into discrete spheres of responsibility, blocking is one area in which actors, directors, stage managers, and designers share an ongoing, if not equal or consistently maintained, interest. Through it, we can index that division of labour and begin to see the hierarchies it involves.

Perhaps because it is such a commonplace feature of modern theatre, blocking can be taken somewhat for granted. Its frequent disavowal by contemporary theatre practitioners could also mislead us into thinking that it no longer matters. As is often the case in theatre, though, there can be a substantial gap between rhetoric and practice – just because an actor or director disclaims blocking does not mean it still does not happen. Blocking has received minimal attention in theatre and performance scholarship, and it tends to be addressed fairly cursorily in practitioner pedagogy (though the ways that it is addressed in such training reveal important things about the division of labour within the theatrical production process and the complex negotiation of power and authority it entails). The 'spatial turn' in theatre and performance studies, along with more recent experiments in performance practice, have not changed this scholarly inattention; while there is now arguably a greater appreciation of the complex spatiality of performance than before and theatre scholars and practitioners have embraced a broader repertoire of spatial forms of performance, there is nonetheless a risk of overlooking some of the less exceptional but equally important spatial practices upon which theatrical production has come to depend.

In this chapter, I view blocking as an industrial practice – one that addresses, at a granular level, the fundamental economic problem of producing and reproducing a performance over time and space. When I characterise blocking as 'industrial', I do not mean it as a synonym for a sector of the economy but instead in the sense outlined by Marx in his early writings, as the process by which labour power is transformed through the creation of things that ultimately stand apart from the workers who made them (even if, as in the theatre, this abstraction is sometimes difficult to discern).[5] As I will discuss in the first section, this is not the way that blocking commonly has been viewed, either in performance theory or in practitioner pedagogy (the two fields where it has received some, albeit minimal, attention). Blocking has commonly been treated as either an aesthetic problem of stage composition or a mechanical problem of stage organisation (as in the hoary, if not wholly incorrect, advice to actors to 'say your lines clearly and don't bump into the furniture'). Today blocking is most frequently discussed within practitioner training, where it is often conceived as a largely uninteresting practice (especially in directing and acting pedagogy) or as a purely technical exercise (as in stage management training). But if we read this training literature from a different angle, we begin to see blocking as an industrial practice – one that reveals the sometimes-fraught divisions of labour on which theatre production processes have commonly come to depend.

In the second section of the chapter, I look at blocking in action. Here, though, I am less interested in the movements of live actors than I am in the forms of notation that blocking commonly involves, which are most obviously found in stage managers' prompt books (though I do discuss the interplay between these two manifestations of blocking in the latter part of the chapter). Blocking has come to entail the creation of increasingly complex forms of notation that are especially important to the operations of modern theatre production and, in turn, to its potential geographical reach. I see this notation as a kind of industrial script – one that is enacted simultaneously with the artistic script that accompanies it (whether in an actual performance or in a hypothetical one in the future). Blocking notation seeks to improve the efficiency of the production process because it abstracts key elements of the work from the worker. It means that the production process does not require the involvement of one actor to transmit the blocking associated with their part to another actor taking over the role; anyone who knows how to read the notation can do this, sometimes far removed in time and space from the original performance. This spatial abstraction also breaks any proprietary relation between an actor and their blocking – once rendered in notational form, it gains a life independent of the actor who originally created it.

Furthermore, blocking notation not only illustrates forms of spatial management in which modern theatre has come to be engaged; it provides the means to *do* this management. It renders the spatiality of production visible in codified form and allows for changes in this spatiality to be tracked over time; it offers a means to verify that production is unfolding as intended; and it supplies the key spatial data necessary to mount further productions of the same show, in other times and places. As I will discuss in relation to two National Theatre productions – the 2000 production of *Noises Off* and the 2011 production of *Frankenstein* – this notation can be both managerially intensive (as in *Noises Off*, which demanded an especially complex coordination of resources for each performance) and managerially indifferent (as in *Frankenstein*, which involved the lead actors alternating the play's two main roles). Blocking notation also offers a way for theatre to reproduce its labour power over time and space efficiently while maintaining managerial discipline – something that is especially important when production expands to the scale of transnational theatre production, where the same show may be in performance simultaneously in multiple locations, and where the licensing of what commercial producer Cameron Macintosh Ltd calls 'replica reproductions' often expressly mandates the replication of a particular staging.

Notation is undoubtedly important to the efficient operation of individual theatre productions, but abstracting all manner of staging from those who originally enacted it also enables the geographical reach of theatrical production to expand exponentially. When the replication of an entire mise-en-scène no longer requires the involvement of the artistic and technical personnel who initially executed it, theatre's productive reach has the potential to grow enormously. Modern theatre, then, has evolved some very considered and distinctive spatial marshalling of its own labour, technologies, and audiences. And these quotidian, often overlooked spatial practices reveal how industrious it can be.

Industry, Blocking, and the Spatial Division of Theatrical Labour

Take, for example, a fairly conventional professional production process in English-language theatre culture. Although there are, of course, variations of this model, a three- or four-week rehearsal period, followed by a run of several weeks, is a fairly common occurrence. Anyone who works on such a show quickly realises how much of its production process depends not on ephemerality or constant innovation but on systems and replicability: finding ways to repeat the performance, in much the same way, over an extended period of time and, sometimes, space. This is the case regardless of whether a run is several weeks or several months or several years long. Producing and reproducing a performance, then, demands an array of techniques to coordinate, instruct, manage, discipline, verify, document, and deploy theatre's constitutive resources (whether human, mechanical, or 'natural'). What is happening here is theatre finding ways to be industrial, though not in the sense of how we might commonly use the term.

At its most fundamental level, industry involves what Marx refers to as the '*exoteric* revelation' of humanity's '*essential powers*' through labour.[6] In other words, industry is manifest 'in the form of *sensuous, alien, useful objects*' (such as theatrical performances and their attendant artefacts) that are created through a process of abstraction – to a greater and lesser degree, and in many possible ways, industry is part of the process by which the work comes to stand apart from the worker.[7] This abstraction is economically and experientially labile; it may be liberating and pleasurable ('creative', even) while simultaneously being exploitative (in that it may involve the commodification of labour). Theatre complicates such 'exoteric revelation', though, because in the theatre event the performance usually appears inseparable from the performer; abstraction is undoubtedly present (the actor and the character remain two different entities) but semiotically and phenomenologically this distinction is not always possible to discern, at least from the perspective of the spectator (though they know in principle that the distinction exists). But as I will discuss, such abstraction is more apparent from other vantage points within the production process.

Industry also implies systematic production and, importantly, reproduction – the ability not only to produce goods and services more than once but also to reproduce the mode of production itself, in the broadest economic, social, and cultural senses. As Marx observes in the first volume of *Capital*, every 'process of production is at the same time a process of reproduction' and, as feminist critics such as Isabella Bakker, Sylvia Federici, and others have pointed out, this is as much a social (and especially gendered) process as it is a strictly economic one.[8] Modern theatre production is no different in this regard, where frequently the goal is not just to make a new performance every night but to repeat the same performance multiple times, and to sustain the production apparatus – human and otherwise – that makes it possible to do this. Industry, moreover, is usually thought to denote some sort of aggregation of activity. Whereas in economic geography this has usually been understood in terms of an aggregation of producers who share broadly similar production methods and/or produce similar goods or services, it is also fair to think of industry in terms of networks of productive practices, in a single place or across space and time (and theatre might be an especially interesting place to track these ways of working). And, finally, industriousness is the quality that makes all of these things happen. If theatre has not commonly been thought of as industrious, this has more to do with flawed hermeneutics than actual practice.

Speaking of theatre in industrial terms, though, seems both to diminish it (since it threatens to subsume its value within an economic and managerial calculus) and misrepresent it (since theatre often does not seem very industrious). As cultural economist David Throsby points out, such sentiments are to some extent a legacy of deeply ingrained, Romantic ideals of artistry, which have inflected thinking about the arts in Europe and North America since the early nineteenth century, and which often valorise the singular creator (the 'creative genius') to whom material needs, especially monetary ones, should be unimportant. The assertion that art and artists might be part of an industry arguably only amplifies this unease.[9] Proposing that art is often industrial risks undermining the romance of artisanal production and the status of the artist as a privileged producer. As a producer working in an industry, the artist begins to look more like either a worker or an entrepreneur (and sometimes both simultaneously). The former bears the taint of collectivity, while the latter bears the taint of commerce. Industry also implies a submission of the artist to systematic production, which undermines the singularity of the artist and highlights the fact that artistry depends on multiple intermediaries between the creator and the artistic product, and that the role of the artist in coordinating this production process is usually heavily circumscribed. All of this risks contaminating the consumer's encounter with the work with the whiff of either money or social relations. While both, of course, are always present in some way or other, neither is seen as wholly desirable. Locating theatre's industry in its 'creativity' does not necessarily address the problem either, since a great deal of theatre's industriousness does not depend on creativity.

Thinking about theatre in industrial terms is also somewhat at odds with familiar discourses arising from within theatre and performance itself, where the ephemerality of live performance has tended to be valued highly: the proposition that a given performance, at its best, offers an intense, transitory experience that will never happen in the same way again (that it will be, to quote the title of one prominent acting guide, 'different every night').[10] It is difficult, however, to set aside the fact that ephemerality still usually depends on some form of systematic theatrical production, whether or not the techniques involved ultimately bring theatre into the sphere of market exchange, and a significant extent of the production process is devoted to minimising variation rather than encouraging it.

The key problem, then, is for theatre to become industrious in the sense Marx outlines, and blocking has become one way to do this. In the *longue durée* of Euro-American theatrical production, blocking is nothing new. Or, at least, one of its fundamental concerns – how to organise performers optimally on the stage – is not new. Performers have always moved on the stage in some sort of coordinated fashion, and these movements have always played an important part in the creation of theatrical meaning. This being said, we can see modern conventions of blocking being practised in British and continental European theatres in the middle of the eighteenth century, and in the nineteenth century blocking is being recorded in a way that is recognisable today (though, as I will discuss, some of the nuances within this bigger picture are important). Although I am not trying to undertake a history of blocking in this chapter (however interesting that might be) it is nonetheless important to acknowledge instances where theatre theorists and practitioners are working out the industrial potential of blocking, even if they do not articulate it in these terms.

While it is difficult to locate a particular source for the term, 'blocking' is commonly thought to take its name from the wooden blocks – each often representing a character – used to work out actors' positions on a stage maquette, usually so that these could then be learned by actors in rehearsal and subsequently reproduced on stage (this practice is depicted in Mike Leigh's 1999 film *Topsy Turvy*, which contains a short scene in which William Gilbert, of Gilbert and Sullivan fame, arranges little coloured blocks on a model of the set of *The Mikado*).[11] Blocking develops during the eighteenth and nineteenth century as a highly flexible practice. It serves the growing desire among some thinkers and practitioners to move away from declamatory acting styles in order to achieve greater versimilitude and increasingly 'natural' (though not yet naturalist) stage compositions from the late eighteenth century onwards. At the same time, it is caught up with increasingly complex and expansive forms of staging that could serve all manner of theatrical spectacles. Such practices were arguably aided by lighting and scenic inventions, such as those developed by Philip de Loutherbourg and installed in David Garrick's Drury Lane in the 1770s, which facilitated greater use of the entire stage, and, later, by the formulation of complex systems of staging notation, which made it easier to document and reproduce a show, both in a particular theatre and, ultimately, in an imagined theatre somewhere else, in the future.

Discussion of blocking, or the spatial concerns underpinning it, has largely been confined to two, quite different, spheres: early modern performance theory, and, to a greater extent, twentieth- and twenty-first-century practitioner pedagogy. Arguably the most notable example of the former is philosopher Denis Diderot's essay 'Conversations on *The Natural Son*' (1757), which was published alongside the script of his play *The Natural Son*. This wide-ranging essay, which consists of a series of imagined conversations between the author and Dorval, the lead character in the play, not only takes up staging but also dramaturgy, genre, mimesis, language, and more (that Diderot's concerns are so wide-ranging is a testament both to his intellectual curiosity and to the fact that *The Natural Son* is a bit of a mess of a play – it is no accident that Diderot is now remembered primarily as a theorist rather than a playwright). As an advocate of verisimilitude, Diderot is displeased with what he sees as an excessive reliance on the *coup de théâtre*, the sudden and unexpected turn of events, in French dramaturgy. He also disdains the staging conventions that underpin the *coup de théâtre*, which he believes undermines the accurate representation of complex sentiments and social relations:

> Can people possibly not realize that misfortune has the effect of bringing men closer together; and that it is ridiculous, especially in moments of turmoil, when passions are carried to extremes, and the action is at its most violent, to stand in a circle, separated, at a certain distance from one another, and in a symmetrical pattern?

As a corrective to these defects Diderot proposes the *tableau*, in which actors would move naturally on the stage and be organised according to the pictorial logic of painting. This, he argues, would enable both greater verisimilitude and more complex forms of visual and aural pleasure for spectators (and would render the contrivances of the *coup de théâtre* impotent and archaic). Characters would now, when friends, 'look each other in the face, turn their backs to the audience, come together, move apart and come together again', much as they would in real life.[12] As Marvin Carlson observes, 'in this major essay Diderot lays the groundwork for the standard compositional practices of the modern stage'.[13]

Today, discussion of blocking is more likely to be encountered in accounts of the rehearsal hall than in performance theory. Even here, though, it is not always the subject of extended consideration. Prominent American director Anne Bogart, for example, barely takes up the issue in either *A Director Prepares* or *And Then, You Act.* William Ball, in turn, treats blocking almost entirely as a preparation exercise conducted within the director's imagination that is then abandoned on the first day of rehearsal.[14] Where it is discussed, the aims of contemporary practice tend to chime broadly with Diderot's: to achieve an appropriate verisimilitude (where actors' movements seem 'truthful' or 'natural' for the character within the fictive world of the play and to the spectator in the social world of the live performance) while realising interesting stage compositions (without too self-consciously mimicking the conventions of painting or appearing overly choreographed – adherence to some degree of verisimilitude is thought to guard against such excesses). As British director Katie Mitchell puts it, 'All the time we are thinking of creating an environment that the actor can use naturally (as the character in the situation) and yet will lead them to position themselves in a way that is aesthetically pleasing and well focused for the audience'. Echoing Diderot, she claims, 'The worst type of blocking occurs when actors are positioned in a nice semi-circle facing downstage, walking sideways like crabs'. Like him, she encourages aspiring directors to 'spend some time studying painters and paintings' since it will 'train your eye in composition' – not in order 'to make the stage look like a painting' but to 'focus the action the audience will see'.[15]

Of course, realising such aims may result in very different types of staging, and some of these may provoke controversy. Mitchell, for example, is more comfortable with spectators finding it difficult to see or hear actors clearly at all times than other directors often are, a fact that has periodically exorcised some reviewers of her productions in the UK (their aversion also likely reflects the long-standing mistrust of the *Regietheater*, or director's theatre, tradition in British theatre, an antipathy exacerbated by one of the leading British exponents of this approach being a woman in a male-dominated occupation). Across a range of directing and acting texts, however, it is notable how much their authors agree about what blocking should involve, and how it should be done: achieving a balance of verisimilitude and visual interest, through a fairly pragmatic, often intuitive process (which can be summed up as something along the lines of, 'if we're working with the text correctly, the play pretty much blocks itself').[16]

Over time, though, there have been some subtle changes in thinking about how these aims might best be achieved in the rehearsal hall. These indicate historical shifts in the division of labour within theatrical production and these shifts, in turn, raise intriguing questions about how the participants within that production process might negotiate them. The consensus that blocking should emerge organically in rehearsal, through a collegial back-and-forth between director and actors, means that a contemporary Gilbert, working out actors' moves in order to transmit them in rehearsal, has been difficult to conceive for a long time – the achievement of a 'natural' stage composition is now thought to correlate to a similarly 'natural' rehearsal methodology. (Of course, 'pre-blocking' has not disappeared; it has simply migrated to other places: as part of the 'bibles' that are the templates for touring productions of popular shows originally produced in large metropolitan centres, and for 'replica reproductions' of West End and Broadway mega-musicals.) To a director like Harold Clurman, whose 1972 treatise, *On Directing*, became a touchstone of American directing pedagogy, pre-blocking might save time in rehearsal but, he implies, it is ultimately immature and archaic, having been abandoned by one of the greatest figures of the modern theatre: 'Stanislavsky said he worked this way as a beginner. He gave it up later.'[17] Insofar as this suggests that Stanislavsky stopped formulating detailed blocking in advance of rehearsals Clurman is not quite correct, since Stanislavsky continued the practice throughout his career (though his process did evolve over time to accommodate actors' contributions more directly, especially through the active analysis and physical actions methods he developed later in his life).[18] The accuracy of Clurman's characterisation is less important, however, than the sentiment it illustrates: the suspicion with which directing methodology came to view pre-blocking by the later twentieth century, to the extent that any non-conforming practices of directing's leading progenitor required retrospective amendment in order to bring them into line with the now preferred way of working.

The approach to blocking commonly advocated today claims to supplant a director-centred model with one based on a more equable negotiation between director and actor, in which the critical eye of the former combines with the character sensibilities of the latter (in a way, blocking is where theatre semiotics and theatre phenomenology intersubjectively combine). Of course, the opposition between a supposedly historical, authoritarian model of blocking and a contemporary, collegial one (where the director's power to command is held in reserve and only used when necessary) risks effacing industrial power relations that may be just as much in play in a contemporary division of theatrical labour as in one centuries ago. Thus Mike Alfreds's almost hyperbolic resistance to blocking in his actor training guide, *Different Every Night* – in which Alfreds proclaims that he is 'totally against' blocking because 'it blocks possibilities of creative change, of spontaneity, of life itself' – can be seen not so much as a defence of artistry as an attempt to advance the cause of actors within the theatrical production process by resisting the spatial techniques of their subjugation.[19] Who decides what the blocking is, when it happens, and when it stops reveals how authority is distributed within any given rehearsal room. The jobbing actor who persists with a particular line of blocking because it 'feels right', against a director's wishes, may very quickly cross a line (usually unspecified until traversed) between being committed to a character and being insubordinate. At the same time, however, the star who dislikes 'table work' and so insists on 'getting the play on its feet' early in rehearsal may successfully defy a director's preferred way of working, and exercise greater control over staging than a less illustrious actor could. Blocking demonstrates that the equability of the collegial rehearsal model should not, therefore, be mistaken for equity.

The key figure usually missing from discussions of blocking is the stage manager. If one learned about blocking solely from directing or acting guides, or from theatre scholarship, one would scarcely guess that this third figure even exists, let alone that it now plays such an important role in making blocking happen. This oversight may arise from the now commonplace separation of theatre work into 'creative' and 'technical' roles, with those doing 'creative' work (such as the director or actor) occupying a superior position within a hierarchy of theatrical labour. The stage manager does not fit neatly into the creative/technical binary, though the occupation has become key to the execution of both creative and technical roles. But it is via stage management that the range of important functions that blocking serves within the theatrical production process is best seen, and it is the artefacts and techniques of stage management that clearly reveal theatre's industriousness.

The stage manager, like the director, is a relatively recent historical development; though, as with many theatrical jobs, it is important to distinguish between function and occupation when thinking about it.[20] As Tracy Catherine Cattell shows in her perceptive history of stage management in the United Kingdom, many of the theatre practices that are now associated with stage management in modern British theatre long predate the consolidation of the stage manager – in the occupational sense we would recognise it now – in the early nineteenth century.[21] Cattell details how the 'book keeper', with responsibility for overseeing the master script and plots (the former being the licensed copy of the playtext and the latter being an outline with key staging information recorded at the appropriate moments), was a familiar figure in British theatre in the early 1600s and points to a range of performance 'support' functions that are arguably antecedents of modern-day stage management practices (though some of these could be considered antecedents of the modern-day director as well).[22] The emergence of these coordinating roles and functions also makes a lot of sense given the growth of theatre companies during the early modern period:

> In addition to the gatherers, scriveners, and refreshment vendors, the playhouses were further staffed by tiremen, who helped the players to dress; stage keepers, who operated live effects, and set and struck any items too large to be carried on by the players in the course of their entrances onstage; heralds, whose trumpets summoned the audience to the playhouse; and musicians, whose live flourishes and fanfares punctuated many characters' entrances and exits in addition to the playing of music integral to the play. With such a collection of assistants, each with individual functions, required to contribute in a co-ordinated way to a performance dependent on their support, a need for cohesive management is implied.[23]

The demands of staging increasingly spectacular and technologically intensive performances not only in the UK but elsewhere in Europe and in the

Americas in the eighteenth and nineteenth centuries would surely only have increased the incentives for such forms of management.[24] Put simply, when production involves more resources – human and otherwise – there is a strong incentive to create specialised roles and techniques for ensuring that production as a whole proceeds smoothly and – crucially for my purposes – undertaking the spatial management on which that production depends.

Notation and the Spatial Management of Theatrical Labour

When the critic Henry Fothergill Chorley visited London's Lyceum Theatre in 1863, he not only marvelled at the advancements in its technological capabilities (which, he thought, would make it possible to achieve more sophisticated and convincing theatrical effects) but also recognised that increasingly detailed stage diagrams made precise theatrical reproduction possible, while, in the process, abstracting staging from its original creators:

> That minute subdivision of this new stage into small separate pieces which has been already spoken of, has another advantage besides that of placing a prodigious number of traps at the manager's disposal. For, these subdivisions being all numbered, an accurate plan can be made of every scene, which, though temporarily put aside, may be wanted some day again. A drawing may be made, so accurate, that a set of carpenters who never were in the theatre before, could by its aid set up the scene in question at any time, exactly as it was originally, with every shrub and piece of rock-work in its place to an inch. Such drawings of all the different scenes occurring in any given play will be laid up in the archives of the theatre along with the prompt copy, and by such means the play can at any time be put on the stage again with the greatest exactness.[25]

It is notable just how comprehensive and expansive Chorley's aspirations are here. He may have been more interested in diagramming scenery than actors, but for the purposes of production (and reproduction), it is barely a step from a 'shrub' or 'piece of rock-work' to a human performer. He also anticipates the possible future productions that such notation could enable – his productive imaginary is both microcosmic and macrocosmic, his theatrical workforce posited as much as actual.

Chorley articulates the notational and managerial aims of his time especially well, and he gestures towards a notational complexity that, as Cattell documents, was increasingly found in the prompt books of his day.[26] He also puts his finger on the extent to which this notation would involve a much greater degree of spatial detail than in the past. As Edward A. Langhans shows, eighteenth-century prompt books tended to be concerned in the first instance with textual rather than spatial management, recording the (often extensive) modifications to a script during its production: 'the evidence ... seems to suggest that most prompters, presumably working with instructions from their managers, began with textual cuts, additions, and emendations'.[27] This is not entirely surprising, since scripts – and authorship itself – were treated with much less reverence at that time than they are today and legal copyright regimes did not yet exist. Langhans shows that what little spatial notation exists in eighteenth-century prompt books is largely devoted to marking entrances and exits, usually through simple abbreviations that indicate an actor's position in relation to that of the prompter (e.g., PS = Prompt Side; OP = Opposite Prompt). Sometimes this notation is refined further (e.g., LDPS = Lower Door Prompt Side; 1ERH = First Entrance Right Hand; From the Top = Upstage) and sometimes notations consist simply of numbers, which usually correspond to a separate call-book (with each number corresponding to a different character). In general, though, Langhans argues that prior to the nineteenth-century spatial notation is inconsistently present and idiosyncratically executed.[28]

By the nineteenth century, however, prompt books were recording more detailed and extensive spatial information. The general trend over the course of the nineteenth century was to record spatial notation in progressively greater detail. Whether or not Gilbert worked out his *Mikado* blocking in the way that Mike Leigh imagines, the results were recorded in a manner that is easily recognisable today. The prompt book for the original D'Oyly Carte production at London's Savoy Theatre in 1885 has many of the same features that contemporary prompt books possess: scenery and properties plots; sections of printed script affixed to one side with a facing page of notes and diagrams on the other (these were most likely executed by D'Oyly Carte's stage manager, W. H. Seymour); entrance and exit cues; script emendations; and character positions and movements delineated in plan form, using a combination of graphical and textual notation (a note at the end of the prompt book also indicates that it was used in later revivals by the company, which reinforces the fact that a prompt book can not only record the staging of an existing performance but a future performance, in another time and place).[29] A contemporary prompt book might be rather more neatly executed but its key characteristics would be very similar.

While contemporary prompt books usually contain a variety of types of information pertaining to cueing a show (and may, in fact, include several different types of book, such as the rehearsal book, the cueing book, and the production book) the most prominent of these now often relate to blocking. As Larry Fazio observes, this blocking notation can serve a wide range of functions:

> The greatest amount of information gathered and entered in the rehearsal script is the blocking of the show: so much so that the rehearsal script is also called the blocking script. *Blocking* is the noting and recording of all the movement, action, and business in the show, as set and agreed on by the director and actors. Blocking is noted on the rehearsal script, first to aid the director and actors, should they happen to forget it at a later time; second, to aid the SM in preparing the understudies and for putting in replacement actors; and third, for a new play, noting blocking becomes a record of the director's creation and invention. It is the historical account kept for the archives, prosperity [*sic*], and in part, for the publication of the play. . . . The actors write their own blocking on their personal scripts, while the SM's rehearsal script has the blocking for every actor or character.[30]

All of these functions are accurate, and more could likely be added. (It is also interesting that Fazio sees blocking as the notation of stage action rather than the action itself, a perception that an actor, say, would be unlikely to share.) But from the point of view of theatrical production, prompt books are economically illuminating for at least three reasons: they demonstrate how microcosmic spatial management is a fundamental concern of theatrical production; they illustrate the extent to which theatrical production now depends on systematically formulated and applied techniques of spatial documentation, verification, and compliance (they are both operational *and* disciplinary); and they assist the reproductive capacity of theatre over time and space – their notation abstracts theatrical work from the theatrical worker and, in doing so, enables the integration of new workers into the production process and potentially extends the geographical reach of theatre and its products.

If prompt books undoubtedly reflect stage managers' personal notation styles, they still tend to look broadly alike. There are several reasons for this: they document much the same information and serve similar purposes within the production process, regardless of the individual show; they need to be legible to another stage manager, should personnel change or the book serve as the basis of a subsequent production; and they reflect the fact that stage managers tend to be trained to relatively common, or at least easily translatable, 'paperwork' templates. The goal is that theatrical production should be able to continue, regardless of changing circumstances, because, as Lawrence Stern and Alice R. O'Grady put it, 'someone else could pick up the promptbook and run the rehearsal or show'.[31] But beyond these basic characteristics, it is the spatial notation found within prompt books that performs key productive functions: codification, verification (along with its counterpart, compliance), and, ultimately, reproduction. In this, theatrical production is no different from any other form of production, regardless of how emphatically theatrical discourse sometimes employs the language of experimentation and originality.

As Gail Pallin observes, prompt books commonly employ a combination of two types of notation: graphic (such as diagrams) and shorthand (such as abbreviations for stage locations or character names).[32] It is also common for stage managers to employ expository notation to some degree, especially where some degree of granularity in documentation is desirable (where, for example, a character not only crosses the stage but executes a specific, detailed action that may not be easily captured by a combination of graphic and shorthand notation). Ideally, this notation should be able to 'be understood by anybody', but it should also condense key information into a form that can be used as quickly as possible by the stage manager; the aim is for blocking notation to be both universally legible and efficiently deployable (at least to and by a stage manager, whether the prompt script has been prepared with the intent of handing it over to a colleague or just in case its author is 'hit by a bus', and another stage manager must step in to run the show).[33] The most common contemporary book style consists of two opposing pages (usually 8½ × 11" or A4 size each) with a page of script on one page and, at least initially, a blank page opposite. This opposing page provides space for diagrams (sometimes including an overhead plan of the stage, with important elements of scenery drawn in) and additional notation corresponding to particular points in the script opposite.

Since I began this chapter with *Noises Off*, it makes sense to return to it to illustrate how this can work in practice. Let's consider the working prompt copy for London's National Theatre production of the play in 2000, directed by Jeremy Sams, which subsequently transferred to Broadway the following year. It contains the sort of information necessary for a stage manager (in British parlance, the Deputy Stage Manager, who is usually responsible for calling the show) to run the production on a day-to-day basis: detailed blocking recorded in diagrammatic, shorthand, and expository form, amendments to the script, lighting and sound cues, and so on. This prompt script is also accompanied by a series of supporting cue sheets for use by onstage DSMs in order to execute some of the play's tightly timed actions. (*Noises Off* depends on a series of precisely executed entrances and exits, and these frequently involve props and scenery that must be choreographed accordingly.)

Seen as an industrial script, this notation codifies the spatial, labour, and technological relations underpinning the show and makes its overall topography comprehensible to those involved in the production process. This is important if – as is usually the case – an aim of production is not simply to invent a single performance on a given night but to plan it in advance and be able to repeat it. Such notation may need only be minimal in order for this function to be carried out successfully, but as the intensity of resources requiring coordination increases, and the ideal that each production should have its own bespoke blocking becomes a common premise of production, having a comprehensive record of those resources' distribution – spatial and otherwise – becomes increasingly useful and, arguably, necessary. This is especially important in a production of a play like *Noises Off*, which would fail spectacularly (as failure to produce, as well as a representation of the failure to produce) without such careful spatial management.

Notation also provides a means of verifying that production is proceeding as intended. Verification is especially important during rehearsals, when actors are learning blocking or items are being integrated into the action; for example, blocking notation enables an actor to check with a stage manager that a given movement is correct, or a stage manager may use a setting plot to restore a piece of scenery to its designated position if it has shifted. Diagrams also supply reference points for recalibrating and encouraging compliance. During the run of a show, when actors' blocking can change, sometimes without them being aware of it, or scenery can subtly shift, spatial diagrams provide points of reference that the stage manager can use to recalibrate in line with previously established compositions (and, by implication, they provide the data necessary for enforcement should there be a failure to comply – stage managers' reports and notes to actors often rely on this information).

Related to this, spatial notation helps improve the efficiency of production, sometimes in small ways but nonetheless with real effect. For example, properties or setting plots not only record where a prop or piece of scenery is to be placed (onstage or, if an actor enters with it, offstage) they often notate precisely how an item is to be angled or any particular way it needs to be prepared. The purpose of these refinements is to ensure that a performer's interaction with the object is as predictable as possible, in order to be able to execute an action the same way each time (which may also have knock-on benefits, such as ensuring that an actor is lit correctly). As any actor knows, the smallest variation in prop or scenery placement can disrupt an action and impact upon other actions with which it is associated. It is likely that anyone who has worked on the run of a show, in whatever capacity, has experienced an incident like the one described here by Copely and Killner:

> An actor running from stage left to right needed to pick up a newspaper folded in a certain way from the prop table as he was running. The paper had been set at the back of the prop table and not folded in its usual way. He hesitated and missed an important entrance which another actor had to react to; there was also a sound cue to her reaction that, as a consequence, did not happen and rather spoilt the scene.[34]

The chair that is slightly out of place, the coffee mug turned the wrong way around, the absent plate of sardines – any of these kinds of minor misplacements can lead to lines being forgotten, entrances being late, and cues being fumbled.

Appropriately enough for a play in which they feature so prominently, the prompt script for the NT *Noises Off* includes separate cue sheets for sardines, as well as for sheets and bathmats. (It also includes a sheet of 'Door Details' that cautions, 'ALL DOORS GET SEVERE ABUSE THROUGHOUT – YOU'VE BEEN WARNED'.) Their cues correspond to particular moments in the script, often with precise actions specified about where or how the sardines need to be placed in order to be picked up by an actor making an entrance (sometimes through a door that, itself, has been prepared in some way). The accompanying daily rehearsal reports are concerned, more than anything else, with prop and scenery management, so that actors' actions can be executed in the right time and place. Thus the sardines must be packed in oil (not tomato), the television must be turned off or on at the correct moment, and the hinges on the kitchen door must be installed in a certain way (on the upstage edge, to be precise) so that the actors can make their entrances and exits in the desired manner and the appropriate staging effect can be realised.[35]

Spatial diagrams also can perform an important pedagogical function, as a way for actors to learn their blocking. In a production with bespoke blocking and a single cast, the need for this pedagogy may not be so great, since actors often learn their blocking as it is created (though they may refer to spatial diagrams – perhaps a combination of arrows and abbreviations scratched in the margins of their own rehearsal script – as a memory aid while they assimilate this blocking). But in a long-running show where actors will leave and join, or where understudies must be able to perform at short notice, spatial diagrams become hugely important. As actor and musician Loren O'Dair points out, in a West End musical that may run for months or years, it is common for an assistant director or member of the stage management team to supervise specialised rehearsal sessions, based on the production bible, to integrate incoming actors into the cast and help them learn the show's already-established blocking.[36] Thus spatial diagrams sustain the continuity of the production process by helping integrate new members without interruption.

Spatial notation, therefore, is an important mechanism to help minimise variation within the theatrical production process. At the same time, however, theatrical production displays remarkable 'tolerance' (in an engineering sense) in that it can normally cope with such variations and continue to function: when changes are made or problems arise, as they undoubtedly will, theatrical production can usually accommodate them without grinding to a halt (in the worst-case scenario, audiences may still be unaware that something has gone wrong, or, if they are, the transgression may, ironically, become a feature of the performance, as Nicholas Ridout has suggested).[37]

Indeed, it may tolerate such variants by ignoring them altogether. Take, for example, another National Theatre production: Nick Dear's 2011 stage adaptation of Mary Shelley's novel *Frankenstein*, directed by Danny Boyle. This production is notable not only because of the high profile of its two male leads, Benedict Cumberbatch and Jonny Lee Miller, but because the actors swapped the main roles – the scientist Victor Frankenstein and the Creature that he created in his laboratory – from performance to performance. Both versions of the show worked with the same script, and with the same general staging, but each actor's distinctive characterisation affected how they executed some of their movements onstage; as the rehearsal notes commented early on in the process, 'although the Script will not alter due to the alternating Creature performers . . . the physical performances and movements might' (and, in the end, they did).[38] Cumberbatch's and Miller's interpretations of their two roles were undoubtedly different: Cumberbatch emphasised Victor's single-minded coldness while Miller stressed his blustering masculinity. As the Creature, Cumberbatch showed the character revelling in his developing powers of language and reason while Miller highlighted the tension between the Creature's destructive impulses and his emotional desires.

The two actors observed broadly common blocking when playing the same roles, but their respective characterisations resulted in subtle differences in movement and action, which consequently produced different nuances in meaning for audiences (in much the way that, earlier in this chapter, Knowles suggests). For example, there was a modest but notable variation in the ways that Cumberbatch and Miller executed Victor's blocking in Scene 26, which takes place after the Creature has killed William, Victor's younger brother, and the Frankenstein house is in mourning. M. Frankenstein, Victor's father, is seated at his desk, reviewing the post that has been brought to him by the servant, Clarice. Victor enters, abruptly dismisses Clarice, and announces to M. Frankenstein that he intends to delay his wedding to Elizabeth and return to England for work. This news greatly upsets M. Frankenstein, who accuses Victor of betraying both his family and his betrothed (the bracketed notation and numbering are taken from the Blocking and Cueing Script, and are inserted at the moment indicated in the DSM script):

> When your mother was dying, I gave you a promise that I would see you wed your cousin Elizabeth [5: MF takes step to V]. That was my wife's last wish – that you might be happily married. You were such a brilliant child, a carefree child, [6: MF xs to V ¾ way] alert and inquisitive, the joy of our days! I came to believe you would do great things, and I would be proud of you. [7: V xs round DSC of room & up to look out of SR 'window' MF turns to watch him] Instead we have this sullenness, this melancholy, this low fog of gloom. You flout my authority; you do not respect the codes by which we live. If you insist on leaving, I cannot stop you. But you may tell your fiancée yourself. [8: MF xs to door & opens it/V turns to MF then turns & steps USR corner of room head in hands].[39]

After this speech, M. Frankenstein leaves the room and Elizabeth enters. In performance, the blocking specified in this passage corresponded almost exactly to that executed by Cumberbatch.[40] Miller, however, did not execute blocking cue 7 as notated. Instead of crossing around down-stage-centre (the production was staged in the Olivier Theatre, which has a semi-circular forestage), he crossed upstage to M. Frankenstein's desk and slumped in the chair. Unlike Cumberbatch, who stood and stared out the window with his back largely to the audience (in part profile to the stage right side of the auditorium) while M. Frankenstein berated him, Miller faced the audience, seated, his tormented expression visible to the entire auditorium. Although a small change, the theatrical effect was notable. By slumping in the chair and facing the audience, Miller forcefully registered M. Frankenstein's denunciation of Victor as wallowing in 'this sullenness, this melancholy, this low fog of gloom'. Cumberbatch's blocking, however, implied that Victor was impervious to such accusations, his mind already elsewhere; literally and figuratively, he had already turned his back on his father and the Frankenstein house.

Such shadings and inflections happen all the time in performance. But it is nonetheless interesting that the variations in the two actors' blocking are not recorded in the DSM's calling script. In fact, one would not know from the DSM's script that different actors played Victor and the Creature in this scene in alternate performances, and executed their stage movements somewhat differently, as the single set of blocking and cueing notation is not tailored to the variances of each actor – it represents an abstracted performer, who may be related to Cumberbatch and Miller but is not reducible to them. From the point of view of the audience, these variations matter, since, as Scene 26 shows, they impinge upon the potential meanings of any given part of the show. From the point of view of production, though, they are insufficiently material to merit notation – they are immaterial not in the usual theatrical sense but rather in a managerial sense, as they literally do not matter for the purposes of sustaining production. The fact that Miller and Cumberbatch executed their blocking differently did not affect the various cues that needed to happen in order to keep the show running as designed: the lighting state was general and constant, so neither actor lost his light by occupying different positions on the stage; the sound cue within the passage was linked to M. Frankenstein's exit rather than Victor's move, so could happen in the same way each time; and M. Frankenstein's exit and Elizabeth's entrance still occurred at the same time regardless of how Victor moved. If the variations of movement introduced by different actors alternating the same roles gave rise to subtle and intriguing semantic nuances, for the purposes of running the show, these were not significant enough to matter.

Thus spatial notation within the theatrical production process reflects not so much an attempt to eliminate variations in working practices outright but rather a means to manage them efficiently, to note required information but omit variations which may be material to an audience's experience of a performance, but not to the production and reproduction of that performance. The precision of such notation – not only in what it includes but what it excludes – acknowledges that variation will occur and provides an objective point of reference to which production can return when it inevitably does. It is spatially specific but not overly so – when trying to keep the theatrical machine running, sometimes a little vagueness works better.

Conclusion

Taken together, these spatial practices reveal the intimate relationship of theatre with industry. But this is not a relationship that is cemented through theatrical creativity. Instead, it materialises through the operation of theatre's own distinctive spatial mechanisms; as blocking shows, theatre has developed, and scaled up, its own highly efficient methods of managing space, time, and material resources, sometimes in advance of the wider economy, for profit or not. These mechanisms also call into question some of the ways that the relationship between theatre and the market might be understood. On the one hand, blocking and its notation demonstrate the extent to which virtues commonly attributed to the theatre – its artistry, its ephemerality, its uniqueness, and so on – are inextricable from the routines, systems, and technologies upon which any production process depends. Indeed, the pleasures of theatre, whether from the position of its creators or its spectators, are derived as much from the latter as the former, since they demonstrate the reassuring industriousness of theatre when theatre has often been viewed otherwise (whether affirmatively by its partisans or, as we will see in the next chapter, with some circumspection by its sceptics). At the same time, spatial techniques that abstract the work from the worker, with all the potential for both ingenuity and exploitation that can entail, are also a precondition for forms of theatrical production – from touring shows to 'McTheatre' – that are often treated with suspicion by theatre critics (if less so by audiences) and which take theatrical production firmly into the realm of the market. As the economic geography of its production shows, theatre has not had to look elsewhere to learn how to be industrious. For better or worse – or better *and* worse – it has been very good at it, for a very long time.

CHAPTER 2

Productivity

> Productivity isn't everything, but in the long run it is almost everything.
>
> Paul Krugman, *The Age of Diminished Expectations*[1]

Shortly after the Royal Festival Hall opened on London's South Bank in 1951, a civil servant attended a symphony concert. The following report subsequently appeared in the Ministry of Transportation *Bulletin*:

> For considerable periods the four oboe players had nothing to do. The number should be reduced, and the work spread more evenly over the whole of the concert, thus eliminating peaks of activity. All the twelve first violins were playing identical notes. This seems unnecessary duplication. The staff of this section should be drastically cut; if a larger volume of sound is required, it could be obtained by means of electronic amplifier apparatus. Much effort was absorbed in the playing of demi-semi-quavers. This seems an excessive refinement. It is recommended that all notes should be rounded up to the nearest semiquaver. If this were done, it would be possible to use trainees and lower grade operatives more extensively. There seems to be too much repetition of some musical passages. Scores should be drastically pruned. No useful purpose is served by repeating on the horns a passage which has already been handled by the strings. It is estimated that if all redundant passages were eliminated, the whole concert time of 2 hours could be reduced to 20 minutes, and there would be no need for an interval. The Conductor agrees generally with these recommendations, but expresses the opinion that there might be some falling-off in box-office receipts. In that unlikely event it should be possible to close sections of the auditorium entirely, with a consequential saving of overhead expense – lighting, attendance, etc. If the worst came to the worse, the whole thing could be abandoned, and the public could go the Albert Hall instead.[2]

The report was soon reprinted, under the title, 'Cuts by the Score', in a 1952 issue of *O & M Bulletin*, the in-house organisational management journal of the British civil service (among such alluringly-titled articles as 'Office

Equipment News' and 'Government in Belgium – Part 1'). An edited and excerpted version was published in *Harper's Magazine* in 1955 under the title 'How to Be Efficient with Fewer Violins'. Although *Harper's* made minor modifications to the text (presumably to conform to their house style), their main amendment was to insert a prefacing sentence – not in the original – that read: 'The following is a report of a Work Study Engineer after a visit to a symphony concert at the Royal Festival Hall in London.' The report was then reprinted, in its entirety but carrying the *Harper's* title and prefacing sentence, in the *Bulletin of the American Association of University Professors* that same year. Finally, in 1966, William J. Baumol and William G. Bowen reproduced the text from the AAUP *Bulletin* in a footnote in one of the key chapters of their landmark study (and arguably the first major work of cultural economics), *Performing Arts: The Economic Dilemma.*[3]

Clearly, the report was initially an in-joke among bureaucrats. At the time of its publication, the British welfare state was trying to adopt new, 'scientific', tools of public administration and industrial management. The post-war Labour government had nationalised large sectors of the British economy, including coal, steel, railways, gas and electricity, as well as created the National Health Service, the universal, publicly-run health system that has remained one of the main preoccupations of life in the United Kingdom ever since. Monumental arts venues, like the Royal Festival Hall and the rest of the planned South Bank development, were part of the wholesale remaking of London's urban fabric, undertaken according to the designs of the 1943 *County of London Plan*. The *Plan* was the first attempt to shape, comprehensively, the built environment of the country's largest metropolis, and the subsequent construction of a series of large arts venues along the southern reach of the River Thames was a sign of the extent to which culture was now caught up with new forms of urban and economic governance. Such radical transformations also demanded that the British state acquire, and then seek to apply, all manner of specialist expertise in the interests of pursuing rational economic, spatial, and cultural management.

Seen in this context, then, it is not entirely surprising that 'Cuts by the Score' could be read in different ways. It was, of course, a wry disparagement of the ascendant cadre of technical experts then joining the civil service, on behalf of the legions of gentleman generalists who had dominated British government and industry since the nineteenth century (the ultimate giveaway is what American publications removed when they cited the report: that it was originally signed 'S. Tone-Deaf').[4] But removed from its original context, and given a different title and author, who practices the newly invented profession of 'Work Study Engineer', the report also reads all too plausibly as evidence of the scientific management *ad absurdum* that was spreading rapidly throughout capitalist countries following the War. 'Cuts by the Score' appeared both nostalgic and prescient.

I highlight this report not to smirk at its seeming eccentricity but rather to observe that, whether a tongue-in-cheek provocation on behalf of an older way of governing or an illustration of an ascendant technocracy, 'Cuts by the Score', and its intriguing citational genealogy, are symptomatic of a much broader and older scepticism about the possibility of live performance ever being economically productive. S. Tone-Deaf puts an intriguing spatial spin on an old economic problem: the folly of trying to submit live performance to an efficiency calculus is only magnified by the monumental arts venue that appears to be the spatial correlate of that suspect economism. Yet there would be no reason to write this missive if the possibility of live performance being subsumed within the ascendant logic of productivity were not real, with the attendant prospect that a development such as the South Bank might help bring it about. Indeed, Baumol and Bowen's treatise is evidence, fifteen years later, that applying a productivity calculus to live performance is entirely possible, even if the results of doing so are not wholly satisfying. And the South Bank did eventually begin to realise its productive potential, albeit much later, and in unexpected ways. However absurd S. Tone-Deaf finds the possibility of such a productive performance, he (for it was almost certainly a he) prefigures it nonetheless.

Productivity – what it is, how to measure it, and how to improve it – is a complex problem that preoccupies many who think about how market economies work. When a centre-left economist like Paul Krugman comments, 'Productivity isn't everything, but in the long run it is almost everything', he illustrates how central the issue is to modern economic thought, and that it is not fixed to a single point on the political spectrum (conservatives and progressives alike have historically been worried about productivity, albeit for very different reasons).[5] Put simply, productivity normally refers to the ratio of input costs or resources (e.g., wages, materials, utilities, taxes) to outputs produced (usually per hour worked). One of the reasons that economists and policy makers have been so preoccupied with it is that rates of productivity growth in a number of advanced capitalist economies have, on average, been slowing for many years. In the UK, for example, there has been long-term stagnation in productivity since the early 1970s, with the period since the economic slump in 2008 being especially poor. The Office for National Statistics reported in 2017 that 'the UK's post-downturn productivity performance has been among the slowest decades of productivity growth since official records began' in 1770.[6] Although London remains the UK's most productive region, its productivity growth stopped in 2007 and, in fact, London has lagged behind the rest of the UK since. As the economics think-tank Resolution Foundation observed in 2018, 'Far from ameliorating the UK's poor productivity growth, London has been a significant drag on productivity' since the 2008 financial crisis.[7] London's reliance on financial services has made the problem worse, as productivity growth in the sector collapsed after 2008. Since then, the largest driver of economic growth in London has been real estate.[8] The picture has become even more uncertain because of the UK's departure from the European Union, whose member states have supplied London's hospitality sector with a sizeable portion of its workforce, and whose financial services 'passport' has allowed the UK's banking sector to operate freely across Europe. (This is one of the reasons London became such a large financial centre – international banks could set up shop in London and then, because of the passport, trade throughout the EU without having to establish national bases in other member states.)

In addition to this concern with productivity writ large, there are long-standing doubts about the productivity of live performance in particular. Seen through the lens of classical economic thought, theatre is inefficient because of its reliance on labour that is, by its nature, unproductive. In Adam Smith's way of thinking, the services that theatrical labour creates are largely ephemeral, and so cannot be wholly commodified and exchanged for profit.[9] Modern cultural economics, in turn, stresses the difficulties of reducing labour costs when the artistic good produced is inseparable from the artistic worker producing it, and when the good being produced can only be re-engineered to a limited degree (one can only cross-cast a performance so far or cut its running time so much before it ceases to be recognisable). Thus it is difficult for live performance industries to realise productivity gains at the same rate as the wider economy, making them especially susceptible to what is known in economics as the 'cost disease' (or 'Baumol's cost disease', after its principal theorist).[10]

These theoretical accounts sit alongside my own experience of theatre-going in London in recent years. By the early 1990s many London theatres – in common with theatres around the country – were in poor repair, having been starved of capital investment for years. But this started to change in the late 1990s, and especially during the first decade of the 2000s, as an influx of money from the recently created National Lottery began to be invested in the refurbishment and construction of theatre venues across the city. (National Lottery funding for the arts has largely been directed towards capital and one-off projects and is, in effect, a way of spending public money on 'good causes' without the national Treasury having to pay for it directly.) Put simply, London's theatre buildings – modest and grand – got a lot smarter and better equipped. At the same time, there was notable growth in theatre happening outside these venues, in places that had never been used for it (and which usually would be used for something else after a show's run had ended). In 2008, theatre reviewer Andrew Haydon jokingly predicted that '[s]oon every theatre will be putting on performances in underground car parks and office spaces and using the main stages for storage'.[11] While producing work outside conventional theatre venues was hardly novel in the UK, what was new – at least in London – was the extent to which this work involved co-productions between small and large arts organisations (such as High Tide and the Old Vic, Punchdrunk, Shunt and the National Theatre, and Blast Theory and the Barbican Centre). And all of these spatial transformations, monumental and modest, depended on London theatre's increasingly integrated position within an ever-shifting landscape of leisure industries, quangos, consultants, government departments, finance companies, and property developers. London theatre's productive infrastructure was more capacious and more extensive – theatrically, politically, and economically – than it had been before.

Yet many of these places of performance promised more infrastructurally than they delivered theatrically. This does not mean that London theatres produced more shows that I found disappointing. Rather, it means that a notable number of performances in some way failed to mobilise fully the infrastructure available to them (even when, as in many 'site-specific' performances, they sought to do precisely that). An infrastructural gap seemed to have opened up between the material resources available and the performances these resources were actually used to produce. In my experience, this gap was often most apparent in venues that insisted emphatically on their spatial uniqueness – I often felt it most acutely in the National Theatre, on the one hand, and in London's recent wave of 'site-specific' performances, on the other.

It is no accident that such accounts of live performance's productivity ultimately find it wanting. Smith, Baumol and Bowen, and S. Tone-Deaf may have markedly different takes on the productivity problem, but they all view it through the lens of live performance's labour process. Seen this way, the problem becomes intractable: performance cannot help but either be inefficient (inherently) or become inefficient (comparatively). My own account of theatrical productivity is also based on a faulty premise: it assumes that the productivity of performance will be realised most fully onstage. But there is no reason why this should necessarily be the case – it could be manifested elsewhere within the theatre or outside the theatre entirely (or some combination of both). The South Bank, today, brings these accounts of productivity come up short. It demonstrates that they measure live performance's inputs too narrowly and, in my own case, mislocate its outputs – taken together, they look at the wrong things in the wrong place. But if we observe performance through its socio-spatial infrastructure rather than its labour process, today's South Bank begins to look rather more productive. These productivity gains have, however, been urban and economic as much as, and possibly more than, they have been theatrical.

In this chapter, I explore the South Bank's productivity. Becoming productive, though, has taken much longer than was ever intended, and a much more extensive urban and political-economic intervention than initially envisaged. The outcome is also not necessarily the one that the South Bank's many creators, over decades, ever anticipated. I examine two adjacent but very different sites in the South Bank's core: the collection of monumental arts centres clustered along the river – especially the National Theatre – and the tunnels (more recently called the vaults) under Waterloo Station that have more recently been refashioned as a venue for short-term theatrical performances, live art events, and club nights.[12] While the South Bank has for decades been defined by its massive, purpose-built vestiges of Britain's welfare state, since 2009 it has been supplemented by a venue only partly repurposed from its former use as a store for railway equipment. The Waterloo tunnels have, in some ways, become the local, 'pop-up' counterpart to the monumental national arts centres that have historically been synonymous with culture on the South Bank.

The connection between these two South Bank sites is apparent in their geographical proximity, to be sure, but also because they constitute different, yet complementary, forms of fixed capital within London's urban economy. A monumental, purpose-built theatre building like that of the National Theatre and a repurposed venue such as the Waterloo tunnels pose radically different sorts of challenges artistically, but, in recent years, they have become coins of the same theatrical currency, each capable of being invested productively in London's increasingly financialised and real estate-driven economy. The monumental South Bank now trades on the massive built form of its welfare state cultural institutions – a built form, ironically, that was originally seen as hostile and alien. And the Waterloo tunnels illustrate how contemporary London theatre might mobilise the social form of performance events, encouraging participants to 'feel productive' in a city where that experience is less and less available to them (even when, as is sometimes the case, this comes at the expense of the show itself). Put simply, then, contemporary London theatre has salved its own productivity worries by spatialising them. And the South Bank suggests that London's productivity problems might in turn be solved, even if only temporarily, by theatricalising them.

Performance and Productivity

Leaving aside the doubtful veracity of overtly ideological anxieties about the economic characteristics of art, the persistent unease about artistic productivity is not wholly surprising. A division between productive and unproductive labour is deeply embedded in classical economic thought and arguably still inflects much popular discourse about art and artists. Adam Smith draws this distinction sharply in *Wealth of Nations*: 'There is one sort of labour which adds to the value of the subject upon which it is bestowed: There is another which has no such effect. The former, as it produces a value, may be called productive; the latter, unproductive labour.'[13] For Smith, labour is productive when it produces capital, by creating commodities, exchanging them, and turning a profit. Use value is irrelevant; while goods or services created through labour may have value to those who perform or benefit from them, these are unproductive unless they generate capital.

One might suggest that, according to Smith's definition, many forms of artistic creation involve productive labour. For example, the commercial theatre aims to generate profits for its owners, and its workforce – actors, directors, technicians, writers, and so on – is employed in order to achieve that objective. But Smith explicitly disallows the possibility of theatrical labour being productive, even under profit-seeking conditions, on the grounds that the service being consumed in live performance is too evanescent to be considered a commodity and thus is unable to assist the process of exchange that creates wealth. For Smith, the actor, like the 'menial servant', offers services that 'generally perish in the very instant of their performance, and seldom leave any trace or value behind them, for which an equal quantity of service could afterwards be procured'.[14] It follows, then, that unproductive labour, whether honourable or base, is ultimately parasitic and indolent (in this discussion we can see, in sharp relief, the deep comingling of the economic and moral realms that characterises much of Smith's thinking, here and in other writings). Labourers may undertake the 'gravest and most important' vocations ('churchmen, lawyers, physicians, or men of letters') or practice 'some of the most frivolous professions' ('players, buffoons, musicians, opera-singers, opera-dancers, &c'.), but they are, nonetheless, 'maintained by a part of the annual produce of the industry of other people'.[15] Smith argues that every country's wealth is determined by the proportion of economic activity characterised by 'industry' (productive labour, or 'capital') as opposed to 'idleness' (unproductive labour, or 'revenue'). Where the former predominates, a country grows wealthy. Where the latter prevails, a country becomes poor. Live performance, which depends on frivolous and unproductive labour, ultimately undermines the wealth of the nation.

Of course, Smith's line of argument relies on a very narrow understanding of productivity – one which, today, even the staunchest advocates for free markets would find excessively constrictive. It also employs a conceptual binary that underplays the complex forms that economic activity may take and the myriad ways that value may be produced (neatly slotting labour into productive and unproductive categories achieves a kind of clarity but this comes at the expense of considerable empirical and interpretive nuance). As a way to think about the economy, though, it has proven remarkably durable, especially during periods of economic strain: witness the deployment of 'strivers versus skivers' rhetoric to justify huge cuts to social programmes in the UK following the election of the Conservative-Liberal Democrat coalition government in 2010 (such rhetoric is not restricted to the Right, since a leading Labour politician proclaimed in 2012 that his party was for 'workers' not 'shirkers').[16] Hoary exhortations for artists to 'do something productive instead' are manifestations of the same logic.

While it is important to resist such lazy moralising, it should also be recognised that live performance nonetheless has an ambivalent relationship with productivity. This is due to the particular economic character of performance industries themselves, which Baumol and Bowen argue are characterised by an 'income gap'.[17] In a move that may seem counterintuitive to scholars of the arts – who often assume, a priori, the exceptionality of their objects of study – Baumol and Bowen argue that the performing arts should be considered as forms of economic activity like any others:

> Here it is helpful to treat the arts, not as an intangible manifestation of the human spirit, but as a productive activity which provides services to the community; one which, in this respect, does not differ from the manufacture of electricity or the supply of transportation or house-cleaning services. In each case labor and equipment are utilized to make available goods or

> services which may be purchased by the general public. In each case there is a technology whereby these inputs are transformed into a finished product.[18]

For Baumol and Bowen, the problem is not that the performing arts are economic or that they coalesce into industries. The problem is why, as industries, the performing arts do not function like most industries do. By placing them in the context of activities that share many of the same features, they suggest, it is possible to determine (or at least achieve a better account of) their economic distinctiveness.

Baumol and Bowen argue that live performance industries are especially susceptible to what has come to be known as the *cost disease*. Today, economists discuss the cost disease primarily in relation to service industries, such as health care and social services, which depend heavily on human labour (Baumol himself was a leading health economist). But it is worth recalling that Baumol and Bowen first developed this theory in *Performing Arts: The Economic Dilemma*. This study undertook the first major analysis of the economics of theatre, dance, opera, and live music in the English language (and it is important to note that Baumol and Bowen restrict their focus to *live* performance – the cost disease does not arise so acutely, if at all, in art forms involving the production of objects that circulate independently of their creators, such as with cinema or many forms of visual art).

The cost disease arises because of the difficulty for live performance industries to realise productivity gains at the same rate as the broader economy, due to fixed costs that inhere within live performance itself. When a product (say, a theatre performance) and the worker who produces it (an actor) are inseparable, the scope for the firm (the producer or company) to either decrease the cost or increase the output per unit of labour is limited.[19] After all, most actors' wages in the theatre are already low, one can only double-cast a production so far, and any efficiency gains achieved by performing faster threaten to render a performance nonsensical. As Baumol and Bowen put it:

> The characteristic of live performance which precludes substantial changes in its mode of operation is that the work of the performer is an end in itself, not a means for the production of some good. ... The performers' labors themselves constitute the end product which the audience purchases. ... The immediate result of this technological difference between live performance and the typical manufacturing industry is that while productivity is very much to subject to change in the latter, it is relatively immutable in the former. Whereas the amount of labor necessary to produce a typical manufactured product has constantly declined since the beginning of the

> industrial revolution, it requires about as many minutes for Richard II to tell his 'sad stories of the of the death of kings' as it did on the stage of the Globe Theatre. Human ingenuity has devised ways to reduce the labor necessary to produce an automobile, but no one has yet succeeded in decreasing the human effort expended at a live performance of a 45 minute Schubert quartet much below a total of three man-hours.[20]

To be clear, Baumol and Bowen do not claim that 'increased efficiency or innovation is totally impossible for the arts or that increases in productivity per man-hour are completely precluded'.[21] Anyone working in theatre is familiar with the constant drive to keep costs low, and 'self-subsidy' is rife within the arts generally. But this can only go so far and, comparatively,

> the arts cannot hope to match the remarkable record of productivity growth achieved by the economy as a whole. Moreover, the performing arts find themselves in this position largely as a result of their inherent technology – something which is out of the hands of their managements and beyond the reach of the efficiency expert.[22]

Over time, this productivity gap is likely to widen to the point where 'market failure' occurs and the live performance becomes economically unsustainable without some form of public subsidy. As a result, it looks increasingly anachronistic within a market economy, especially in a historical moment (like now) where private industry is lionised and public expenditure is usually looked upon with great suspicion (insofar as it bears the taint of social welfare – insofar as it is corporate welfare, that is quite another matter). In this context, the fact that performance does not seem very productive becomes an especially acute problem.

Although it is a canonical text of cultural economics, Baumol and Bowen's work has received minimal attention in theatre research until recently, but it is the cost disease that has resonated most with theatre scholars. (This is not entirely surprising; *Performing Arts: The Economic Dilemma* is a book written by economists for economists, and whatever its merits, the relatively short section of the book on the cost disease is more accessible to non-specialists than, say, the statistical data that informs the bulk of the authors' analysis). Hillary Miller and Jenny Hughes both use the cost disease to help explain how crises in theatrical financing play out in relation to broader political-economic turmoil (in Miller's case, in 1970s New York, and in Hughes's, in 1980s London).[23] These judicious applications of Baumol and Bowen should not, however, distract from some of the potential pitfalls of recuperating their work for the present day. First, there is a risk of treating the cost disease as more of an existential problem than

Baumol and Bowen think it is – they argue that the cost disease can be addressed fairly straightforwardly through public subsidy of the arts, which effectively redirects a minuscule portion of the proceeds attained through productivity gains elsewhere in the economy towards a sector whose existence is nonetheless of social value. There is also the potential of abstracting the theory too far from the empirical research base underpinning it, since the live performance industries Baumol and Bowen (exhaustively) analysed in the 1960s no longer exist in those forms and, as Derek Miller points out in relation to Broadway, theatre producers have been able to find efficiencies to a greater extent than is sometimes recognised. For example, Miller suggests that cross-casting has resulted in more widespread efficiency gains than are commonly credited, and notes that the rise of the 'triple threat' performer – actor, dancer, and singer in one – is an important economic as well as artistic innovation.[24] Finally, it is all too easy for the cost disease to justify lapsing into an overly narrow calculus of theatrical productivity, with the consequence of overlooking forms of productivity that might be occurring elsewhere.

If the labour technologies of live performance are problematic in relation to productivity, its spatial technologies are not, though, at least not in this particular historical moment. Insofar as the productivity of live performance is a legitimate concern (or, at least, enough of a recurring preoccupation that it bears further examination) performance sites have become places to address it. In the first instance, the monumental South Bank – with the National Theatre as its pre-eminent cultural institution – has become (perhaps surprisingly) a way to mitigate long-standing concerns about the urban economy of the southern reach of the Thames. In the second, the Waterloo tunnels have illustrated how agglomeration might be not only an industrial characteristic of live performance but also an experiential benefit of it. Taken together, these two sites not only 'solve' a problem of theatrical productivity that would otherwise appear endemic; they spatially transform theatre into an exemplary, productive agent within London's urban economy.

The South Bank and the Promise of Productivity

London's South Bank stretches for approximately three kilometres along the southern side of the River Thames between County Hall to the west and Blackfriars Bridge to the east. (These boundaries are not hard and fast, since some would extend the South Bank's eastern boundary to London Bridge, and the section between Blackfriars and Southwark bridges has also been called Bankside.) It straddles the border between the boroughs of Lambeth and Southwark and is most notable today for the collection of iconic arts venues built along the river after the Second World War: Royal Festival Hall (which opened in 1951), the National Film Theatre (1957), the Queen Elizabeth Hall (1967), the Hayward Gallery (1968), and the National Theatre (1976).[25]

These were joined later by the reconstructed Globe Theatre (1997) and Tate Modern, the modern art museum constructed within the shell of the then disused Bankside Power Station (2000). The Young Vic Theatre, which reopened after major renovations in 2006, is located nearby on The Cut, as is the Old Vic. Alongside these arts venues, there has been significant growth in other entertainment industries (particularly in film, television, and advertising).[26] Since the early 2000s, the South Bank has also become an increasingly popular tourist destination, with shops, restaurants, and hotels opening to cater to the millions of people who visit the area each year.

The South Bank, in its form recognisable today, arguably entered the realm of London's urban governance in 1943. This can be seen in a seemingly minor, but in actuality enormously significant, instance: the outline of a theatre building on the south bank of the Thames on planning maps contained within the 1943 *County of London Plan* (where Royal Festival Hall is now located).[27] The *County Plan* was commissioned by the County of London, the metropolitan level of government responsible for overseeing the area now usually referred to as 'inner' London, at the bequest of the national Ministry of Works (a *Greater London Plan*, which addressed surrounding areas, followed a year later).[28] It attempted to imagine the new London that would emerge from post-war reconstruction, explicitly positioning itself as the spatial counterpart to William Beveridge's recently published proposals on social security: 'Sir William Beveridge has talked of giants in the path of social security. There are giants too in the path of city planning'.[29] German bombing had destroyed many of the buildings on the southern bank of the Thames, and so the authors proposed 'a great cultural centre, embracing, amongst other features, a modern theatre, a large concert hall and the headquarters of various organisations' as part of their plans for the spatial transformation of central and south London.[30] That there was historical precedence for a cultural district in south London chimed with their aspirations, which were to resuscitate both the arts and the city through urban planning:

> In earlier times the south bank [*sic*], with its Globe Theatre, Paris Garden, and its other centres of attraction, was a vital and popular district of

> London. There is little reason why it should not recapture some of its former lively spirit. The scheme we have prepared should provide the necessary impetus.[31]

The *County Plan* includes a picturesque illustration of the South Bank from 1647 placed next to photographs of the same, bomb-damaged, area in 1943, and invites the reader to imagine that the new scheme would restore the South Bank to its former glory as a 'popular entertainment centre of London'.[32] Of course, this rewrites the theatrical and urban history of south London. At the time of the original Globe, the area south of the Thames was outside London proper, and, though 'vital and popular', it hardly conformed to modern planners' desires to integrate the area into central London (if anything, the area's 'lively spirit' in the late sixteenth and early seventeenth centuries depended on its exclusion from London, rather than any contiguity with the city). And the planners elided what was perhaps the area's most vibrant period as an entertainment district – from the late eighteenth century (beginning in Southwark) through the nineteenth century, when Lambeth was the home of a network of large theatres and music halls that provided entertainment for thousands of spectators each night.[33] But this omission signalled that the way of understanding the relationship between the arts and the city had now reversed. By the middle of the twentieth century, cultural industries were no longer seen as problems for the urban governance of south London (as they had been at different times in the nineteenth century).[34] Moreover, the delineation of a theatre on the maps within the *County Plan* signalled that cultural venue-building was no longer just a long-standing rhetorical ambition, it was now integrated into the fine-grained planning of the city (even if the National Theatre wound up being the last venue built on the South Bank, to the east of Waterloo Bridge).

Realising the aims of arts advocates and urban planners, however, required the creation of a governance apparatus that could coordinate intensive state investment in the built environment. This, in turn, brought the arts more firmly within the ambit of modern political-economic governance, and it made possible the construction of arts venues in the United Kingdom in a way that was previously unachievable. When Beveridge demanded that the national state take responsibility for the economic and social security of the United Kingdom, he not only called for the creation of individual enterprises such as the National Health Service and increased state intervention in national economic management, he and his political allies offered a rationale for a new model of political-economic governance.[35] Beveridge (along with allies like the Fabian Society and elements within all major political parties) reconceived the political, economic, and cultural spheres in which the British state could legitimately intervene and for which it should claim ultimate responsibility. This most directly involved the commanding heights of industry and social welfare, but it rapidly extended to other realms, like the arts, that appeared to share the ethos of social citizenship that the British welfare state would attempt to cultivate and for which it aimed to serve as guarantor ('social citizenship' should be understood here in the sense of T. H. Marshall's classic left-liberal formulation, in which he argues that a full sense of citizenship can only be realised once the state augments its historical concern for civil and political rights with the economic right to 'live the life of a civilized being according to the prevailing standards of society').[36] Expanding the role of the national state also necessitated the development of a governance apparatus that could actually implement the welfare state agenda and broker agreements with civil society organisations to finance and coordinate the delivery of public goods in the most efficient manner possible. It is in this light that the creation of the Arts Council of Great Britain in 1946 can be seen, as an agent and instrument of governance that could help coordinate relations between the national and local state, arts organisations, charities, and more. That the first chairman of the Arts Council was Keynes, who had led the British delegation at Bretton Woods in 1944 as well as provided much of the economic rationale for Beveridge and the post-war Labour government's programme, only emphasised the degree to which the arts had become part of the political-economic governance of the United Kingdom. As Clive Gray puts it, these changes 'depended not so much upon conditions within the arts world itself as it did upon changed conceptions of the role of the state and the management of the resources of society'.[37] The arts – and the monumental cultural-venue building programme undertaken on their behalf – were deeply implicated in establishing and extending welfare state governance, in both urban and political spheres, and public investment in them elaborated the logic of efficient investment that underpinned the welfare state.

Seen together, it is remarkable how much the buildings comprising the South Bank scheme articulate, through their built form, the ascendency of the British welfare state and the role of the arts and the state in spatially securing it. They testify to a compact between the state and civil society and give physical form to a public good that this compact sought to promote. Their scale – these are large buildings that cost a great deal to build – illustrates the state's newly developed fiscal capacity and its will to demonstrate it. They show the utility of the scientific planning techniques through which public spending was coordinated. And they spatially cultivate national and artistic prestige through their location and monumental architecture. (Their importance is signalled by their proximity to landmarks of church, state, and commerce across the river: the houses of Parliament, St. Paul's Cathedral, and the City of London.) The monumental South Bank spatially legitimised the economic logic of the welfare state, along with the technical apparatus necessary to achieve it.

Yet it could still be argued that the South Bank remained stubbornly unproductive, at least from the perspective of the built form and orientation of its cultural venues. The scheme treated the bomb-damaged riverside as *terra nullis*, as an urban test case of modern planning doctrines. Realising planning aims such as separation of use (where residential, industrial, and commercial areas are segregated to greater and lesser degrees) required the displacement of remaining industries along the Thames and a more sharply differentiated relationship between the South Bank and surrounding residential areas.[38] This provoked conflict from the start: the South Bank's 1951 development plan drew more than five thousand objections, many from businesses still operating in the area, that balked at the wholesale appropriation of such a large part of the riverside. But the London County Council (LCC) held firm: its view was that the South Bank should no longer be treated as part of south London but instead should be integrated into the cultural and commercial area across the river. In response to an objection to the planned expropriation and demolition of a modern wharf building used for waterside commerce, the LCC responded curtly: 'South Bank area proposed as southward extension of central area of London. This part of area suitable for public buildings and cultural purposes – logical extension of the area between County Hall and Waterloo Bridge.'[39] Later, in the 1980s, there was enormous resistance to the dominance of commercial interests and cultural industries on the South Bank, as the Greater London Council (the LCC's successor), the boroughs of Lambeth and Southwark, and residents' groups fought to maintain some measure of residential housing in the area.[40]

The style of many of the South Bank's cultural venues has also been attacked. Prince Charles, no fan of modernist architecture, infamously commented that the Denys Lasdun–designed National Theatre (now a Grade II* listed building) was 'a clever way of building a nuclear power station in the middle of London without anyone objecting'.[41] This antagonism was only amplified by the development's orientation towards the river, since the South Bank's arts venues present their public faces north:

the main entrance to the National Theatre is from the riverbank; the south side of the building is clad in plan brick instead of the dramatically sculpted concrete that faces the river; and the theatre's electronic billboard, which announces current productions, is best seen from the other side of the Thames. This orientation made the South Bank venues appear as though they had, almost wilfully, shunned their immediate neighbours (such as the working-class residents of Elephant and Castle, which itself experienced a highly contentious programme of post-war reconstruction). As Marvin Carlson observes, 'The South Bank was a bold scheme to reclaim some of the river', but it came 'at the cost of ignoring the blighted areas further to the south, on which the present complex resolutely turns its back.'[42] For much of its existence, then, the South Bank scheme has been a source of recurring conflict between nearby residents, London borough governments, urban planners, social commentators, and the national state.[43] Indeed, 'fixing' the monumental South Bank's problems has been a preoccupation of many, almost from the construction of its first building – partly for artistic reasons, but even more to realise the urban and political-economic aspirations that motivated its construction in the first place.

Monumental Productivity

Now, the political-economic picture is entirely different from what it was at the time of the monumental South Bank's conception, and the way we tend to think about the role of cultural districts within cities has changed as well – for better and worse. Much current thinking about the relationship between cultural districts and cities focuses on the extent to which arts practices and environments are both symptoms of and agents within a contemporary, globalising urban economy.[44] This implies that cultural districts play a role in positing London as a cutting-edge creative city that competes with other 'global' cities in a world of ostensibly free-flowing capital. That the monumental South Bank is still caught up with changing forms of urban governance is hard to dispute, but its role today is a much more sympathetic one than in the past.

It is undoubtedly the case that the monumental South Bank has in recent years been caught up with London's shift towards, as cultural economist Alan J. Scott puts it, a 'cognitive-cultural economy' that 'is being driven forward by key sectors like technology-intensive manufacturing, services of all varieties (business, financial, personal, etc.), fashion-oriented neo-artisanal production, and cultural-products industries'.[45] As these activities tend to be concentrated in particular urban zones, cultural districts, including the South Bank, have proven effective in undertaking the 'place-making' that increasingly marks the competition between cities under global capitalism (though 'new economy' rhetoric should not obscure the extent to which cultural districts such as the South Bank are today's urban, service sector, and middle-class analogues to older 'enterprise zones' periodically advocated by the Right – like enterprise zones, they are populated by tax-sheltered industries in which employment is precarious and low wages are endemic, albeit largely for the White children of the bourgeoisie rather than the racialised working class). Susan Bennett also argues persuasively that the South Bank has become a kind of contemporary 'tourist stage', in which 'places, cities, regions, and countries in the tourism context are all composed as performances so that they might attract visitors' spectatorship, increasingly a lucrative part of the economy, and, in very many cases, a primary engine for employment'.[46] Since the Globe and Tate Modern opened, the South Bank has seen a marked increase in visitor numbers and, as Bennett observes,

> now boasts the extended trappings of a tourism economy: five hotels, clusters of restaurants (including the Globe's own popular eating venue), retail and service stores, as well as the Millennium Bridge, the city's first new pedestrian bridge across the Thames in more than a century, linking the South Bank back to the City of London (and another premier tourist destination, St. Paul's Cathedral).[47]

The efficacy of this performance (which, as Bennett highlights, is as much an urban and economic one as it is a theatrical one) hinges on the South Bank's position within a dense web of governing relations encompassing a large number of institutions: multiple departments within the national state, the Greater London Authority, the Mayor of London, Lambeth and Southwark councils (although local authorities are less important than in the past), urban planners, the Southbank Centre, individual arts organisations, global corporations, local and national businesses, media companies, and more.[48] These networks contribute, in turn, to ongoing efforts to maintain London's position as a global city and secure its pre-eminence as the world's leading centre of finance industry (in spite of the particularly severe effects of the financial crisis in the UK, owing to London's large and politically influential finance sector).[49]

The South Bank, though, is very much a legacy of welfare state cultural and urban planning, and this history does not simply disappear with its integration into the operations of neo-corporatist capitalism (and its associated forms of production, consumption, and governance). In fact, the South Bank's productive potential today depends on the reanimation of the welfare state governance apparatus that shepherded the original scheme into existence, and the rehabilitation of the built forms that exemplified that older political-economic regime. As criminologist Mariana Valverde points out, each new mode of governing tends to position itself as a revolution from the mode that came before. Nonetheless, she argues, contemporary modes of urban governance rely significantly on 'techniques' adopted from past governance regimes that they have ostensibly supplanted, deploying a continually shifting array of governing practices, both new and old.[50] But if Valverde is primarily concerned with legal techniques and forms, there is no reason why these techniques cannot be architectonic as well. London's prominence among major financial centres has involved the rehabilitation and redeployment of the South Bank's welfare state legacy – and especially the built form it takes – to serve contemporary political and economic ends. While the South Bank has become increasingly popular in recent years, this is, in part, because its current iteration salves long-standing anxieties about the welfare state urban and cultural planning apparatus that was installed in the UK in the 1940s and elaborated over subsequent decades (recall that when S. Tone-Deaf expressed his distaste for Royal Festival Hall, it was not only the building that displeased him but the political-economic system that produced it). The South Bank was an instance of that apparatus but never central to it, with the result that it was widely seen as a failure in urban planning terms and too exclusive in artistic terms. Its monumentality has also been treated with some scepticism – and occasionally outright hostility – by popular and academic commentators alike.

The current success of the South Bank hinges, then, on a rehabilitation of this welfare state legacy through the district's integration into transnational forms of consumption and production, which, crucially, are supported by neo-corporatist forms of urban governance. The South Bank also provides a repository of spatial and planning tools, conceived by and for the welfare state, that are being redeployed within contemporary urban governance networks that seek to secure London's position as a leading centre of finance capital. Today, the South Bank is an integral part of London's urban and economic life, nearly seventy years after it first emerged (and whether its cultural institutions are too exclusive is far less of a concern now than in the past, since cultural exclusivity is a key selling point for London today). Ironically, though, this has been achieved by mobilising the built form and technocratic inheritance of the welfare state itself, which the South Bank's arts venues, individually and collectively, embody on a monumental scale. This monumentality, which seemed by the 1980s to symbolise all that had gone wrong with post-war urban, cultural, and economic planning, has become something much more amenable with the passage of time. The South Bank now exemplifies how productive cultural districts can be within urban economies, and it demonstrates that this does not entail a wholesale repudiation of the welfare state that 'neoliberalism' seeks to supplant. Rather, it involves a more extensive application of the welfare state's spatial legacy, albeit in better ways to serve different ends.

Whereas the efficacy of the monumental South Bank's urban performance was once compromised by its association – politically, economically, spatially, and artistically – with the welfare state, it now hinges on the rehabilitation and redeployment of welfarist built forms. The architecture of the monumental South Bank's arts venues is especially important here. Although each has its own design, most of the cultural venues share a brutalist architectural vernacular that was commonly employed for public arts buildings in many countries following the Second World War (the exception here is Royal Festival Hall, which draws more on the sleeker International Style than on rough-hewn brutalism). In the UK, brutalism is almost exclusively associated with the public sector, placing the South Bank's arts venues within a repertoire of public infrastructure built between the 1960s and 1980s that includes social housing, government buildings, and educational institutions. The architectural design of these buildings, executed in poured concrete, emphasises rectilinear forms and mass (the English term 'brutalism' is commonly thought to derive from the French *béton brut*, or 'raw concrete'). The South Bank's monumental venues are serious and substantial, and their almost obdurate built form suggests the possibility of resisting – or at least slowing – the passage of time and the speed of social change in a city where both often seem disorienting and frequently threatening.

After a long period during which they were widely disdained, the South Bank's arts venues have eventually come more into fashion. This is partly due to changing popular tastes (brutalist architecture has come back into vogue to some degree in the UK) and it undoubtedly has a great deal to do with judicious renovation (of which there has been plenty). But it is also because, spatially, they perform an important palliative function within a city that otherwise prioritises the pursuit of finance capital. The National Theatre, the most elegantly realised design among the South Bank's arts centres, is exemplary in this regard. When the National Theatre opened in

1976, commentators not only assailed its design; they worried that its architecture expressed the widely-perceived political and economic decline of Britain as a whole. One American observer commented that the new National Theatre was a 'fortress theater' that seemed like 'the last glory of a troubled Britain'.[51] Indeed, it is easy to see how the new building could seem out of step with Britain in the mid-1970s, not only because of its design aesthetics but because of its architecture's political-economic valences: as a massive, purpose-built cultural institution, the building appeared not so much to be cutting-edge cultural infrastructure but rather a dying gasp of an increasingly rickety welfare state (not empire, as the American commentator suggested; Figure 2.1). Within months of the National Theatre's opening, the Labour government of the time – which had proclaimed itself to be both author and guardian of the post-war welfare state – would negotiate an emergency loan from the International Monetary Fund that required it to impose a punishing combination of public spending cuts, tax increases, and interest rate rises. In this febrile political-economic context, it is not surprising that the National Theatre's built form could seem at best anachronistic and at worst the theatrical last stand of the *ancien régime*.

Figure 2.1 National Theatre under construction, London, 1975 (Getty Images)

One of the ironies of financialisation, however, is that it has unexpectedly helped rehabilitate an architectural style previously despised as statist and inhuman. While all places are comprised of absolute, relative, and relational elements, contemporary London, as a major hub in the global financial network, privileges relativity and relationality to an almost bewildering degree.[52] The unyielding brutalist architecture of the South Bank's cultural venues, and the historical association in the UK of brutalism with the welfare state, is now increasingly reassuring in a financialised urban economy predicated on flows of capital. The National Theatre, in particular, serves as a concrete counterpoint to the gleaming glass spires – such as Renzo Piano's Shard nearby – that epitomise the architecture of contemporary global capital. While it would be naive to infer that the built form of the South Bank's arts venues make the district a bulwark against globalisation (as Bennett shows, it is clearly implicated in globalisation), the sheer heft of the National Theatre implies both fixity and durability, spatio-temporal qualities that are tremendously important to the successful management of global cities and the theatres within them – without these sorts of anchors, the National Theatre implies, London would disappear in so much flow. In an era of extraordinary financial liquidity, the National Theatre's built form is reassuringly and productively illiquid.

This being said, the monumental South Bank's rehabilitation has also been assisted, and its current role advanced, by the fact that its arts venues have accommodated quite significant transformations to their built form while retaining the obdurate qualities that defined them in the first place. This has entailed not only a series of architectural updates but a long-term scenographic intervention in London's cultural and urban fabric, the effects of which are quite different today from when it began. Now, the built form of the monumental South Bank's venues sends much more sympathetic signals than it did at the time of these buildings' creation. These resonate not only in London's tourist economy but in the city's political economy writ large.

Given the building's architectural iconicity it is easy to overlook the fact that Lasdun's original design for the National Theatre has been subtly modified several times since its initial construction, while still preserving its general form. Many of these renovations have served to integrate the building more seamlessly into the riverside, while expanding and, importantly, making visible these increases in the infrastructural capacity of the National Theatre. For the first two decades of its existence, a one-way road surrounded the building, so that theatre-goers could be delivered by car and dropped off at the front entrance. This design, however, amplified the building's sense of isolation vis-à-vis its surroundings. Renovations in 1997 removed the road, which opened up space to create Theatre Square – an open area for public events, especially in the summer – in front of the building. It also linked the building better with the riverside (Figure 2.2). Additional glazing was also installed into the *porte-cochère*, which made space for a new bookstore and expanded the foyer and box office space; together these alterations made the front entrance more visible from the riverside (even if, as theatre architects Haworth Tompkins noted, they distracted from the 'dramatic raking struts supporting the overhanging terraces above' and altered the symmetry of the Lyttleton Theatre's foyer at the front of the building).[53] A 'Watch This Space' summer programme of events in Theatre Square was inaugurated in 1998, and the building's exterior would even be used for public art: in one high-profile installation in 2007, artists Harvey and Ackroyd covered the riverbank surfaces of the enormous Lyttleton fly tower in growing grass (and many of the building's vertical surfaces – including its two huge fly towers – are now, strikingly, illuminated at night).

Further, extensive renovations were undertaken between 2008 and 2015. These, designed by Haworth Tompkins, removed a service car park at the building's northeast corner in order to create another public square along the

Figure 2.2 National Theatre main entrance, including Theatre Square, London, 2019 (Getty Images)

river walk. They also included the installation of additional glazing throughout the building, which made its public-facing walls more transparent – it was now easier to see directly into the heart of the building from the outside, not only from the riverbank but from across the Thames. Haworth Tompkins expanded the capacity of the building further by adding the Max Rayne Centre, a substantial extension on the south side containing new scenery and production facilities, and rebuilt the Cottesloe Theatre to updated specifications (the Cottesloe was subsequently renamed the Dorfman Theatre, after one of the National Theatre's major donors, the founder of the Travelex foreign exchange company). Haworth Tompkins added a 'new public viewing route' that, as they put it, allowed 'the life of the updated workshops and back of house spaces to be seen, giving an insight to the scale and sophistication of the NTs' production capacity'.[54]

Perhaps the most eye-catching addition during these renovations was the Temporary Theatre, which opened in 2013 in Theatre Square and was dismantled in 2016. The Temporary Theatre (initially called the Shed) provided a third performance space for contemporary theatre while the new Dorfman was being built (Figure 2.3). This new space was clad in bright red timber, each corner topped with a tall, square chimney (which

Figure 2.3 National Theatre with the Shed/Temporary Theatre, London, 2013 (Alamy Stock Photo)

made it seem a little like a child's drawing of a factory, an apt evocation given the improvements to the National's 'plant' as a whole). Although the eye-catching design of the Temporary Theatre was intended to communicate the building's transience, it was nonetheless symbolically backstopped by Lasdun's monumental edifice. The Temporary Theatre's bright-red styling and use of recycled materials were intended to be the architectural analogue to the contemporary work that the National Theatre planned to programme within it, but absent the main building the Temporary Theatre could have appeared as just another one of the trendy 'pop-ups' that have become so familiar in London as the cost of commercial leases in the city has spiralled. In part, this was due to the fact that the Temporary Theatre's site – in Theatre Square in front of the main entrance to the permanent building – meant that Lasdun's structure wrapped around the Haworth Tompkins-designed box on two sides. This gave the Temporary Theatre the appearance of being sheltered by the permanent building. The Temporary Theatre's bright red cladding, made from rough wood planks, also mimicked the horizontal detailing on the permanent building's concrete façade (which bears the imprint of the wood forms pressed into its still-wet concrete during construction). More than three decades later, it almost looked as if these same forms had been brought out of storage and used to erect the Temporary Theatre. It also implied that Lasdun's brutalist building was not only the Temporary Theatre's architectural point of reference but also its progenitor and guarantor. Rather than rebuking the brutalism of Lasdun's design, the Temporary Theatre actually demonstrated its subtle plasticity and publicly testified to the original building's ongoing productivity.

The built form of the National Theatre, then, illustrates theatre's ability to manage change over time in a city where all that is solid threatens to melt into air. Along with the monumental South Bank as a whole, the National Theatre has come to model highly attractive forms of urban productivity, and this modelling is arguably even more important following a financial crisis than it otherwise would be. The National Theatre is efficient; it is affluent; it is flexible; it is entrepreneurial; it is sustained through the benevolent stewardship of many partners (public, private, and not-for-profit); it houses cultural producers, so uncomfortable oppositions like labour and capital seem not to apply in it; and it is persistent, even at a time of political-economic upheaval. The National Theatre and the monumental South Bank are productive today because they are both amenable to financialisation and help manage its otherwise intractable contradictions.

Social Productivity

The Waterloo tunnels lie roughly 600 metres south of the National Theatre, beneath Waterloo Station, one London's oldest rail stations and the largest and busiest rail terminus in the UK. Like many rail stations in south London, Waterloo's trains arrive and depart on elevated viaducts (unlike most trains in north London, which more commonly travel in trenches below street level). The Waterloo tunnels occupy one part of a larger network of vaulted brick tunnels that extend beneath the station, which was historically used for railway storage and offices (some parts of the network still are). Since their opening as a performance venue in 2009 the tunnels have been home to the Old Vic Tunnels – when the Old Vic programmed part of the space between 2009 and 2013 – and, in an adjacent section, The Vaults ('London's home for immersive theatre and alternative art'; Figure 2.4).[55] The Old Vic Tunnels were subsequently taken over by skateboard and leisure clothing company Vans, and turned into the London branch of House of Vans, a 'place where imagination lets loose over concrete bowls, art installations, workshops and concert stages'.[56] The tunnels' nineteenth-century industrial aesthetic, combined with the fact

Figure 2.4 Waterloo Tunnels, including the entrance to The Vaults, London (Getty Images)

that their side-street entrances can be difficult to find, make the venue an undeniably evocative – and, in spite of its location in the heart of London, almost secretive – place in which to encounter performance.

Historically, Waterloo Station has been the main way for train and London Underground travellers to access the South Bank. Unlike the monumental South Bank, though, the Waterloo tunnels came into existence as a performance venue for reasons that had little to do with either culture or urban planning; the venue emerged as a result of the unusual way that the UK runs its passenger rail network, on the one hand, and rising rents in London's commercial property market, on the other. Waterloo Station is owned by Network Rail, the state company that manages Britain's rail infrastructure (Network Rail was born out of the collapse of Railtrack – a privately owned conglomerate that went bust in 2002 following a series of managerial failures and train accidents – and the train services themselves are franchised to publicly-subsidised private operators, a complicated arrangement that evolved out of the privatisation of Britain's rail system in the mid-1990s). The UK government substantially reduced its annual grant to Network Rail in the company's 2007–8 budget year, which put additional pressure on the company to maximise its revenues through increased commercial activities. Network Rail began to lease out more of its estate, over and above the retail units commonly located in its stations, and sought to capitalise upon London's high-priced commercial property market to a greater degree than it had in the past. To be sure, the rail network had rented out parts of its property holdings for a very long time (the image of the ramshackle automobile repair shop located under a railway arch is a familiar one in Britain). But when stylish new restaurants started to open under railway arches in cool neighbourhoods in east London, and a large performance venue opened under Waterloo Station, it was a clear sign that the city's historical infrastructure was being put to use in ways that would have been difficult to imagine only a few years earlier (fittingly, Network Rail sold the bulk of its commercial property assets to a partnership between property investors Telereal Trillium and private equity group Blackstone for nearly £1.5 billion in 2018 – the sell-off was a condition laid down by the Treasury in 2015 on Network Rail for receiving additional public funds for infrastructure improvements).[57]

Unlike their monumental counterparts nearby, the tunnels are invisible at ground level. Their built form is undoubtedly part of their performance aesthetic but, unlike the National Theatre, this aesthetic is almost entirely interior – their presence barely registers within the urban environment of the South Bank. Nonetheless, when this nineteenth-century railway architecture was appropriated by contemporary performance events – and I use the word 'appropriated' advisedly here – new productive possibilities began to open up. If only for a short period of time, spectators could feel productive in a city where that experience was less available to them than in the past.

This economic logic emerged in one of the earliest theatrical productions staged in the Waterloo tunnels: the High Tide/Old Vic co-production of Beth Steel's *Ditch* in 2010.[58] The play was first performed in April 2010 as part of the High Tide Festival at The Cut, a community arts centre in Halesworth, Suffolk, in a small, end-on auditorium. The production transferred the following month to the Old Vic Tunnels, in co-production with the Old Vic Theatre. *Ditch* is set in Britain, in the near, but unspecified, future. The country is in a state of civil war after an environmental catastrophe, with a fascist government trying to subdue a restive population through military repression and forced labour. Much of Britain is socially and environmentally devastated. As one character proclaims to another: 'You let it get to this! You let the sea rise and flooded cities, burst river banks and destroyed our houses. You used up oil, made cars stop, forced us inta towns. You made us share rooms, put us in factories, fed us rations, let us get sick.'[59] The play is set in an isolated military outpost in the Peak District, the beautiful but sometimes forbidding range of hills and moors in central and northern England. On the lookout for insurgents and refugees, the characters' existence is lonely and savage: food is scarce, living conditions are poor, and moments of hope (as when two younger characters fall in love and one becomes pregnant) are extinguished by death (both characters are killed, the young man in battle, the young woman murdered). *Ditch* is a dystopian portrait of a bleak future, a warning about the need for ecological stewardship and the dangers of authoritarian politics.

Audiences attending the Waterloo *Ditch* first had to locate a scarcely-marked entrance down one side of Waterloo Station. They then encountered the tunnels, which were gloomy, dirty, and most noticeably, smelly: the damp was palpable and the mustiness powerful. In High Tide's staging, there appeared to be blood on the dirt-covered ground. Pools of light and patches of darkness framed installations composed under the old brick arches: stretched animal skins hung from the roof; an old wooden wheel, no longer in use, was engulfed by vegetation; a small deer (stuffed, it became apparent) stood, isolated, in an antechamber (because spectators encountered the deer after passing by the animal skins the deer appeared as though it could be a hunter's next target). All the while, the trains rumbled immediately overhead, the background noise sounding like rolling thunder or, more ominously, distant artillery fire. The scripted play had yet to begin, but the audience was already immersed in the fictional world of the play.

The rest of the event, though, was located in what was very much like a conventional, end-on theatre auditorium (supplemented by a very conventional theatre bar constructed under an adjacent arch). This auditorium spanned the width of one arch and was immediately familiar to a theatre-goer: there was a stage at one end, risers of theatre seating faced it, and stage lighting hung overhead. At the same time, however, the auditorium amplified the atmosphere of the play more than a conventional theatre auditorium could – the stage floor was mud, there were old panels of rusting corrugated steel on the underside of the arch above the audience, and the strong smell of damp persisted. (This would become even more conspicuous when it rained onstage and the mud that covered the playing area thickened.) The performance space reiterated the post-apocalyptic register of the play more than a conventional theatre space could, yet it also offered the customary features of a theatre auditorium. It was evocatively fictive but reassuringly familiar.

The Waterloo *Ditch* sought to capitalise upon spatial and theatrical relations that the tunnels made possible, but which could not be realised in a conventional theatre space like The Cut. The production's effects (and affects) depended on an interplay between the particular architectonic qualities of the tunnels, the diegesis of the script, and the socio-spatial configuration of the playing and spectating areas. In this way, it was like many other instances of theatre companies taking over infrastructure originally built for other purposes and remaking it as performance venues, whether temporarily or on a longer-term basis. (In London these days, any theatrical use of non-theatrical infrastructure tends to be called 'site-specific', though this is really just a catch-all term for theatre taking place outside already established performance venues – in most cases, there is little 'specific' about it.) But the show's productivity also operated according to a logic that was not only artistic but economic. The Waterloo *Ditch* was an instance of what might be called *monopoly performance*, a distinctively theatrical economic form that brings together an uneasy mix of features that are normally thought to be in tension, if not outright contradiction, with each other in market economies (and some of which are usually seen to be inimical to productivity in the first place). There is, first, the problem that theatre industries tend towards 'monopolistic competition' because of the nature of the products they produce. At the same time, the Waterloo *Ditch* translated the distinctively agglomerative industrial characteristics of theatre (and the particular social and spatial forms these predominantly involve) into experiential benefits of the performance event to an unusual degree. Complicating the picture further, though, was the fact that the production was also symbolically rent-seeking, in that it extended theatrical dominion over a portion of the urban environment and then sought to capitalise upon spatial elements found there that could not be replicated elsewhere (or at least that would be difficult to do so). Theatrical productivity, then, depended on some fairly sophisticated management of these economic tensions. But it was through this management that the production modelled forms of theatrical, economic, and urban productivity that are especially attractive in London today.

In his analysis of 'cognitive-cultural capitalism', Scott observes that cultural industries, although comprised of 'a rather incoherent collection of sectors', nonetheless have a number of shared features that distinguish them from other industries.[60] 'First', he claims, 'they are all concerned in one way or another with the creation of sign-value or symbolic value. Second, they are generally subject to the effects of Engel's Law, meaning that as disposable income expands, consumption of these outputs rises at a disproportionately higher rate'. Third, and most importantly here, 'they exemplify with special force the dynamics of Chamberlinian or monopolistic competition'.[61] Monopolistic competition, which was first theorised by E. H. Chamberlin and, separately, by Joan Robinson, is a form of 'imperfect competition'. It arises when there are multiple producers of the same general type of products but these products cannot satisfactorily be substituted for each other (this scenario is different from an outright monopoly, where a single producer dominates). As a result, producers are less likely to set prices through reference to other, similar products; although millions of people eat breakfast cereal every day, loyalty to Cheerios rather than Corn Flakes means that General Mills does not have to compete as keenly with Kellogg's on price as it otherwise would.[62] In the context of theatre, and in a large cultural metropolis such as London, monopolistic competition arises because although there are many performances on offer, when (say) *The Seagull* is sold out, *The Lion King* is not usually a straightforward substitute. Indeed, theatre industries are especially susceptible to monopolistic competition because producers often do not see each other as true competitors in the first place and, more importantly, the appeal of a given show is predicated on its presumed, and emphatically proclaimed, uniqueness (to a degree than would seem excessive in relation to breakfast cereal but which, in the theatre, seems entirely appropriate). For a spectator, it is not so much that *The Seagull* is preferable to *The Lion King*, or that Chekhov is better than Disney (though the choice between them may be expressed in terms of a taste hierarchy). It is that the experience each show offers is understood to be radically incommensurable with the other.

This monopolistic tendency is counterposed by the fact that theatrical production tends to be agglomerative, particularly in large urban centres like London. According to classical economics, there is a contradiction here, since monopolistic competition is usually thought to be inefficient but agglomeration economies are seen as being predominantly efficient. In the most basic sense, agglomeration economies occur when firms of similar types cluster in particular locales (and often in identifiable districts within those places).[63] As Michael Ball and David Sunderland point out, they do this in order to reduce costs by operating in close proximity to their workforce and the consumers of their products (the latter may happen by appealing to a local consumer base or, as is often the case in theatre, by drawing audiences to a given performance).[64] Modern cultural industries generally, and theatre industries especially, are highly agglomerative. Not only have theatres historically tended to cluster in cities (as well as districts within those cities); theatrical performance is unusual in the extent to which production and consumption of its products predominantly happen at the same time, in the same place. This significantly shortens the economic circuit of production and consumption, to a degree that happens in few other industries.[65] Indeed, the Waterloo *Ditch* was distinctive because of the extent to which agglomeration characterised the economic geography of its production *and* was a key experiential feature of it as an event (through the co-presence that it involved). Rather than resolve the tensions of imperfect competition, then, the performance found new ways to make them spatially productive.

Part of the appeal of being a spectator in the Waterloo *Ditch* was the promise that 'being here together' would pay off in ways not possible in most performance events, and, by extension, other economic contexts. The Waterloo *Ditch* sought to translate agglomeration to the diegetic and phenomenological registers of the performance more fully than a spatially conventional event could. The playing area installed in the tunnel became a less privileged diegetic space within the event than it otherwise would have been – instead, diegesis appeared to be produced by the total performance environment and all of the agents within in it (including, but not limited to, the spectators of the show). This environmental diegesis was assisted by the sense-perceptual intensification that moving *Ditch* into the tunnels involved: the military outpost in the play is dirty, damp, and smelly – and so were the tunnels.[66] In the Waterloo *Ditch*, agglomeration was not only an industrial and social characteristic of theatre writ large; it was a narrative and experiential benefit of spectatorship within the individual performance event.

Moreover, the productivity of the Waterloo *Ditch* was contingent on the extent to which it offered spectators a new type of encounter with a place that would, in the absence of performance, be unlikely to happen. In this way the production verged on rent-seeking; its theatrical exploitation of a particular portion of the environment operated according to a logic that owes as much to capital as it does to creativity. But its productive potential depended on theatrically overturning the negative economic valences of rent-seeking. In economics, rent is the difference between the price paid for a resource to its owner and the cost (land, labour, and capital) of keeping that resource in circulation. The problem of rent has concerned economists since its most notable theorisations in the nineteenth century by David Ricardo and, subsequently, Karl Marx.[67] But there is a difference – discernible in theory if not always in practice – between profit-seeking and rent-seeking; the latter involves unproductive economic activities that generate profits but at the expense of wealth creation in the broader economy. Economist Robert Shiller's account of the problem is perhaps the best-known today:

> The classic example of rent-seeking is that of a feudal lord who installs a chain across a river that flows through his land and then hires a collector to charge passing boats a fee (or rent of the section of the river for a few minutes) to lower the chain. There is nothing productive about the chain or the collector. The lord has made no improvements to the river and is helping nobody in any way, directly or indirectly, except himself.[68]

If, in the classic formulation, rents and rent-seeking arise in relation to land, more recently rent-seeking has arisen in relation to phenomena such as intellectual property, capital gains, the buying and selling of patents, and some of the more complex features of the global financial system – like credit default swaps – that featured in the 2008 financial crisis (though land has not disappeared from the equation, as the volatility of international real estate markets in recent years illustrates). As David Harvey observes, rent-seeking tends to arise today in two main situations: when social agents 'control some special quality resource, commodity or location which, in relation to a certain kind of activity, enables them to extract monopoly rents from those desiring to use it'; and when there is what economists call an 'inelastic supply' of resources (either by design or historical consequence), which results in the value of those resources being greater than would be the case if they were more widely distributed through the economy or could be created easily by others.[69] Financialisation and rampant property speculation mean that London audiences are intimately familiar with rent-seeking (some may even have participated in it) whether or not they think of real estate in this way. And it is not hard to see how such conditions might arise with special force in the world of theatre, where the value (broadly defined) of theatrical products depends to an unusual degree on both their uniqueness and rarity. This specialness is only intensified by performing in unusual places such as the Waterloo tunnels, whose appeal hinges on their spatial uniqueness vis-à-vis more conventional events and venues.

Economically, rent-seeking is usually considered a bad thing. But theatrical rent-seeking was an important reason why the Waterloo *Ditch* could model forms of productivity that are tremendously alluring within theatre itself and within London's broader urban economy, but which are very difficult to realise in both. The production brought together and appeared to resolve – again, however temporarily and symbolically – some quite difficult theatrical, economic, and urban problems: of theatrical efficiency, of private property, and of spatial disuse, respectively.

The Waterloo *Ditch* traded on the privileging of private property ownership as the ideal economic relation between social subject and space under modern capitalism. Private property ownership creates a monopolistic relationship between social subject and place, in that it elevates an owner's claim to a particular parcel of space over competing claims. In the Waterloo *Ditch*, spectators were invited to 'purchase', through the performance, temporary 'ownership' over a non-replicable time, place, and experience. This played out a fantasy of property ownership that is difficult to realise in the broader urban economy of a city like London, where access to property ownership is restricted by high costs of entry, in large measure because property has become an increasingly important store of wealth at a time when real wages are stagnant and deferred wages – in the form of pensions – have sharply declined. The performance encouraged spectators to imagine themselves, if only briefly, as productive economic subjects of a particular kind: the property-owning bourgeoisie. This role is especially seductive when it is progressively less available outside the theatre.[70]

Finally, the Waterloo *Ditch* took disused (or not optimally used) urban spaces and put them back into production. This was attractive for several reasons. The idea that the arts can play an important role in urban renewal is one that has gained particular currency in the past decade, among theatre practitioners, politicians, and public policy-makers.[71] *Ditch* brought what would otherwise be an unproductive space back into (legitimate) use and, if only for a short time, integrated that space within London's urban economy. It also helped cultivate the sense of 'place difference' that is key to distinguishing cities from each other under transnational capitalism and making them more attractive places for capital investment, as well as for individual capitalists themselves.[72] *Ditch*, then, modelled two related, and highly appealing, forms of urban productivity through its use of the Waterloo tunnels: it appeared to improve London's productivity as a place in itself, and it ostensibly contributed to London's ability to compete successfully with other cities under global capitalism.

Conclusion

So, theatre's productivity problems are solved, as are London's. Not quite. There is a difference between modelling productivity and completely achieving it (even if this difference is not always clearly apparent, and even if sometimes modelling is enough). However ambivalent one might feel about the South Bank's current mix of culture and consumerism, it would be churlish to deny that the area is more vibrant than it was in the 1980s and 1990s. It is therefore tempting to see many of the area's productivity problems – theatrical and urban – as having disappeared. If this seems an appealing proposition, it is not because financialisation has finally put the monumental South Bank's welfare state legacy to rest. In fact, the reverse is true: to the extent that the South Bank works today – both in itself and in its wider contribution to London's urban economy – it is because of that legacy (and has little to do with, for example, the performances staged within the National Theatre, which, in my experience, are too often dull and unimaginative). The South Bank's productivity today depends not on a repudiation of welfarist built forms and attendant governance techniques, but, instead, on their rehabilitation and more strategic application.

The South Bank today also shows that there is no such thing as absolute productivity – some material must inevitably be externalised in order to realise a productive performance. This can even include elements of theatre itself. In spite of the impressive spatial choreography that the Waterloo *Ditch* involved, the experience of it as a spectator was rather dissatisfying. The event tried hard to do spectators' interpretive work for them – during the show the tunnels assumed a reiterative function, just in case spectators failed to 'get it'. Thus the production betrayed an anxiety about how spectators might undertake their interpretive labour within the Waterloo tunnels, even if their participation was necessary to realise the economic performance happening at the same time. Staging *Ditch* in the subterranean tunnels was very atmospherically evocative but it arguably misread the script, which repeatedly draws attention to its location on the open spaces of the Peak District. In this case, theatrical productivity was achieved at some semantic, if not economic, expense.

If S. Tone-Deaf were to return to the South Bank today, what would he make of it? He would likely be astonished at the network of cultural venues built since his time, and he would almost certainly marvel at the huge number of people enjoying the area's amenities, day and night. Although he would recognise elements of the monumental South Bank, he would probably be struck by its scale and durability, especially when seen against the glass spires of the City of London. At the same time, the idea – let alone the practice – of performing regularly under a working train station would have seemed extraordinary. It is not at all clear whether S. Tone-Deaf would have found today's South Bank marvellous, alarming, or both. But he would surely have to reconsider his original dismissal of its productive potential.

CHAPTER 3

Citizenship

For God's sake bring me a large Scotch. What a bloody awful country.

Reginald Maudling, British Home Secretary, after his inaugural visit to Northern Ireland (1970)[1]

It has now been more than twenty years since the signing of the Good Friday Agreement in 1998. Also known as the Belfast Agreement, the Good Friday Agreement is popularly heralded as marking the end of the Troubles in Northern Ireland. As I write this, though, the Northern Ireland Assembly has only recently been restored after having been suspended for more than three years because the Democratic Unionist Party and Sinn Féin, the largest political parties in Northern Ireland, were unable to agree a new power-sharing deal following Assembly elections in 2017 (which were themselves precipitated by the collapse of the multi-party Executive after a corruption scandal within a DUP-led government department). Even though the Assembly has been restored, the broader political and economic climate in Northern Ireland remains uncertain.

Furthermore, the departure of the United Kingdom from the European Union – prompted by the 2016 referendum in which a narrow majority of the UK voted in favour of exiting the EU, while a clear majority in Northern Ireland voted to remain – has especially serious consequences for Northern Ireland, which is the only part of the UK that shares a land border with another EU member. The threat of reinstating some sort of 'hard border' with the Republic of Ireland, after so much effort to dismantle it as part of the peace process, has hardly been conducive to the political and economic stability of Northern Ireland, and the impact of the withdrawal agreement – which hived Northern Ireland off from Great Britain into a (de facto if not de jure) separate Irish customs territory in order to avoid border checks with the Republic, over the objections of Northern Irish unionists – could be severe.

If recent events have led unionist parties to cry betrayal (ironically, after a period when a minority Conservative government in Westminster depended on the support of the DUP's ten Members of Parliament), it is not as though the UK government had been much help in the lead-up to Brexit anyway. When she was named Secretary of State for Northern Ireland in the lead-up to Brexit, Karen Bradley gave an interview in which she blithely remarked, 'I freely admit that when I started this job, I didn't understand some of the deep-seated and deep-rooted issues that there are in Northern Ireland. I didn't understand things like when elections are fought, for example, in Northern Ireland–people who are nationalists don't vote for unionist parties and vice versa.'[2] As political commentator Marina Hyde acerbically put it in *The Guardian*, 'I mean . . . ideally, you would start understanding these things some decades before you were the cabinet minister with operational responsibility for arguably the most highly sensitive region of the United Kingdom.'[3] Bradley later caused a political firestorm by casually remarking in the House of Commons that members of the police and military bore no legal responsibility for their role in killings during the Troubles, at a time when the Public Prosecution Service was in the process of deciding whether or not to lay criminal charges against former British soldiers for shooting dead fourteen participants in a march against internment on Bloody Sunday in 1972. She was quickly forced to recant, saying, 'It's factually wrong, it's not what I believe and I have apologised.'[4] The journalist Susan McKay, assessing the debacle in the *Irish Times*, commented acidly: 'Bradley has already won herself a reputation as the stupidest and most inept secretary of state anyone can remember.'[5]

It was not supposed to work out like this. Indeed, the institutional dysfunction that has frequently characterised the two decades following the Good Friday Agreement risks obscuring how remarkable it was that the Agreement was secured in the first place, let alone the fact that the DUP and Sinn Féin were ever in government together. It is also easy to forget just how (warily) optimistic many in Northern Ireland were at the time of the Agreement, and in the years immediately following it. After many failed attempts to broker peace deals during the Troubles, the Good Friday Agreement marked a sea change in political relations and aspirations in Northern Ireland.[6] The British and Irish governments not only signed up for it; so did most of the North's political parties and its major paramilitary groups. While the Agreement was not solely responsible for subsequent events in Northern Ireland – it exemplified political and cultural shifts that were already underway – its approval by simultaneous referenda in North and South and its statutory codification in the Northern Ireland Act 1998 cemented the difficult peace process that had been triggered by republican and loyalist paramilitary ceasefires four years earlier, and it set in motion the process of transforming Northern Ireland's political institutions.

The recurring institutional difficulties in Northern Ireland should also not distract attention from just how fluid the politics and economics of the Agreement period were, and the extent to which this period involved an extensive cultural working through, awkwardly and incompletely, of what 'peace' might entail. The Agreement itself was only one element – albeit a very important one – within this broader negotiation. The conflict in Northern Ireland is popularly imagined, at least by many outside Northern Ireland, to arise from sectarian enmity between Catholics and Protestants. It would be more accurate, however, to describe it as having arisen, at least in part, from a struggle over state and economic power and the forms of social (and not only legal) citizenship that might be possible in relation to them. Since Northern Ireland was created through the partition of its six counties from the newly independent Irish Free State in the South in 1922, it has been a contested state whose residents claim citizenship of different countries: the North is constitutionally part of the United Kingdom but a significant minority of its population aspires to a united Ireland. Those born in Northern Ireland are also entitled to citizenship of the UK and may claim Irish citizenship on the same terms as those in the Republic (and which passport one acquires tends to reflect one's views on the existing constitutional arrangement in the North).

The Agreement is notable for its combination of nuts-and-bolts constitutional mechanics and high-minded civic aspirations. It restored a devolved legislative assembly to Northern Ireland for the first time since 1972, administered by a power-sharing executive comprised of representatives from the larger parties in the Assembly. (It was not all that long ago that a significant part of the unionist political class favoured either a majority-governed Northern Irish parliament or the full integration of Northern Ireland into the political structures of the United Kingdom, while Sinn Féin refused to participate in any form of Northern Irish legislature.) The British and Irish governments also agreed that the future political affiliation of Northern Ireland – whether it would remain part of the United Kingdom or become part of the Republic of Ireland – would be determined by those in the North themselves, and this involved the removal of the Republic's claim of sovereignty over the six counties from its constitution. Furthermore, the British state agreed to reduce its military and political presence in Northern Ireland and, with a large caveat about its continued visibility in areas with a history of intense conflict like west Belfast and south Armagh, its security apparatus has been shrinking ever since. Finally, the Agreement expressed a renewed, if somewhat ambiguously defined, emphasis on the civic realm in Northern Ireland. It suggested that a less state-delimited, and more determinedly social, type of citizenship might be imagined, and held out the possibility of a more fully representative form of democracy than had previously existed in the North.[7]

It is, of course, impossible to abstract these rather lofty civil ideals from the long-standing divisions that still define political institutions and everyday life in Northern Ireland, even if some of these antagonisms are no longer expressed through armed conflict to anything like the extent that they once were. The economic aspirations with which these civil ideals have been linked have also only partly been realised. The political-economic figuration of peace in terms of a 'dividend' has been a central part of political discourse in Northern Ireland since the paramilitary ceasefires were first called in 1994. The phrase 'peace dividend' did not arise first in Northern Ireland; instead, it came to prominence at the end of the Cold War, as a way to describe the economic returns that would ostensibly result from reallocating public expenditure on the military towards more socially beneficial activities – spending money on butter instead of guns. In Northern Ireland, it has usually meant something a little different: the economic benefits that would flow from ending the Troubles, since a peaceful and stable Northern Ireland would presumably be more attractive to private investors. (Northern Ireland's economy has historically been much more dependent on public expenditure than other parts of the UK, in part because of extra defence and security spending due to the Troubles but also because of additional social welfare spending due to the economic difficulties that accompanied the conflict.) To some extent, a peace dividend seems a slightly crude aspiration, as if the main justification for ending the Troubles were realising economic benefit rather than halting a decades-long conflict that killed nearly four thousand people and injured many more. This said, Northern Ireland's historically poor economic performance was clearly inextricable from the Troubles, and even if too many of the benefits brought by the cessation of the conflict have been concentrated in low-wage industries, and largely failed to spread to Northern Ireland's poorest postcodes, the hope that peace – and the new political institutions it involved – might economically improve the lives of those living in the North was not misplaced.

Indeed, parts of Belfast today are almost unrecognisable from the decades during which armoured military vehicles patrolled its streets and soldiers in full combat gear were a common presence in the city centre. Now, Belfast features excellent restaurants, stylish bars, and up-to-date arts and leisure facilities. Tourism – almost unheard of during the Troubles – has become an important industry in Northern Ireland. And high-profile cultural events, such as Derry's year-long UK City of Culture festival in 2013, have sought to conjoin peace promotion with economic development, arguably with some success.[8]

This peace dividend has, however, been fitfully and unevenly achieved. As Colin Coulter points out:

> The single most recurrent pledge that informed official discourse on the peace process was that if paramilitary organizations were to maintain their cease-fires, there would be an influx of multinational capital, especially from the United States, that would lift Northern Ireland out of its seemingly perennial condition of under-development.[9]

Some of this investment did arrive, particularly in the late 1990s and early 2000s, and unemployment in the region (which had historically been the highest in the UK) began to approach, and at times drop below, the UK-wide average. Northern Ireland also saw a sharp rise in residential property prices for possibly the first time ever, and, not surprisingly, this was 'widely interpreted in political and media circles as both emblem and agent of a renewed economic vitality in the region'.[10] But US investment dropped sharply after 2005–6 and has never reached the same levels since.[11] Furthermore, much of that investment was directed towards low-wage industries such as call centres, and unemployment in areas most affected by the Troubles – such as west Belfast – remains stubbornly high.[12] While there have been some improvements in the overall situation, the proportion of the workforce considered 'economically inactive' (which includes groups like students and the retired but also, more worryingly, people who have dropped out of the workforce altogether) continues to be considerably higher in Northern Ireland than in the rest of the UK, and overall employment remains comparatively lower as well.[13] The property boom that seemed to signal newfound prosperity also went bust after the global financial crisis of 2008, pushing large numbers of mortgage-holders into negative equity as the value of their properties dramatically fell.[14] To the extent that a peace dividend has materialised, it has often fallen short of the returns touted and its proceeds have been unequally distributed.

If Northern Ireland has undergone a profound social transformation during the past two decades, this change has been marked by a notable gap between political-economic aspirations and realities. Put simply, there is an efficacy shortfall here: the insistence on a set of tightly entwined political, economic, and institutional aspirations (some admirable, some markedly less so), but the ability to give them only partial effect. While such a gap exists in most polities, the distinctive history of the conflict in Northern Ireland means that it has arisen here in an especially acute form. The period around the Good Friday Agreement was especially fluid: on the one hand, there was widespread relief that the ceasefires appeared, for the most part, to be holding and that political and economic progress might be made; on the other hand, there was deep scepticism, borne out of decades of bitter experience, of the ability of the process to bring about anything more transformative than a 'cold' peace. Both, it turned out, would be the case.

In this chapter, I am interested in how theatre has intervened, spatially, to fill this efficacy gap. Since the time of the Agreement there has been a notable increase in spatially reflective arts practices that reflect, sometimes obliquely and sometimes directly, upon the changing political terrain of the North. This work includes that of theatre companies and practitioners like Tinderbox Theatre Company, Marie Jones, Sandra Johnston, and Martin Lynch, as well as that of visual and live artists like Phil Collins, Rita Duffy, Liam Gillick, Philip Napier, Mike Hogg, and Susan Philipsz.[15] It has often involved conscious interventions in the North's built environment, where the physical and symbolic landscape of Northern Ireland – which records the history of the conflict in its topography – has become a resource for artists to ask what types of social citizenship might be possible in a political and economic environment that has been trying to move beyond the Troubles, but is still heavily circumscribed by them.

Some of the most significant theatrical interventions in this regard have been by Belfast's Tinderbox Theatre. Perhaps its highest-profile production was *Convictions*, a collection of short pieces written by seven playwrights, in Belfast's disused Crumlin Road Courthouse in 2000. The Courthouse was the location of many of Northern Ireland's highest-profile paramilitary-related trials and had recently been closed as part of the peace process. Spectators were led in small groups into such places as courtrooms, a jury room, a judge's office, toilets, and the holding cells. In each place, they witnessed a performance, usually no more than ten or fifteen minutes in length, that in some way referred to the properties of that place. In Gary Mitchell's 'Holding Room', for example, spectators squeezed in through steel doors and huddled beside prisoners' cells, the scene taking place in the narrow patch of floor remaining available. At the conclusion of the scene, the prisoner was placed in his cell, a steel door was closed behind the spectators, and the lights were extinguished before the audience was released and led to the next scene. The audience's passage between places in the Courthouse was often marked by art installations which alluded to the building's past use: a collection of women's hats suspended from the ceiling of a hallway recalled the formality of dress once required of women attending trials and cited a time when this requirement (sometimes fulfilled with competitive relish) did not contradict a shabby, near-derelict building. When a character spoke derisively about the 'state of this place' in Daragh Carville's 'Male Toilets', he was responding not only to the present physical condition of the Courthouse but was also reminding the audience that the building was once the place of the British state and that its disrepair was a commentary on that state's heavily circumscribed legitimacy in contemporary Northern Ireland. A major part of *Convictions*' appeal lay in the fact that it offered the spectator an experience of state space that was previously inadmissible and unimaginable.

Given its striking location, it is not surprising that *Convictions* attracted considerable attention from audiences, popular commentators, and theatre scholars alike (including, at the time, from me).[16] But looking back at the period that followed the Agreement, an earlier Tinderbox production is at least as intriguing: the company's staging of Stewart Parker's *Northern Star* in the First Presbyterian Church in Rosemary Street, central Belfast, in November 1998 (Figure 3.1). *Northern Star* was first performed in Belfast's Lyric Theatre in 1984, which at the time occupied a functional but uninspiring building in Stranmillis, South Belfast. (In 2011 the Lyric opened an architecturally striking new and larger building, located on the same site but now oriented directly towards the revitalised banks of the River Lagan.) The action of the play is set during the 1798 rebellion led by the United Irishmen, a non-sectarian movement for an independent Ireland that involved the leadership of a number of Northern Protestants. (Parker named the play after the Belfast newspaper that one of the rebellion's leaders, Henry Joy McCracken, edited at the time.) The First Presbyterian Church, whose current building dates from 1783, was an evocative place in which to stage *Northern Star*: the play's main character, McCracken, was born a few hundred metres from the Church and lived close by; a number of the historical figures represented in the play likely worshipped there; the Church represents a lineage of radical, ecumenical Presbyterianism that the Troubles largely foreclosed; and the play explicitly

Figure 3.1 First Presbyterian Church, Belfast (Alamy Stock Photo)

invokes the streetscape immediately outside the Church. Parker's script also addresses its audience with a refrain that had especially forceful, but ambiguous, resonances in November of 1998: 'citizens of Belfast'. Voters in Northern Ireland and the Republic of Ireland had overwhelmingly approved the Good Friday Agreement in simultaneous referenda the previous May, and elections to the newly created Assembly had been successfully held in June. But the widespread, if cautious, optimism about the possibility of peace had been subsequently shaken by the horror of the Omagh bombing in August, when a breakaway republican paramilitary group, the Real IRA, detonated a car bomb in the town centre on a busy Saturday afternoon, killing twenty-nine people and injuring more than two hundred.[17] The play's refrain about citizenship also anticipated the first meeting of the Assembly, which would be held the following month. Through a distinctively self-reflexive use of the city's built environment, in the two hundredth anniversary year of the 1798 rebellion and during the uncertain period following the Agreement, the production suggested that being a citizen of Belfast might finally be possible, in the theatre at least.

In this chapter, I return to the 1998 Tinderbox production of *Northern Star* in the First Presbyterian Church and view it in relation to the 'peace dividend' that has been widely promoted since the early days of the peace process but has at best been fitfully realised. One of the recurring problems of realising the peace dividend is that although it appears to be a single political-economic entity, it is, in fact, two separate elements conjoined through a presumed causality – that is, sort out the political institutions and the investment will follow. History has shown, though, that there is a massive gap between these two components, with the result that a peace dividend has been very difficult to experience in a unified form, in a single time and place. Site-specific theatre also comes with its own problems; in many cases, its theatrical aspirations are unfulfilled in practice (and this failure can seem especially frustrating to audiences when a production seems to be trying so hard, spatially). Nonetheless, when Henry Joy McCracken stepped forward and addressed the audience in the First Presbyterian Church as 'citizens of Belfast' in 1998, he realised a peace dividend in a very material and immediate form, to an extent that the state and the market have never convincingly been able to do in Northern Ireland.

In making this argument, I take seriously the proposition that, under certain circumstances, a single theatrical production might achieve a greater return than either the state or the market can. This is not because the Tinderbox *Northern Star* stood apart from politics or economics, or metaphorised them; rather, it is because the production temporarily conjoined politics with economics more effectively than the state or the market could. Tinderbox's staging of *Northern Star* in the First Presbyterian in 1998 gave the play's civic rhetoric new and special force – the production's ideological efficacy was strengthened by not only by its historical contingency but also by its spatial efficiency. In the process, it provided a living model of what a non-marketised peace dividend – a 'citizen of Belfast' – might look and feel like, and posited theatre as the ideal (and possibly only) place to find it. For a brief period in November 1998, the Tinderbox *Northern Star* proposed that the greatest dividend of peace was to be a citizen of Belfast. And a citizen of Belfast was, ultimately, a spectator of a highly efficient theatrical performance.

The Civil Economies of Site-Specific Performance

Part of the appeal of the Tinderbox *Northern Star* is that it acted as a spatial 'supplement' to, as David Lloyd and Paul Thomas put it, 'a state perceived to be not yet equal to its ethical idea'.[18] Lloyd and Thomas argue that an important function of aesthetic culture in Europe and North America since the late eighteenth century has been to serve as 'exemplary objects of pedagogy' through which to cultivate the ideal of a citizen: a political subject capable of sublimating its own partial interests and participating fully in institutions of civil society and representative democracy.[19] The 'ethical idea' to which the state may not yet be equal, in their formulation, is one where it can represent – and thereby enfranchise – all of its citizens. Both ideals are fundamental to modern liberal democracy, which, unlike autocratic models that dominated pre-Enlightenment Europe, aspires to a form of statehood whose legitimacy rests on its universal representation of 'the people', and whose citizens can move easily between the institutions that comprise civil society, the market, and the state itself.[20]

The actual historical practices through which this process has occurred have been, of course, complex, messy, and never fully realised. But it is also the case that the conflict in Northern Ireland compromised the possibility of recourse to such ideals of citizenship and representative democracy to a greater extent than in many western European countries. The Good Friday Agreement seeks to address, in a very tentative way, this long-standing political history and geography (which extends well before the Troubles and is tied up with hundreds of years of British political involvement in the island of Ireland).

The political potential of theatre has often been grounded in the distinctive social and spatial relations its events usually involve. There is a long-standing Euro-American ideal of theatre as a deliberative civic institution, with the spectator as its favoured political and theatrical subject. Strands of this way of thinking are visible in the work of a range of theatre critics and practitioners. In a Habermasian vein, David Wiles stresses the civic potential of a theatre that is not only public but that demonstrates '*public* reasoning and communicative interconnectedness involving the mutual recognition of truth claims'.[21] Jill Dolan, in turn, argues that theatre offers a forum in which 'people constitute themselves as citizens' and also 'model civic engagement in participatory democracy'.[22] Helen Freshwater claims that theatre 'can illuminate our hopes for other models of social interaction . . . and our perception of our roles and power (or lack of it) within the broader public sphere'.[23] Paul Makeham argues that theatre 'enables citizens to invent – through memory, imagination and desire – new ideas about themselves and their relationships with the urban landscape'. Urban performance, in particular, aspires 'to foster and value partnerships between the polis and its people' and provides the 'shared civic space' that makes such affiliations possible.[24] Even a more circumspect treatment of the relationship between performance and citizenship – that offered by Darren O'Donnell – accepts as axiomatic a strong affiliation between theatre and civic engagement.[25] And, of course, these thinkers are extending a long tradition of modern thought that views theatre and citizenship in a mutually affirming relationship (as in, for example, the work of Friedrich Schiller, Alexis de Tocqueville, Percy MacKaye, and St. John Ervine).[26]

These accounts tend to start with the premise that theatre is generally a good thing (institutionally, aesthetically, politically, affectively, and so on). They also tend to presume that theatre has a special ability to cultivate positive forms of social and political relations, especially where other social institutions, such as the state and the market, fall short. Here theatre is thought to supply a privileged space for political subject formation and debate outside the purview of the state, and to supply the formalised communicative conventions to undertake this debate. This deliberation is intended to model, simultaneously, some sort of change in the social world outside the theatre. On the one hand, the spectator's participation in the theatre event is seen as a civil practice, in that this participation involves sublimating prior political identities and affiliations in the hope of realising a form of community that may be inflected by these allegiances but which ultimately supersedes them. The theatre event becomes a model deliberative forum through which this transformation might be achieved in the present. On the other hand, the performance event is a formalised way to imagine a citizenship that will ultimately be practised in another place: it is a rehearsal for a performance to be given in the future, somewhere else. Thus the theatre event is both civically constitutive and prefigurative.

As a site-specific performance in Belfast in 1998, Tinderbox's *Northern Star* put a distinctive – and more ambiguous – ideological and economic spin on these civil operations. The production's efficacy hinged on a double movement: it simultaneously aimed to respond to a perceived ideological problem within the public sphere while capitalising upon the economic geography of site-specific performance. In Baz Kershaw's foundational analysis of the politics of performance, theatre's efficacy is secured through its special potential to bring about ideological change. In fact, Kershaw's account of ideological efficacy models a performance that is both Northern Irish and site-specific.[27] Kershaw outlines a hypothetical community performance in a Northern Irish town that seeks to question the Protestant ideological dominance expressed through local commemorations of the Twelfth of July (which has historically been celebrated by some Protestants to commemorate the victory of the forces of Protestant William of Orange over the Catholic Jacobite armies at the Battle of the Boyne in 1690). That Kershaw's example happens to be Northern Irish is no coincidence. The Troubles resulted in an unusually codified visual iconography and set of ceremonial practices that emphatically signify the contours of the conflict, whether the British union flag versus the Irish tricolour, Twelfth of July parades versus St. Patrick's Day celebrations, or others. These signify clearly within the performance event, and miscommunication or misreading is less likely to occur when this is the case.

That Kershaw's hypothetical performance is site-specific is hardly accidental either. Although he does not frame it in quite this way, the theatrical and ideological efficacy of Kershaw's proposed community performance is secured through a homologous relationship between performance, politics, and place, where these three elements appear to resonate with each other more tightly within the site-specific theatre event than they would in an event where the site itself were not so self-consciously at stake. This chimes with Richard Schechner's early take on what he called 'environmental theatre' (but which today would probably be called 'site-specific performance', or similar): that performing in a place not already coded as theatrical endows the performance with an aural of the real, thereby nearly slipping the bonds of representation itself; that the 'reality' of the place of performance enhances the intensity of the theatrical experience for all participants at a phenomenal level; and that the close proximity of the place of performance to places invoked within the fiction of the play sustains the diegetic success of the performance.[28] Kershaw gives this a more explicitly ideological slant but his logic is similar: performance, politics, and place must 'authenticate' each other in order for the event as a whole to become ideologically effective. Of course, this does not necessarily mean that friction between these elements will not occur, since some friction is necessary for critique to happen. But each element ultimately enhances the persuasiveness of the other, and the event as a whole achieves effect (and affect). As Kershaw puts it, the performance

> must employ authenticating conventions/signs to discomfort or disturb the ideology of the community in ways that do not cause a riot or other kind of insuperable schism. To put this rather gnomically, the Ulster flag would somehow need to be damaged but not destroyed. . . . Moreover, in order to achieve inescapable significance for the audience the closer the flag gets to being destroyed – the more fundamentally the community ideology is challenged – the greater the likelihood that the performance will become efficacious within the networks of the community.[29]

Such homologies may not always be wholly harmonious, but the conjunction of performance, politics, and place never completely disrupts the event itself. Indeed, quite the opposite: this resonance deepens the experience of 'eventness' that makes the site-specific performance appealing and intensifies the spectator's awareness of their simultaneous membership of theatrical and political communities.[30]

It is also the case, however, that the ideological efficacy of site-specific performance can depend on a logic that is economic as well as political. Perhaps more than any other theatrical form, site-specific performance dramatises property relations, in that throws into relief how portions of the environment are owned and their use regulated, formally and informally (and in my experience, this property drama has often been more interesting than the fictional drama that accompanied it).[31] But site-specific performance's economic inflection does not arise solely because its creation means dealing with economic forces that are exogenous to itself. This inflection also emerges within site-specific performance's own spatial operations, and the Tinderbox *Northern Star* showed how this happens.

Like many site-specific performances, the Tinderbox *Northern Star* sought to address a sense – whether acknowledged explicitly or not – that the optimal operation of the theatre event is diminished when the spatial elements of that event are not fully capitalised upon. Most theatre events treat their places of performance as spatially unremarkable, bracketing them as, for example, scenographic challenges to be addressed through successful stage design. The Tinderbox *Northern Star*, however, drew attention to the way that place is both a constitutive element of the entire theatre event and a set of spatial resources to be deployed vis-à-vis other material within that event. It implied that, unless the theatre machine is using all of its spatial components fully, it is not firing on all cylinders – what would otherwise be waste must be turned into fuel. Thus, performing a play about the events of 1798 in the place where its lead character's real-life analogue likely worshipped – and in a historical moment where the political and economic future of Northern Ireland was very much up for grabs – was not only a clever staging choice; it recognised the fortuitous availability of untapped spatial resources. Mobilising these resources – taking up existing material (Parker's script), appropriating new spatial inputs (the First Presbyterian Church), and transforming these into arresting theatrical outputs (the live performance) – also entailed a refashioning of the spectator's role within the event created. To be a citizen of Belfast was not only to be a civic subject, or a participant in a theatre event, but a productive political and economic agent as well.

What these ideological and economic inflections of site-specific efficacy share is their preoccupation with the theatre event itself as much as the world beyond it: in the first instance, seeking to deepen the experience of the event in order to posit an ideological change that is difficult to achieve outside the theatre; and in the second, seeking to optimise that event's spatial operations. In Tinderbox's *Northern Star*, the former was inextricable from the latter – its ideological efficacy depended on its spatial efficiency. But rather than reaching beyond the theatre, Tinderbox's *Northern Star* achieved its peace dividend – becoming a 'citizen of Belfast' – by turning in on itself. Realising this dividend was possible precisely *because* it was difficult, and perhaps impossible, to achieve elsewhere.

Citizens of Belfast

Northern Star takes place on a single night in 1798. Henry Joy McCracken, a leader of the rebellion that sought to unite 'Protestant, Catholic, and Dissenter' in an armed struggle for an independent Irish republic, is hiding out with his partner Mary in a broken-down cottage on Cavehill, overlooking Belfast. McCracken has played a key role in anti-imperial politics in Ireland for a number of years. He has served as editor of the *Northern Star*, the radical newspaper based in Belfast, and has been a leading figure in the United Irishmen. McCracken is conscious of the fact that he is likely about to be caught and hanged by the British state for his role in the rebellion (as, indeed, the real-life McCracken was). The play's action proceeds through a series of flashbacks in which McCracken's political activities and ideals are enacted and critiqued, and the contemporary audience is invited to read the history of the 1798 rebellion against the modern-day conflict in Northern Ireland.

Early in the play's first scene, McCracken turns to the spectators and addresses them directly: 'Citizens of Belfast, the story so far'.[32] This refrain – 'citizens of Belfast' – is repeated throughout the play; characters greet each other as citizens, and McCracken prefaces a number of his direct addresses to the audience with 'citizens of Belfast'. The phrase is significant for several reasons. 'Citizen' is a mode of address used between characters within the fictional frame of the play but it is also a mode of address that temporally and spatially bridges the fictional realm of the play and the social realm of the audience. Being a citizen is a condition of being a political agent in *Northern Star* (regardless of whether the political project pursued is ultimately successful) and the characters not only understand each other as such, McCracken self-consciously positions the audience as spectators and citizens simultaneously. Framing spectators as 'citizens of Belfast' also calls into question the extent to which this political subjectivity is mediated through the geography of the city. Moreover, 'citizens of Belfast' must be understood as a performative and subjunctive form of address – McCracken's use of the term is as much about bringing this political subject into being through its theatrical and urban articulation as it is about acknowledging any a priori existence of that subject. Finally, 'citizens of Belfast' has to be understood within the context of the play's urban geography, which is simultaneously utopian and deeply ironic.

McCracken, in effect, theatrically issues what sociologist Vikki Bell characterises as a 'call to Peace [*sic*]'.[33] For Bell, 'Peace cannot be observed, being defined only negatively, as an absence of something else: It has no mode of presence.'[34] Instead, it is a 'performative that orientates itself to a newly imagined future', not by breaking with the past but rather by recalling and then dissociating itself from the past in the hope of delineating new forms of civic participation through which a new type of citizen subject might be imagined. It is only through these civic performatives that peace can be glimpsed, and 'Justice' apprehended, in however fleeting and fragmented a way.[35]

Northern Star's call to peace, however, is specifically a theatrical performative and, as such, is heavily overdetermined by theatre's historical position as a civil institution, and its attendant claim to its spectators being exemplary citizen-subjects. In other words, when McCracken addresses the audience as 'citizens of Belfast', his call is amplified by the theatrical event and institution in which it is spoken. This was undoubtedly true in the play's first production at the Lyric Theatre in 1984. But the 1998 production in the First Presbyterian Church, staged at a historical moment in which peace seemed less conjectural than in the past and in a place that could plausibly give it social form, made the proclamation with special force. At the same time, though, the 1998 *Northern Star* complicated the (already slippery) temporality that a call to peace entails, since its spatiality called into question the futurity that a call to peace involves. Where and when is this civic performance happening?

Northern Star's rhetoric of citizenship is highly appealing because it theatrically suggests to spectators that they are more than simply theatre-goers and that the event to which they contribute is more than just a performance.[36] Instead, this is a model public sphere, with participants serving, *pace* Dolan, as 'microcosm' of a broader, but as yet unrealised, 'civic audience' that is desired for the wider political realm.[37] This appeal goes beyond theatre's claim to be an exemplary public sphere, however, and it is intensified by the distinctive political history of Northern Ireland. *Northern Star*'s civic rhetoric is attractive precisely because it recuperates an autochthonous civic discourse that was once viable in Northern Ireland (and which, implicitly, might be viable again). This discourse was not organised around the now-familiar poles of nationalism versus unionism, or republicanism versus loyalism. As such, it represents a way of thinking about politics – and one's own political subjectivity – in Northern Ireland that is at once old and new again.

Such civic modelling, though, is not without its challenges. Although McCracken addresses spectators as urban citizens, grounding a sense of citizenship in Belfast is deeply problematic, both within the fictional frame of the play and within the contemporary audience's lived experience. Belfast is a city where the practice of civic politics has been heavily delimited by a centralising British state whose locus is elsewhere. The modern political lineage of citizenship – illustrated by the French revolutionary variant that so influenced the United Irishmen – is also tightly tied up with national state formation and legitimation in ways that are difficult to assert in a region whose sovereignty is disputed, and in ways that potentially undercut the civic politics the play advocates. And if being a citizen of Belfast is a pre-condition of the type of non-sectarian republicanism the play endorses, it is nonetheless a political subjectivity rooted in a city that is, as McCracken characterises it, 'a place of perpetual breakdown, incompatible voices, screeching obscenely away through the smoky dark wet'.[38]

For a play that appeals so openly to an audience's urban and political ideals, such complex political terrain is difficult ground in which they might gain purchase. That they did, however, is illustrated by novelist Glenn Patterson's recollection of the 1998 production:

> As the audience left the church that November night with [McCracken's] final soliloquy ringing in our ears ('Why would one place break your heart more than another? A place the like of that?'), there was a palpable sense that we had reclaimed not just the city – these were streets best avoided at night before the ceasefires – but something also of our heritage as its citizens.[39]

But how did the spatiality of the 1998 production of *Northern Star* make the play's appeals to a new form of citizenship so persuasive? At least part of the answer lies in the way that, as a site-specific performance, it intensified homologies between politics, theatre, and place already present in the play. The performance succeeded by making the play's already-established conjunction of political ideology and theatre practice newly and distinctly productive.

As a play, *Northern Star* attempts to recuperate a non-sectarian, non-nationalist Irish republicanism, in the interest of resuscitating a political subjectivity that the modern conflict in Northern Ireland has largely effaced. McCracken, along with a number of other leaders of the 1798 rebellion, was both Northern and Presbyterian. Now, it is easy to forget that agitation for Irish independence was once an ecumenical project and that Belfast was very much its locus. (When the British government declared martial law in Ireland in 1798, its brutal counter-insurgency campaign especially targeted Ulster, partly because the northern province was a hotbed of political unrest and partly as a strategy to discourage the kind of non-sectarian alliances that the United Irishmen most prominently represented.) *Northern Star*, therefore, seeks to overturn an equation of republicanism with Catholicism and nationalism that has been naturalised since Daniel O'Connell's parliamentary-led campaign for Catholic emancipation in the early nineteenth century. It highlights a historical period when an independent Irish republic of thirty-two counties was an aspiration shared by those from a variety of faiths and backgrounds within what is now Northern Ireland, and in Belfast especially.

The political subjectivity that McCracken proposes, and which the play attempts to resuscitate, can be seen as a kind of civic republicanism. Although there may be some degree of romanticism in its recuperation by Parker, there is nothing historically fanciful about civic republicanism itself. Historian I. R. McBride argues that the portion of the Irish independence movement that came together in the United Irishmen and led the 1798 rebellion depended on the recasting of a 'denominational group' (a radical Presbyterian one) into a 'civic community' that was understood to be the basis of a non-sectarian (though not secular) and independent Ireland.[40] McBride argues that the northern part of Ireland was characterised by a 'rich associational culture which included Masonic lodges, constitutional clubs in Lisburn, Belfast, and Newtonards, and the lively democracy of the Belfast town meeting'.[41] The liberal ideals of the American and French revolutions, which influenced the United Irishmen greatly, were mediated through experience of these civic institutions and civic political discourse. The patriotic rhetoric of the United Irish, therefore, was not an expression of the type of nationalism that would become entrenched during the nineteenth century under leaders like O'Connell, but rather reflected an allegiance to a vision of an independent Ireland that was the macro-level version of the civic communities of which many of the United Irishmen had intimate experience and which they valorised. While the ideals of a civic political subject and a civic republican Ireland were largely extinguished in the years following the imposition of union between Britain and Ireland in 1800, *Northern Star* points to a moment in Irish history where such ideals were actively debated and practised.

Civic republicanism, as McBride observes, emphasises participation and is heavily associational; that is, civic political subjects and communities are understood to be outcomes of participation in the public sphere rather than pre-conditions for it. Moreover, its legitimacy does not depend on sanction either by the private individual or the state in the last instance. Quite the opposite, as Gerard Delanty notes, '[t]he challenge for civic republicanism is to preserve as much of the autonomy of the political field as possible, to prevent politics from becom[ing] privatistic or statist'.[42] Delanty argues that civic republicanism 'is about participation, not merely rights and duties. As a private person one has rights and duties but only in public action is citizenship a meaningful category . . . . [It] is a communitarianism of participation, with identity playing relatively little role. Rather than identity or loyalty to an abstract ideal it is more a question of commitment to achieving a common goal.'[43]

The potential viability of civic republicanism is amplified in any production of *Northern Star* by the social form and (imagined or actual) deliberative potential of the theatre event itself. Put simply, the theatre event looks like the political forum the play privileges, and its spectators look like the citizens it models. Moreover, theatrical citizenship has tended to be conceived along similar lines to civic republicanism, where theatre is commonly understood to function in contradistinction from the national state (statutory national theatres aside) or in opposition to it.[44] And its efficacy has also tended to hinge on the transformative potential of participation and the virtues of association: theatre is very adept at producing communities out of those who do not necessarily have much in common, and membership in these spectatorial communities may be deeply felt, even if, as is usually the case, they only exist for a short time.

The persuasiveness of *Northern Star*'s civic appeal does not hinge on its empirical verifiability, though. It relies, instead, on the extent to which political and theatrical spaces and subjectivities appear to mimic each other socially, rhetorically, and affectively. The distinctive spatiality of the 1998 production only intensified these political and theatrical homologies. The potential efficiency of the production emerged at the typological level (through site-specific performance's distinctiveness from other performances that are not spatially self-reflexive) and in this particular instance (through performing *Northern Star* in the First Presbyterian Church in 1998).

The 1998 *Northern Star* actively cultivated this recognition on the part of the spectator. As a playscript, *Northern Star* proposes that a citizen will come into being by imaginatively walking the streets of Belfast. The elaboration of this proposition involves using Belfast's streetscape in order to conjure an ironic geography of Belfast that is simultaneously utopian and deeply ambivalent about the city itself. As McCracken puts it in the final speech of the play, which he addresses directly to the audience:

> Why would one place break your heart, more than another? A place the like of that? Brain-damaged and dangerous, continually violating itself, a place of perpetual breakdown, incompatible voices, screeching obscenely away through the smoky dark wet. Burnt out and still burning. Nerve-damaged, pitiable. Frightening. As maddening and tiresome as any other pain-obsessed cripple. And yet what would this poor fool not give to be able to walk freely again from Stranmillis down to Ann Street ... cut through Pottinger's Entry and across the road for a drink in Peggy's ... to dander on down Waring Street and examine the shipping along the river, and back on up to our old house ... we can't love it for what it is, only for what it might

> have been, if we'd got it right, if we'd made it whole. If. . . . (*by the rope at the top of the stairs*) There is of course another walk through the town still to be taken. From Castle Place to Cornmarket, and down to the Artillery Barracks in Ann Street. And from thence back up Cornmarket to the scaffold. So what am I to say to the swarm of faces? *He places the noose around his neck.* Citizens of Belfast. . . . *The lambeg is loudly beaten, drowning out any further words along with the singing of Mary and the blackbird. Fade lights to black.*[45]

McCracken's repetition of the word 'if' (both at the start of a series of subordinate clauses and, for emphasis, as a stand-alone sentence) is both backward and forward-looking. Although he laments a victory that did not happen, he implies that it could still happen in the future, and illustrates this with recourse to an urban metaphor: the streets of Belfast itself. The streets that McCracken names still exist, and a Belfast audience, in particular, would know them well. He aspires to 'walk freely from Stramillis down to Ann Street', to 'dander on down to Waring Street'. In walking these streets he maps out a way to make the city whole, each stride knitting its urban fabric together and geographically producing himself and the audience as citizens of Belfast.

This utopian psychogeography is haunted, however, by the spectre of death and defeat. McCracken delineates a second walk through Belfast, but this one ends at the gallows, the political ideals endorsed by the play deferred. The last line of the play – 'citizens of Belfast' – is a symbolic passing of the baton: which walk will be taken? But it is also a reminder that each walk will always be haunted by the spectre of the other that could have taken place, where the citizenship posited by the play will go unrealised. The civic politics of *Northern Star*'s script, then, are deeply ambiguous.

But performing the play in the First Presbyterian Church diminished the ambiguity of McCracken's final speech by shifting its spatio-temporality to the present. In doing so, it spatially remade the cultural politics of the play. This is because the place of performance now superseded McCracken's uncertainty through its proxemic and phenomenal density. In a feature on the 1998 production in *The Guardian*, Michael Billington described the First Presbyterian Church as 'not only the starting point for the play but the hub of the radical culture it describes. Short of seeing Hamlet at Elsinor, you could hardly find a play that comes closer to home'.[46] Leaving aside the geographical inaccuracy of Billington's comparison – *Hamlet* is no more about the actual Danish castle than anywhere else, whereas *Northern Star* is at least concerned with the urban environment in which it was performed – he (perhaps unintentionally) points to the way that the production invoked an acute sense of spatial propriety and appropriated the play's 'radical culture' to itself. The First Presbyterian Church became an ostensibly more appropriate venue for *Northern Star* than, say, the Lyric: the Church embodies the Dissenting, pluralist tradition the play endorses (the congregation was one of the few in Belfast that never subscribed to the 1646 Westminster Confession of Faith, with its fierce anti-Catholicism); it is likely that many of the Belfast leaders of the 1798 rebellion actually worshipped there; the elliptical interior architecture of the Church suggests a less oppositional configuration of political and performance space than much church architecture of the time and, by extension, a more inclusive politics than that implied by the end-on arrangement of the Lyric; the Church is located in the city centre, in what was a security zone for much of the Troubles – the performance brought people to an area of the city at night that they were beginning to use again, and use again in the absence of heavily armed British troops walking the pavements.[47] The play's radical culture was no longer something that needed to be recuperated or prefigured, it was now insistently present, in this place.

Moreover, early in the play, McCracken refers to his home on Rosemary Lane; the First Presbyterian Church is around the corner on Rosemary Street. When McCracken names the streets through which he walks, these streets are in the immediate vicinity of the Church.[48] *Northern Star* invites audiences to walk the streets of Belfast imaginatively with McCracken, but to do so in a particularly evocative and affirmative way – we do not just walk, we dander. And given that the Troubles have riven the urban geography of Belfast to the extent that passing through it can sometimes be a challenge, it is not hard to understand the appeal of a rhetoric that symbolically knits the fractured, and immediately adjacent, geography of the city back together at a historical moment when that suturing might just begin to be possible. Here spectators were not so much *flâneurs* as urban developers.

This urban efficiency was also assisted by the production's inclusion within the Belfast Festival. A theatre festival makes monopolistic claims about time that mediate a festival-goer's engagement with the place of the festival. The combination of 'Festival time' and site-specific performance implies that a distinct place requires special attention for a limited period and that the particular experience of that place is only available through theatre and will no longer be available once the festival has ended. Transforming *Northern Star* into a site-specific performance during the Belfast Festival at Queen's intensified the play's phenomenal and geographical registers and changed the temporality of the play's political imaginary: *Northern Star* was no longer about recuperating a lost form of citizenship for an indefinite political future, it became, instead, about participation in the theatre event as an exemplary form of citizenship in the present. The production made itself the privileged instance of the radical political culture the play recuperates from history, but posits for a time and place yet to come. The 1998 production of *Northern Star* proclaimed, instead: this is what being a citizen of Belfast feels like, right here, right now.

Conclusion

The ability of Tinderbox's *Northern Star* to realise a peace dividend depended on a self-conscious, and largely successful, attempt to tighten the homology between the play's representational geography and its economic geography at a historically opportune moment. But modelling a citizen of Belfast in this way was hardly straightforward, and many of the ambiguities it entailed arose from the production's site-specificity. The civic republicanism that the Tinderbox *Northern Star* so effectively recuperated would be almost impossible to practise anywhere else in Northern Ireland today, and, indeed, that is partly the point: this politics has a past, it might have a future, but it is absent in the present (at least outside the theatre). The potential for the 1998 production of *Northern Star* to posit new political subjects and spheres was contingent, therefore, on the production's spatial appropriation of politics to itself in the present, within the walls of the First Presbyterian Church (with the promise of a higher politics outside the performance event appearing only as a phantasm). Thus the transformative potential of Tinderbox's *Northern Star* was ultimately contained within the theatre and its persuasiveness depended on both a feint and a circumscription: it became less about political-economic efficacy in the world outside the theatre, in the past or in the future, and more about practising an increasingly efficient and affectively intense form of spectatorship within it, in the present. In the Tinderbox *Northern Star*, spectators gave a model civic performance and, in the process, realised a peace divided that has proven stubbornly elusive elsewhere. Indeed, it is doubtful that this civic performance would be possible anywhere else.

CHAPTER 4

Security

When I come into the theatre I get a sense of security.
Commonly attributed to Vivien Leigh[1]

On the night of 6 February 2010, Roland 'Buzzy' Roy, a sixty-nine-year-old pharmacist living in Derby Line, Vermont, called Steve's Pizzeria and ordered a large smoked-meat pizza for pickup. After collecting his order Roy returned to his Main Street drug store via Church Street, passing the local library and theatre along the way. Not far from reaching his store, Roy was stopped by a police officer, who admonished him for using Church Street and told him that he was required to use Main Street instead. Roy protested and eventually the officer let him go. Wanting to press his point, Roy walked back down Main Street and returned, again, via Church Street. He was stopped and warned a second time by police officers. Once more he argued that he was permitted to use Church Street, and the officers allowed him to return to his drug store. Fed up with being stopped twice, Roy stubbornly repeated his circuit a third time: down the hill on Main Street and up again on Church Street. This time the police had had enough: they handcuffed him, put him in jail, and gave him a $500 fine.[2]

At first glance, this story appears unremarkable. Minor disputes between residents and law enforcement are a nightly occurrence in small towns across the United States, and Roy is hardly the first person to spend a few hours in jail after an argument with the local police. But two underlying facts make these events noteworthy: Steve's Pizzeria is not in Derby Line, Vermont, but in Stanstead, Quebec; and Church Street spans an international boundary. Roy had been fined for illegally crossing the US-Canada border.

Derby Line and Stanstead are small towns straddling the Vermont-Quebec border, approximately 300 kilometres northwest of Boston and 160 kilometres southeast of Montreal. Stanstead has a population of roughly 3,000 people, while Derby Line is home to about 800 residents.

Historically, the distinction between the two communities has been blurry, and residents have lived and worked closely together since Derby Line and Rock Island (as this part of Stanstead was known before Quebec reorganised municipal government in 1995) were settled in the 1790s.[3] The towns' streetscapes blend into each other, with a largely contiguous street grid spanning both sides of the border. Municipal services are shared between them: sewers, emergency services, and the local library and theatre are operated through a partnership between both towns.

When Buzzy Roy undertook his impromptu border protest in 2010, it was not simply (or only) because of irascibility on his part. Rather, he was insisting on crossing the border in the way that residents of Derby Line and Stanstead had done for as long as they could remember. Until relatively recently, residents were able to move between the two towns with little hindrance, only needing to report subsequently that they had done so at the appropriate border checkpoint on either side. After the attacks in the United States on 11 September 2001, however, the American and Canadian governments markedly increased security operations along the entire length of their shared border. Undertaking these ambitious securitisation programmes proved especially challenging in Derby Line and Stanstead, since it is the only place in the United States and Canada where the border runs through two contiguous, populated communities. Local residents also had close friends and families in both towns, and border-crossing was such a quotidian act that it hardly bore thinking about. In 2009, however, the United States Border Patrol and the Canadian Border Services Agency blocked off streets connecting Derby Line and Stanstead and mandated that all members of the public – residents included – use the border stations on Main Street to move between the two towns. Through its Operation Stonegarden programme, the US Department of Homeland Security significantly increased the police presence in Derby Line, resulting in much greater surveillance of the border from the American side. And, due to changes in law, initially in the United States and then in Canada, those crossing the border also required passports for the first time (before this Canadian and American citizens could be asked to present identification when seeking to enter each other's countries, but this identification did not have to take the form of a passport).

The only place in the two towns where the border can now be crossed legally without using a checkpoint is the Haskell Free Library and Opera House, which straddles the international boundary (Figure 4.1). Built in the early twentieth century as a testament to international cooperation and in memory of a local industrialist, the Haskell houses a public library on its

Figure 4.1 Haskell Free Library and Opera House, Derby Line, Vermont and Stanstead, Quebec (Michael McKinnie)

ground-floor and a 400-seat proscenium arch theatre on the floor above. The northern part of the building – which includes the stage, most of the auditorium, and a portion of the library – lies in Canada. The southern part of the building – which features the main entrance as well as the remaining parts of the library and theatre – lies in the United States. Notably, when local residents assembled for a 'Free Buzzy' rally following Roy's arrest, it was at the Haskell that they staged their protest.

The Haskell has received public attention periodically since it opened in 1904. In these accounts, the Haskell is commonly figured as a quixotic vestige of a kinder age (a figuration that residents of the two towns wear with notable grace, even if, when I visited, a Canadian border official remarked wearily that he was tired of people – like me – asking about the building).[4] It is perhaps not surprising that the Haskell continues to attract attention, or why such interest has grown in recent years. Many living in the Americas have experienced – in decidedly varied ways – the consequences of expanding global trade regimes and intensifying state securitisation programs. Border panic, while hardly a new feature of political and economic life in the Americas, has been mobilised especially forcefully since the election of Donald Trump as US President. In a feature on the Haskell in 2017, *Architectural Digest* magazine commented, 'As President Trump asks architects to start turning his campaign rally chant – "Build the Wall" – into something that *might actually materialize* along the US-Mexico border, it seems a good time to consider other more uplifting ways for architecture to engage national borders.'[5]

The Haskell memorialises a historical period before the US-Canada border was secured to the extent that it is now, and it appears to embody gentler and more self-consciously civic forms of international relations than seem possible today. This peaceable image is enhanced by the fact that Canada, in contrast to Mexico, is often imagined in the United States to be an essentially benign neighbour. (This perception is undoubtedly racialised, where Canada is either presumed to be a much Whiter country than it actually is or, mistakenly, a country characterised by an almost frictionless multiculturalism – it is also the corollary of the racist image of the US southern frontier, beyond which Trump's infamous 'shithole' countries lie.) The Haskell is also arguably the only place left on an American border, where high-minded forms of international relations continue to appear viable and, as a result, it seems to embody an alternative geopolitics to one ever more circumscribed by state power and paranoia.

In this chapter, I explore how the Haskell has become both an exceptional and exemplary civic institution in a time of increased securitisation. But I mean a civic institution in a particular sense here: as a local institution that promises to ameliorate geopolitical and geoeconomic antagonisms, but from a position within these realms rather than outside them. As I will show, the Haskell's civic promise is an effect of political economy and historical geography and is the result of more than a century-long process of securitisation (which I see as a particular form of marketisation, of which the current period is only the most recent iteration). Seeing how this has happened, though, and understanding why it might be appealing now, requires adopting a fairly expansive – and admittedly complex – theoretical and historical frame. The Haskell's civic promise depends not so much on its equidistance from the state and the market but on a deeply embedded relationship with them. The Haskell was also constructed at arguably the last historical moment possible, opening just before the American and Canadian governments began the long drive to make their shared border a visible space of state governance and authority; before the International Boundary Commission was created in 1908, the Canada-US border was a much more porous entity than it subsequently became. Furthermore, when the Haskell was built, it was unusual, but not rare, for buildings to straddle the border. The Haskell's exceptionality is partly the result of these buildings being demolished over time, so that its potential analogues ceased to exist.

While media stories about the Haskell have tended to frame it as an amiably eccentric enterprise, they nonetheless betray a continued attraction to, and social investment in, the type of civic institution that the Haskell embodies. This investment has only intensified with the failures of neoliberal securitisation and the nationalist authoritarianism that has arisen in response to it. The appeal of the Haskell is rooted in the fact that it appears to offer the only remaining space in which to practise forms of social relations that have been systematically foreclosed outside its walls, and to feel secure in doing so. (Recently, it has become a way for Iranians living in the US to see members of their families living elsewhere, who cannot enter the US because of the Trump-imposed 'travel ban' but can acquire visas to enter Canada.[6]) That the Haskell is comprised of a theatre and a library only amplifies this appeal, since theatres and libraries are both institutions historically understood to have privileged roles in cultivating 'place patriotism' and a healthy civil society.[7] Theatre, in particular, supplies bounded places and formalised events in which to model civil relations in ideal form (however solipsistically, as I argued in the previous chapter). The Haskell is seductive because it ostensibly provides not only a refuge from securitisation but also supplies a working hypothesis of how a reassuringly quotidian, but intensively transnational, model of civil society might operate within a security regime. It offers a place to feel secure, without feeling securitised.

Yet the Haskell also illustrates the tensions and ambiguities that such a proposition entails. My aim in this chapter is not to make a 'false consciousness' argument about theatrical security, where the places of performance somehow lull participants in the theatre event into a mistaken sense of their own autonomy ('So you think you're secure in the theatre? You're not, really'). Nor do I wish to make a normative argument, where theatre should, or should not, be a distinctively secure place, a refuge from the political and economic worlds outside its walls. (Ironically enough, the highest-profile iteration of this sentiment in recent years came from Trump, when he tweeted 'The Theater should always be a safe and special place' in response to the cast of *Hamilton* addressing Vice-President-Elect Mike Pence from the stage after a performance in New York in November 2016.[8]) Instead, I aim to show how the Haskell's civic appeal is a consequence of securitisation rather than a rejoinder to it and, as the history of the Haskell and the US-Canada border shows, this has been the case to some degree or another since its inception. Seen this way, the Haskell becomes a distinctively theatrical – and distinctively social – technology of political-economic governance: it localises social bonds that state-secured marketisation threatens to disperse and, in doing so, it retrieves social exchange from its wholesale appropriation by the state and the market. So if, like Vivien Leigh, we often get a sense of security in the theatre, the Haskell reveals something more complex and politically ambiguous than she admits: that theatrical security, in this time and place at least, is secured through a deep and intimate relationship with the state and the market.

Security, Government, and Civil Society

Security is one of the main reasons why states exist: to ensure the safety of the population within their borders vis-à-vis other states, and to regulate the movement of people and goods across borders. The emergence of the welfare state though, gave security a particular sort of political-economic inflection – 'social' security involved the state guaranteeing at least a minimum of economic welfare, and social security programmes became an important way for states to manage the volatility inherent in market economies (since these programmes often function as 'automatic stabilisers' during economic slowdowns, by helping to maintain aggregate demand in the economy at a time when it has weakened). But the coordinated attacks in the US on 11 September 2001, followed by the series of military and political conflicts that have occurred since, prompted many countries to undertake new (and expand existing) programmes of securitisation, and these meant something quite different. These political programmes have ranged from high-profile military interventions by the United States and its allies in Afghanistan and Iraq to the implementation of numerous subtler measures of border management (such as advanced electronic forms of passenger screening at airports and border crossings). But it is important to stress that securitisation also attends to economic interests, where security has come to be understood in terms of the free market: the freedom to trade without impediment, the assurance that this freedom will be upheld and promoted by governments of different political stripes, and the safety from state intervention in the exchange of goods and services. As Matthew B. Sparke observes, security now conjoins a *geopolitical* concern about 'homeland fortification' with a *geoeconomic* concern about free trade and economic interdependence.[9] Securitisation also depends on an array of institutions and 'technologies' (to use Michel Foucault's terminology) to shepherd the process and manage the tensions and contradictions that inevitably arise from it. Securitisation is a distinctive form of marketisation – and its political and economic shape shifts over time – but a form of it nonetheless.

Although governments in North America have made a series of political and economic proclamations about continental security since 2001, these have rarely been realised in practice. For example, the Security and Prosperity Partnership of North America, launched with great fanfare by the US, Canada, and Mexico in 2005, was moribund within a few years. Subsequent attempts to revive its ambitions, through various Canada-US 'Action Plans' (which notably excluded Mexico) were hardly a roaring success either. The election of Donald Trump, and the growing strength of conservative nationalist movements elsewhere in the world, also illustrate that the security consensus is less secure than it perhaps seemed to be.

This political-economic sense of security is not one commonly entertained in the modern theatre. Security is more likely to arise theatrically in one of two, loosely defined senses: as a condition for creating the inclusive theatrical communities on which the successful operation of certain types of theatre events is thought either to depend or to produce (as in some applied or socially engaged theatre work); or, conversely, as a bourgeois theatrical sentiment that should in some way be disrupted (as in the work of Antonin Artaud).[10] The conjunction of theatre with security has been more firmly, if metaphorically, made in recent years within the realm of surveillance and border security as opposed to within the institutional theatre. 'Security theatre', a term first coined by technology writer Bruce Schneier in 2003, refers to measures that give the appearance of security without necessarily making anyone any safer.[11] Having to remove one's belt in order to pass through an x-ray station at an airport, clothing civilian border agents in military-style uniforms, displaying decoy surveillance cameras, and encouraging vigilance by posting warning notices in travel facilities – all of these are instances of security theatre. Not only do these techniques often give the appearance rather than the substance of security; they have the propensity to misfire badly, sometimes in ways that highlight the deeply racist foundations of the security mise-en-scène. For example, passengers have been forcibly removed from flights after speaking to each other in Arabic. In one incident in 2016, an Italian economics professor working in the United States was removed from a domestic American Airlines flight because another passenger thought he was writing something suspicious on a notepad. It turned out that he was travelling to an academic conference and was working out mathematical equations by hand.[12]

Although the notion of security theatre accurately highlights the performative logic of securitisation, there is no doubt that 'theatre' functions ambivalently in this context. While border security depends on things not always being as they appear, and appearances not always corresponding with effects, the operations and effects of such mimesis are much less secure in the realm of the state than they are in the theatre auditorium. But the conjunction of security with theatre is hardly reassuring within the world of performance either, since it entangles theatre with the state and the market, and appears to call into question the viability of theatre's civic promise: that, as an institution and place, it can resolve, or at least manage, political and economic antagonisms that seem endemic in the world outside the theatre.

The Haskell can also be seen as a type of border performance, a category that includes not only theatrical performances but other forms of artistic intervention, choreographed public display, and cultural and political institutions. Crucially, analyses of border performance often stress both the theatricality and liminality of borders. For geographers Louise Amoore and Alexandra Hall, the border is 'a political stage for the performance of control, a showy set of symbolic gestures' through which 'the sheen of security and controllability is conjured'.[13] It is also an in-between space where '[r]ights of passage intertwine with rites of passage, a radical indeterminacy that the border produces even as it seeks resolution through sovereign distinctions between categories of mobile bodies'.[14] Border performances intervene in this political mise-en-scène by disrupting the operations of the security technologies on which the border relies. As Amoore and Hall put it:

> [A]rtists can intervene on the border in ways that exceed 'the symbolic', or the manipulation of signs. In producing theatre from the border, or revealing the border as theatre, or reworking its rituals, artistic interventions are able to reconfigure or transform the space that is created through the border and its technologies of security.

Put simply, the border's security theatre is undone by the artistic theatricality of border performance.

The appeal of this hermeneutic is not hard to grasp. Theatre is not only an apt metaphor for the types of display that borders often involve but also a useful way to account for the fine-grained operations of border security – it both delineates and denaturalises security technologies. And if the concept of liminality emerges from anthropology, its widespread migration to other disciplines and fields means that it resonates with scholars across cultural geography, international relations, and theatre and performance studies (among others). The liminality trope may be especially attractive to performance studies scholars, since, via its adoption by Richard Schechner in his early work, it is one of the founding concepts of the field. (For a performance theorist, to characterise a socio-political phenomenon as performative and liminal is not only a familiar critical gambit but almost a pledge of allegiance to one's own field.)

The Haskell shows that this way of thinking about border performance has its limitations, though. These lie not so much in the use of theatricality or performativity to account for border security – as useful as these critical frames are in this context – but reside instead in the liminality trope, both conceptually and in its application. Characterising borders as liminal spaces runs the risk of confusing a binational (or, in some circumstances, multinational) space with an extranational, extraterritorial one. As the Haskell illustrates, the border is not always a space between but a material fact that demands to be dealt with, not by blurring or deferring it but by managing it better. And although this management is theatrical we should not assume that it is transformative per se, or at least not transformative in the normatively resistant sense articulated previously. Indeed, the civic appeal of the Haskell's border performance depends not so much on its theatrical resistance to security as on its theatrical intimacy with it.

At the same time, the Haskell also highlights the limitations of how civil society, and theatre's relationship to it, has commonly been viewed. The civic scene that I outlined in the previous chapter is largely a liberal democratic one, with a healthy amount of communitarianism mixed in. In this scene, civil society stands in contradistinction from the state, and theatre's imagined role is to model forms of social citizenship – and social relations writ large – outside of the state's purview. (In spite of their institutional affinity in many countries, the state has historically been treated with a large dose of scepticism in modern Euro-American theatres, and this suspicion is intensified by what Christopher B. Balme characterises as the common, if historically inaccurate, presumption that theatre is an essentially oppositional institution.)[15] It is also a scene that is presumed to be deliberative rather than economic (and this bifurcation arguably reflects a latent ambivalence about theatre's own economic character). In order to grasp the Haskell's civic exceptionalism, though, a more *governmental* understanding of civil society is helpful, since the Haskell's civic promise depends on its deep imbrication with political-economic governance and the market economy that governance is intended to serve, rather than theatre's autonomy from governance or its liminal relationship to it. This promise also rests not so much on the operation of individual theatre events but on the Haskell's built form and institutionality, and the forms of spatial management that have historically sustained them.

In Michel Foucault's influential thinking about 'governmentality', which he first sketched out in a series of lectures on biopolitics at the College de France in 1979, he (typically opaquely) characterises his inquiry as a 'study of the rationalization of governmental practice in the exercise of political sovereignty'.[16] Governmentality, as Lloyd and Thomas put it, is concerned with 'the process by which, in the general emergence of the "policing" of societies, a population becomes subject to bureaucratic regimes and disciplines'.[17] These include 'modes of bodily discipline – hygiene, regulation of labor, incarceration or education – and the scientific disciplines – demography, criminology, medicine, and so forth – by which a population can be categorized and regulated in manageable groupings'.[18] In teasing out some of the complexities of Foucault's thinking (hopefully more clearly than he sometimes does himself), my goal is not so much to extend the concept of governmentality, or to undertake an especially Foucauldian analysis of the Haskell; for all its hermeneutic utility, the historicity of governmentality can be imprecise, and if Foucault's emphasis on the heterogeneity of governmental institutions and practices is broadly welcome, he sometimes underplays instances of hegemonic, coordinated state power. Nonetheless, Foucault theorises the relationship between the state, the market, and civil society in distinctive and useful ways. He helps open up a more embedded account of the Haskell's civic role than we might otherwise formulate.

To adapt Foucault's language, the Haskell 'exists in a complex relation of exteriority and interiority vis-à-vis the state'.[19] It is clearly not in a *dirigiste* relationship with the American or Canadian national states (in which case it would be an instrument of state power) and yet its existence and operations have been heavily overdetermined by them. As a place of performance, furthermore, the Haskell offers a distinctive way to manage a spatial contradiction at the heart of liberal civil society that securitisation would otherwise threaten to explode altogether: it localises bonds between social subjects in distinctive ways, and this role has become ever more important as analogues elsewhere are abolished and border panics recur.

Throughout his lectures on biopolitics, Foucault explores how the ascendency of laissez-faire capitalism, as a political and economic ideal in the eighteenth century, radically changed what the proper domain of government was understood to be and the forms of governing that should be practised within it. Liberal government, according to Foucault, draws its legitimacy from society rather than the state, and, as a result, it conceives of the sphere of government and the act of governing in entirely new ways. Whereas under absolutism the state was supreme and the project of government was the achievement of its objectives, liberal government (or governmentality, as Foucault often calls it) 'starts instead from society': it emerges in reference to, and gains its authority from, social subjects and the relations they conduct with each other.[20] But because these subjects and relations are conceived as fundamentally capitalist in nature – society is comprised of 'economic men' engaged in market exchange – government should ideally happen in such a way as to be laissez-faire: the state should 'leave be' the economic agents who inhabit its dominion. Liberal governmentality thus reconfigures the relationship between the state, government, and society. If, before liberalism, government was the means by which the sovereign exercised its authority over its subjects, now government aims to advance the interests of society (figured as a market) through the state. Laissez-faire governmentality thus subordinates the state to the market, but it paradoxically produces a great deal more governing, albeit in different and more diffuse ways than before. Liberal government demands the creation of a whole new battery of governing institutions and practices in order to serve market interests and, at the same time, demonstrate the limits of the state's agency and coordinating power. As a result, the project of governing is shot through with doubts about its own legitimacy:

> Liberalism ... is imbued with the principle: 'One always governs too much' – or at least, one should always suspect that one governs too much. Governmentality should not be exercised without a 'critique' far more radical that a test of optimization. It should not only question itself about the best (or least costly) means for achieving its effects, but also about the possibility and even legitimacy of its project for achieving effects. The question behind the suspicion that there is always the risk of governing too much is: Why, after all, is it necessary to govern?[21]

The answer to this question, at least in part, is 'in order to serve the market'. But as Foucault repeatedly points out, doing this is no easy matter.

In lectures eleven and twelve, Foucault turns to one of the key challenges for liberal government, which is how to govern once society is comprised of beings that are first and foremost economic subjects. As he puts it, 'the art of government must be exercised in a space of sovereignty – and it is the law of the state which says this – but the trouble, misfortune, or problem is that this space turns out to be inhabited by economic subjects'.[22] Why are these economic subjects such a challenge to 'the art of government'? Foucault argues that a new and revolutionary figure emerges in the latter half of the eighteenth century: *homo œconomicus*, or economic man. For Foucault, *homo œconomicus* appears as an exemplary figure in the philosophical and economic thought of the Scottish Enlightenment, most notably in David Hume's *Enquiry Concerning the Principles of Morals* (1751), Adam Ferguson's *Essay on the History of Civil Society* (1767), and Adam Smith's *The Wealth of Nations* (1776).[23] *Homo œconomicus* cannot be identified as the 'subject of right of juridical thought'.[24] In other words, when the social subject is conceived first in economic rather than legal terms, that subject possesses interests that exist only for itself and that are beyond the reach of the sovereign; *homo œconomicus* is, in Foucault's words, 'irreducible, non-transferable [and] atomistic'.[25] This new subject is the base unit of the market economy, which ideally operates not through subjects acting according to their collective good, but through the aggregate effect of subjects acting according to their self-interests (this logic is best articulated, of course, by Smith in *The Wealth of Nations*). The market is predicated on the multiplication of individual interests, not the pursuit of shared interests.[26] Indeed, collective benefit depends on agents' interests being invisible to each other (the 'invisible hand', in Smith's formulation).

The appearance of *homo œconomicus* constitutes a major challenge to older, juridical conceptions of government, in which the sovereign's interests ultimately determine the subject's rights, including its economic ones. Under absolutism, to govern is to express the full reach of the sovereign's authority over its subjects. Liberalism, however, constrains the sovereign's power, since it involves governing subjects who are, by definition, not fully governable – not because they are actively rebellious but because, as *homo œconomici*, they can never, by definition, be entirely subjected to the sovereign's rule. There are two possible responses to this governmental quandary, Foucault suggests. The first is for the state to retreat, to establish a 'frontier' beyond which the market operates and the state does not seek to govern. In this model, the law remains the preserve of the state, but the economy is ceded wholly to the market; government proceeds, but with the economy subtracted from its purview.[27] The second possible response is to retain the economy within the realm of government but for government to become subordinate to the market. This preserves the historical sphere of government but changes the nature of governing, which becomes simultaneously a more passive operation (the state sublimates its own interests to those of the market) and a more diagnostic one (the state keeps vigilant watch over the market, not to control it but to help it function optimally).[28]

Although the second model of government was clearly ascendant from the late eighteenth century onwards in European and American thought, Foucault argues that 'neither of these solutions was able to be any more than a theoretical and programmatic virtuality which was never really applied in history'.[29] The aspiration, though, was clear: 'for the art of governing not to have to split into two branches of an art of governing economically and an art of governing juridically, in short, to preserve the unity and generality of the act of governing over the whole sphere of sovereignty'.[30] Realising this aim – making this 'virtuality' a reality, in however embryonic a fashion – required the creation of a new 'domain' and 'reality' on which governing would subsequently be based: civil society.[31]

For Foucault, *homo œconomicus* and civil society 'are two inseparable elements'. Civil society is 'the concrete ensemble within which these ideal points, economic men, must be placed so that they can be appropriately managed'.[32] This involves a different understanding of civil society from that often employed in popular political discourse, where it stands apart from the state and the market – not necessarily untouched by them, but with some autonomy nonetheless (the phrase 'civil society organisations' now usually denotes non-governmental and not-for-profit groups that often have some contact with the state and the market but are not part of them). Foucault, however, warns against seeing civil society as 'an historical-natural given which functions in some way as both the foundation of and source of opposition to the state or political institutions'.[33] Seeing it in this way would, for him, risk obscuring the extent to which civil society emerges not in opposition or contradistinction to government but as a key part of modern government, with all of its juridical and economic concerns (and seeing theatre, as a civic institution, along these lines would obscure its historical proximity to modern government, which in Euro-American theatres has been established not only through statute but also through the realms of urban planning, funding regimes, tax policy, and so on). Ultimately, civil society is a way to resolve the problem of governing the ungovernable, without appearing to do so.

Foucault suggests that this model of civil society is best expressed in Adam Ferguson's *Essay on the History of Civil Society*. According to Foucault, Ferguson's civil society is 'actually the concrete, encompassing element within which the economic men Smith tried to study operate'.[34] It is defined by four main characteristics. First, civil society is 'an historical-natural constant'.[35] There is nothing before civil society, and even if something existed, it is impossible to know what this would be because it would be completely divorced from what makes us human beings: our sociability. (Foucault points out that Ferguson's reasoning is rooted in a utopian view of society prevalent in the eighteenth century.[36]) Second, the bonds of civil society are formed through 'spontaneous synthesis' between individuals, but this involves no delegation of natural rights to others or determination of shared interests.[37] Rather, social bonds are the result of individuals acting according to their own self-interest, indifferent to the interests of others. While social relations cannot be reduced entirely to an economic calculus, civil society 'has the same form as the immediate multiplication of profit in the purely economic mechanism of interests'.[38] The contents may be different from the economy but their shared form allows *homo œconomicus* to function: civil society is 'much more than the association of different economic subjects [but] the form in which this bond is established is such that economic subjects will be able to find a place and economic egoism will be able to play its role within it'.[39] Third, civil society may be social but its operation does not depend on collaboration or equality. Quite the opposite, in fact: it is a highly differentiated sphere constituted through clear divisions of labour and an unequal distribution of authority. Spontaneous synthesis, then, is accompanied by spontaneous subordination. Fourth, and finally, civil society is 'the motor of history'.[40] Because civil society appears to form spontaneously, we imagine 'that we are dealing with a stable equilibrium' whose existence must be transhistorical.[41] The reality, though, is much more unstable and ad hoc, since 'the egoism of power' ensures that the bonds between members of civil society are as much dissociative as they are associative.[42]

The difficulty with Foucault's theory of governmentality is that it appears nowhere more perfectly than in his account of it. (This is somewhat ironic, given that the concept describes technocratic instruments that tend to conceive social subjects and practices as ideal forms rather than messy actualities.) And if he is conscious that civil society has a geographical dimension, in that it localises social bonds between economic subjects that would otherwise disperse, he offers little sense of how this spatiality might actually be manifest in practice. Nonetheless, Foucault's model has merit, both on its own terms and in how it might invite us to think again about theatre's civic form and its civic potential, while taking into account the political-economic relations that have delineated these in the first place. While I would not want to overstate it or take him too literally, Foucault's vision of civil society is closer to how theatre usually operates than we might sometimes want to admit: whatever theatre's civic promise, it cannot transcend theatrical and political-economic relations that are themselves often highly differentiated, egoistic, and of limited durability (even though the promise itself involves holding out the possibility of that transcendence). At the same time, however, theatre is also very good at making such tensions productive rather than destructive, both institutionally and spatially. This would be important at any time, but it is especially appealing at times of increased securitisation.

The Haskell and the Border

The Haskell opened in 1904, its construction prompted by a combination of turn-of-the-century private philanthropy and distinctive local geography.[43] Like many public buildings built in the United States and Canada at roughly the same time (most notably the many libraries sponsored by industrialist Andrew Carnegie), the Haskell owes its existence to the patronage of a well-to-do business family. The Haskells had become wealthy through Carlos Freeman Haskell's ownership of a number of sawmills on the American side of the border. Carlos was an American citizen; his wife, Martha Stewart Haskell, was a Canadian. After Carlos's death, the Haskell family decided to build a public library and theatre directly on the US-Canada border, so that residents of Derby Line and Rock Island could share equally in the building's services. The Haskells' sponsorship of the building's construction neatly illustrates the way that international relations in this particular time and place bridged political, economic, and familial interests, and in this, they were not atypical.

Architecturally, the Haskell is styled in the vernacular of late-nineteenth and early-twentieth-century public buildings in central Canada and the midwestern and northeastern United States. This civic infrastructure, which commonly included libraries and town halls, was often executed, like the Haskell, in a neo-classical style, albeit on a modest scale that was adapted to local building fashions and materials – in smaller towns, at least, these were buildings designed to impress but not impose. The Haskell is clad in yellow brick and local grey granite and was designed by a local architect with a Boston-based partner. The simultaneous display of high-mindedness and paternalism found in many buildings from the same period can be seen in the Haskell. On the one hand, its library was designed with open stacks and a comfortable, well-lit reading room – people, the new thinking of the time suggested, should be able to browse books as they saw fit, and read them in a relaxed environment. On the other hand, the elaborate woodwork on display throughout the building – featuring an unusually wide range of high-quality woods in floors, wainscoting, doors, architraves, ceiling work, and more – clearly reminded the Haskell user that construction of the building had been made possible through the beneficence of a local lumber baron.

The opera house is a scaled-down version of the grander proscenium arch theatres commonly built in many larger, urban centres in North America during the late nineteenth century (across North America in the nineteenth and early twentieth centuries the term 'opera house' was commonly applied to venues used for a wide variety of theatrical performances rather denoting a grand building intended specifically for opera). Seating is on two levels: a gently curving, lightly raked main block of seats on the floor, with a smaller number of seats in a shallow, horseshoe-shaped balcony above. The original wooden seats are still in use today, although several have been removed to allow wheelchair and disabled access. The stage, at the north end of the building, is framed by a proscenium arch, with a small apron extending through its aperture. Although the theatre is hardly ostentatious, its decoration nonetheless betrays an attempt to achieve a modest grandeur: the balconies and proscenium frame are embellished with ornate plasterwork and gilt; the wall surrounding the proscenium arch is painted with cherubs; and the original, painted scroll-drop curtain features a decorative image of Venice. (The original drop stage sets, also painted by noted Boston-based artist Erwin LaMoss, are among the few intact examples of their kind in North America from this period.) As in the library downstairs, a thick black line is painted on the floor to mark the US-Canada border (Figure 4.2). The stage and most of the auditorium's seating are in Canada; the balcony and the remaining seats are in the United States.

The opera house opened on 7 June 1904 with an engagement by the Columbian Minstrels, a 'grand revival of old-time black-face minstrelsy', and a musical revue based on local topics called *The Isle of Rock*.[44] The opera house was built to tap into the summer popular entertainment touring circuit that operated along the railway network linking Quebec with the northeastern US, with important hubs at Boston and Montreal. (This part of Quebec's Eastern Townships has historically been largely English-speaking, and the Townships have been a summer holiday destination for affluent, predominantly anglophone Montrealers and New Englanders since the nineteenth century.[45]) The initial intention was that profits from the opera house would subsidise the operation of the library

Figure 4.2 Haskell Free Library and Opera House, theatre auditorium with border marked on floor (Michael McKinnie)

downstairs, but this plan became impractical as cross-border theatre touring waned during the early twentieth century. The fact that its opening show included a 'grand revival of old-time black-face minstrelsy' also demonstrates that the high-minded civic internationalism that the Haskell espoused was not seen to be compromised by the suspect politics of minstrel shows. If anything, the opening night programme reveals that those civic ideals could comfortably be articulated through, and not undermined by, the racist performance tropes of minstrelsy, and it suggested that border-crossing – which was being viewed with increasing suspicion in both the US and Canada at the time – might (at least temporarily) be rehabilitated through the public performance of Whiteness.

The building was subsequently bequeathed to Rock Island and Derby Line by the Haskell family and is still operated jointly by local trustees drawn from both sides of the border. It has also been designated a historical site by Canada, the United States, and Quebec. The library, today, is much like any other local public library, and the opera house, in common with many other small-town theatres in North America, offers a summer stock programme of amateur and semi-professional performance. The fact that the Haskell combines a library and opera house is not completely eccentric when seen from the perspective of the early twentieth century: libraries and opera houses were important elements within the repertoire of civic facilities constructed in small towns and larger cities in North America at the time, and it was hardly a huge leap to combine them in a single building.

The appeal of the Haskell is rooted, at least in part, in its rematerialisation of a local way of life practised before the international border between the United States and Canada was secured to the extent that it is today. Ironically, the Haskell resuscitates a historical period when the border was, in many ways, immaterial to residents of Derby Line and Rock Island; in Craig Robertson's framing, this was a time when the two communities shared a highly porous boundary line rather than an (ostensibly) sealed border.[46] Although this distinction is as much heuristic as empirical, it usefully highlights a historical fact largely forgotten in on both sides of the border today: that at the turn of the twentieth century the international boundary between the US and Canada was not generally understood as a 'space of exclusion' by the American and Canadian states in the way that it has been for roughly the past century.[47] Americans and Canadians could cross the border much more freely than they can today; not only was showing one's identity papers rare, in many places along the boundary it would have been difficult to find a border post at which to present them. But modern border governance – with its attendant checkpoints, documentation, and surveillance – has sought to make a 'hard' border between the US and Canada seem both a political inevitability and a transhistorical constant, however folksy the spin put on this fact by its guardians might be. As the International Boundary Commission characterises it:

> An effective boundary allows residents of Estcourt, Maine, and Pohénégamook, Quebec, to know that their porch is in the United States while their kitchen is in Canada. It allows moose hunters in Maine and golfers in southern Saskatchewan to know that their next shot may take them on an international venture. It also allows crab fishermen in Boundary Bay to know which set of fishing regulations to respect. It does what people need a boundary to do: it defines our space.[48]

The 'our' in this final sentence depends on the nationality of the reader, of course. But this rather populist rationale for the US-Canada border should not distract from the fact that the border is overseen by large and well-armed agencies from both countries, and the movement of people and goods across it is tightly controlled.

At the time of the Haskell's construction, however, the international boundary impinged on everyday life in Derby Line and Rock Island, and the US and Canada, very differently from how it does now. In border communities and regions, it was common for economic, familial, and cultural networks to span the line, and for their members to cross back and forth almost at will. As Matthew Farfan comments:

> The culture north of the border was very much an extension of that to the south. Members of extended families lived on opposite sides of the line. Trade functioned almost as though there were no border at all. People traveled freely back and forth. Settlements in the Eastern Townships were served by preachers from Vermont. Popular attitudes and traditions were almost indistinguishable.[49]

Farfan captures the permeability of the border in the late nineteenth century well, but the actual social relations of the time were rather more politically and economically complex, and less symmetrical, than he implies. In an arrangement that is almost the complete reverse of the situation today, the flow of labour across the border in the latter part of the nineteenth century was more significant than that of goods.[50] Canadians and Americans were legally permitted to live and work on either side of the border without being subject to the sort of stringent residency and employment restrictions that residents of both countries now take for granted. Trade, though, was less straightforward, with high tariffs on imports imposed by both the US and Canada. These tariffs simultaneously discouraged cross-border movement of goods and encouraged migration of people. (This migration was almost entirely southward – few Americans made the equivalent trip north.) Migration occurred despite growing resentment from American organised labour groups about Canadian workers seeking employment in the US and the related spread of anti-immigrant political discourse south of the border. (Bruno Ramirez highlights an especially ugly example of French-Canadian migrants being described as the 'Chinese of the East' in an 1881 report by the Massachusetts Bureau of Labor Statistics, because of their supposed willingness to accept lower wages than American-born workers.[51]) US protectionism, perhaps unintentionally, assisted the rapid growth of cross-border labour markets, particularly in the Great Lakes Basin and between Quebec and New England, as tariff-sheltered American industries expanded and sought out new supplies of Canadian workers. The McKinley Tariff of 1890 effectively blocked Ontario's agricultural exports to the US but, in doing so, it prompted large numbers of Canadian farm workers to cross the border in search of work. As a result, David R. Smith observes, it 'contributed to the movement of Canadians across the border while unwittingly also satisfying US manufacturers' need for labor'.[52] Quebec also provided a significant part of the workforce for the textile mills of Massachusetts, and evidence of cross-border mobility can still be seen in the large number of French surnames in Vermont and elsewhere in New England. It was common for Canadians to move back and forth between the two countries multiple times as, without the hassle of needing to seek naturalisation to live and work in the US on an extended basis, there was little incentive to apply for permanent resettlement.[53] They could move between the two countries as work and life demanded.

Cross-border life was not only defined politically and economically, though. The Haskell family itself, which spanned both sides of the line, exemplified the types of kin networks commonly found in northern Vermont and southern Quebec (with the notable difference that, unlike most families in the Northern Kingdom and Eastern Townships, the Haskells possessed the wealth to build a civic monument to them). Vermonters and Quebecers would also have had theatre in common. An English-speaking resident of the Eastern Townships, which was served by the Montreal-Boston touring circuit, would have had greater shared theatrical experience with someone living in New England than with someone living in southern Ontario (who, in turn, would have had more in common with someone in Michigan or Illinois, as they would have been served by the same Toronto-Chicago theatre circuit). Although the Haskell may have celebrated international cooperation, it was not so much testifying to abstract political principles as it was idealising, in built form, political, economic, and theatrical relations that were contested, but nonetheless still part of people's everyday lives.

The Haskell was constructed at almost the last historical moment before the programmatic creation of a securitised border began. The modern-day understanding of the border as a space of systematic state governance arguably dates from 1908, four years after the Haskell opened, when the United States and Canada formed the International Boundary Commission. The IBC was created to provide 'for the more complete demarcation of the boundary from Atlantic to Pacific and the preparation of accurate modern charts throughout', and it still performs this function today.[54] Securitising the border was a mammoth task: at nearly 9,000 kilometres in length, the US-Canada border is the longest between two countries anywhere in the world.[55] In practice, this meant undertaking accurate surveys of the border across huge expanses of water and through dense woodlands. It also entailed making the border more visible, since such visibility was a prerequisite for enforcement: how could border-crossing be regulated, and the border itself be policed, if it could not be seen?

During the 1920s, the ideal of an impermeable border began to be translated into material reality. As Robertson points out, the motivations for securing the border in the early twentieth century were primarily two-fold. In the first instance, it attempted to respond to American concerns about widespread and often highly organised smuggling of alcohol across the border at a time when Prohibition was in force in the United States but not in Canada.[56] It was also seen as a way to control 'back door' immigration to the United States from Canada after the US government, in response to virulent anti-immigrant campaigns, introduced strict overseas immigration quotas in the 1920s. Although Canadian citizens were exempt from the quotas imposed under the US Emergency Immigration Act of 1921, and were eligible for newly created residency visas, non-Canadians living in Canada were not. Border enforcement now involved differentiating between these newly legal and illegal immigrant groups (and in 1924 the US Congress created a national border patrol to help do this). But distinguishing legitimate from illegitimate migration was only possible by subjecting every border crosser to scrutiny, of a type and to a degree previously unknown. Not entirely surprisingly, all forms of migration from Canada fell, meaning that American nativists ultimately accomplished administratively what they had not legally.[57]

Border demarcation accelerated in 1925 after the IBC was made a permanent commission and when the United States, in particular, wished to entrench the border more emphatically. At sea, this often entailed placing buoys at key points in shared waterways. On land, it involved installing thousands of additional border markers. These often took the form of short posts, constructed out of granite, concrete, or metal, that were firmly embedded in the ground. (One of these is positioned next to the Haskell.) The IBC also cut six-metre-wide clearances through the many long, forested stretches of the border, leaving a three-metre-wide strip of each country on each side. The name chosen by the IBC for these clearances – 'vistas' – reiterated its desire for border visibility. Many new border stations were constructed, and requirements to report at those stations began to be more strictly enforced.

Where the border crossed through populated areas – as it did most commonly in Quebec and Vermont, as well as in New Brunswick and Maine and British Columbia and Washington – 'line houses' were identified and complex rules introduced to address them. Line houses were buildings, such as the Haskell but more commonly private residences, built across the boundary line. Robertson documents how the border's bisection of a line house was often marked by nailing large brass tacks into the building's exterior; the location of the front door determined which country assumed powers of inspection. Stories about line houses, figuring them as quirky spectacles, began to appear in American newspapers and magazines.[58] The fact that such stories appeared in the first place was a sign that what was once unremarkable had become now both a threat to 'the integrity of national territory' (in Ramirez's phrase) and, for Robertson, a sign of both the 'historic lack of interest in locating the line and enforcing it as an international border', and the newfound 'oddity of the international as a lens through which to apprehend the everyday'.[59] Most line houses were eventually demolished, leaving the Haskell as one of the few – and most notable – remaining anywhere along the border.

The more visibly the border was secured, then, the more exceptional the Haskell became. As the movement of labour across the US-Canada border was regulated increasingly strictly over the course of the twentieth and twenty-first centuries, and the movement of goods and services became progressively (if slowly) freer, the Haskell remained the only place where people could cross the border without the permission of either state. But the Haskell's exceptionality (and newfound idiosyncrasy) was in fact secured by those states, in 'hard' and 'soft' ways: from Department of Homeland Security surveillance outside its front door to the use of its image by the IBC for public promotion of its border maintenance programme.[60] While one might have the privilege of crossing the border without state surveillance inside the Haskell, this privilege was only secured through extensive state securitisation outside the Haskell. And it meant that the Haskell was a product of a security regime that increasingly equated visibility with surveillance while, simultaneously, offering alternative forms of visibility that seemed to dissent – or at least demur – from this regime.

When local residents gathered at the Haskell to protest the detention of Buzzy Roy, they demonstrated the extent to which the American and Canadian states now delimited their congregation (practically speaking, the Haskell was the only place residents of both countries could easily meet). At the same time, however, they forcefully reasserted the symbolic value of the Haskell itself. Their gathering signalled an investment in a form of civic life in which the local and the international were deeply intertwined in quotidian ways that are largely unavailable in North America now, and which, from the position of the contemporary security state, would be deeply undesirable if widely practised. What better way to reassert the value of such civic practices than through the maintenance of cultural institutions – a theatre and a library – that embody them through their built form, their institutional histories, and the forms of sociality they encourage? The Haskell allows visitors to practise a kind of civic transnationalism that is only possible in proximity to the building, even though they do so within a strictly securitised binational space.

As I argued earlier, civic spaces are important because they promise to localise social bonds that political and economic conditions might otherwise threaten to disperse (though, of course, this is a highly ambiguous promise). The somewhat trickier question is how the Haskell, in particular, does this at a microcosmic level, so that it becomes possible to sit in the United States and watch a play being performed in Canada. It is no accident that this scenario has been commonly invoked in coverage of the Haskell, since it seems to epitomise both the building's peculiarity and its performativity. It also illustrates how the civic sphere can be constituted through a conjunction of theatre and governance but, at the same time, supply forms of social exchange that the state and the market cannot themselves instantiate (and, in fact, are trying to foreclose).

Any theatrical event staged in the Opera House is made possible in the first place by complex forms of spatial management that only amplify the Haskell's appeal. Even the most cursory visit to the Haskell quickly reveals some of the practical complications that operating such a unique facility entails. For example, the black line indicating where the border bisects the building is not simply a curiosity to entertain tourists, though it does also perform that function: visitors touring the building are kindly prodded by staff to have their photographs taken with one foot on either side of the border, American and Canadian flags in hand, as a memento. (When I appeared slightly sheepish about performing this ritual, I was cajoled into doing so by a smiling local resident who, while returning her books, commented, 'Don't worry, everybody does it'.) The black line also reminds the visitor that the Haskell is not a space that blurs the border but, instead, insists emphatically on that border's governing presence and material effects.[61] It draws attention to the many cross-border considerations that must be taken into account on a daily basis in order for the Haskell to operate and its success in negotiating them: building regulations differ in Quebec and Vermont, so a tradesperson may only be able to work on one side of the building; movement of labour between the two countries is restricted; tax regimes are significantly different in Canada and the United States; the two countries do not share a common currency; fire codes are different on either side of the border; Quebec law requires that all signage include French as well as English, but this requirement only applies on the north side of the building; book titles in English are commonly printed from the top down on book spines, but the reverse is often the case in French – and so on. Although users of the Haskell may move easily – and pleasurably – between the United States and Canada, their ability to do so depends on a great deal of day-to-day management of the international border that takes place behind the scenes. Indeed, it is this constant negotiation between international free passage and micro-spatial governance that makes the Haskell so seductive, and its rarity and success in doing it mark it out as exceptional and exemplary. But this sort of spatial governance also makes theatre's own cross-border efficacy possible. In order to transcend border governance theatrically, theatre itself must be deeply embedded within it.

It is notably rare in coverage of the Haskell – recent or past – for any particular theatrical performance to be invoked. Theatre-going is, but not an actual show. This recurring elision suggests that the theatrical scenario has greater force as a generic, sometimes imagined, event than as a particular performance (though the place of performance must remain unique in order for this event to succeed). Part of the appeal of this generic event is that it appears, at first glance, to demonstrate theatre's power to dissolve political-economic boundaries while simultaneously instantiating an intensely localised theatrical community within the walls of the auditorium. While one might be conscious of the black line dividing the theatre space, the cross-border theatrical scenario implies that, when the lights come up and the show begins, that line becomes immaterial – what matters is not the border between the US and Canada, but the new civic sphere constituted through the operation of the theatrical event (which itself has the extraordinary power to transcend international borders). Thus, if the Haskell's civic promise depends on its theatricality, that promise is made nowhere more emphatically than in its theatre, since this is where border governance itself appears to vanish, if only temporarily, and new forms of social exchange are made possible theatrically (or older ones are imagined to be viable again – it is hard to tell which scenario applies, but either is attractive).

The opera house also remakes the meaning of visibility itself. One of the consequences of the securitisation of the US-Canada border (like borders elsewhere) has been a deepening equation of visibility with surveillance. The residents of Derby Line and Stanstead (and before that Rock Island) have historically occupied an unusual position vis-à-vis surveillance regimes. On the one hand, the longstanding tolerance of everyday border crossing meant that residents of the two towns had generally received some degree of dispensation from state border surveillance, to an extent that others in the US and Canada had not. On the other hand, when residents became newly subjected to an expanded surveillance regime in the early 2000s, the revocation of this historical privilege, combined with the geographical fact of the towns' unique cross-border topography, meant that they felt this subjection especially acutely. Residents of Derby Line and Stanstead were now arguably more visible to the US and Canadian governments than they were to each other, and this development was understandably unsettling.

A theatre, though, remakes the meaning of visibility and temporarily retrieves it from its appropriation for the purposes of surveillance. The opera house is a space where residents can gather face-to-face, conduct social relations in plain sight, and cross international borders at will, but within formalised events in an intensively managed venue (the Haskell shows, again, that theatre's institutional, social, and spatial forms are as important as its repertoire and sometimes more so). The opera house, along with the library downstairs, offers the space to rematerialise – temporarily but highly visibly – forms of intensely local social exchange that securitisation has progressively foreclosed.

Conclusion

From its inception, the Haskell has not only existed in relationship to the border, it has been constituted through it. Its appeal has only deepened as border security programmes became, historically, more extensive and familiar; indeed, it is only through the normalisation of securitisation that the Haskell might begin – and continue – to be as unusual and intriguing as it has come to be. Rather than being external or hostile to theatre, the Haskell shows how political-economic governance may instead be something on which theatre's civic performance depends. And to the extent that theatre might appear to offer a refuge from securitisation, especially at a time of border panic, the Haskell shows how this can result from a historical position within border governance, rather than in opposition to it. The Haskell also usefully undercuts any reluctance to think of theatre as an institution in the first place, let alone one in proximity to other institutions, especially those of the state and the market.[62] And it illustrates that theatrical events, however contingent they may be on broader forms of political, economic, and spatial relations, possess a social and mimetic force that can easily result in a kind of amnesia about theatre's own imbrication in them.

The Haskell, then, is a civic institution born not as the expression of an autochthonous local community but rather through a nexus of international political and economic relations. It has always been caught up in the historical practices and process of border governance – one does not need to metaphorise security as theatrical or performative in order to make this connection, when an actual theatre will do. Going to the theatre to 'get a sense of security', in the context of the Haskell, means using theatre as a way to understand how securitisation has historically functioned – in large and small ways – and asking what sort of security technology theatre itself might be. It is not so much an issue of feeling secure (or insecure) in the theatre, but getting a sense, through theatre, of what border governance means in a particular time and place. The Haskell suggests that we may go to the theatre not so much to be secure, but to grasp something much more complex and ambiguous: what political economy is in a given time and place, and how deeply theatre is caught up with it.

CHAPTER 5

Confidence

> The most leftie opening ceremony I have ever seen – more than Beijing, the capital of a communist state! Welfare tribute next?
>
> Aidan Burley, Conservative Member of Parliament, on Twitter while watching *Isles of Wonder* during the opening ceremony of the 2012 Olympic Games in London[1]

To be fair, Aidan Burley was never one of David Cameron's most dependable foot soldiers. The year before his Twitter outburst during the London Olympics' opening ceremony, the MP for Cannock Chase had been dismissed as a ministerial aide for helping to organise a Nazi-themed stag party – including buying an SS uniform worn by the groom on the night – at a French ski resort. (Wearing a Nazi uniform is illegal in France, and newspaper photos of the groom resulted in his being fined by a French court.) But Burley was clearly on a bit of a roll during *Isles of Wonder*, the theatrical performance that was the star of the opening ceremony. He followed up his initial comment by denouncing the show as 'leftie multicultural crap' and hoped that the rest of the ceremony would '[b]ring back red arrows [the Royal Air Force's acrobatic display team], Shakespeare and the [Rolling] Stones!'[2] After a media uproar over his tweets, Burley doubled down, directing particular opprobrium towards 'Second to the Right, and Straight on Till Morning', a scene that included a rousing tribute to the United Kingdom's National Health Service (Figure 5.1). 'We all love the NHS', Burley remarked, 'but really for all the people watching overseas, 20 minutes of children and nurses jumping on beds, that seems quite strange'. (He topped this off with some highly suspect remarks about the prominence of 'all these rappers' in a later part of the show.[3]) Burley's comments were swiftly disavowed by Number 10 Downing Street, the office of the Prime Minster.[4]

Staged by Danny Boyle, the theatre and cinema director best known for his Academy Award-winning film, *Slumdog Millionaire*, *Isles of Wonder* was

Figure 5.1 'Second to the Right, and Straight on Till Morning', *Isles of Wonder*, Opening Ceremony, London 2012 Olympic Games (Getty Images)

the set-piece of the three-and-a-half-hour opening ceremony. The show was performed by a professional and community cast of more than 7,500 in the newly-built, 80,000 seat Olympic Stadium in Stratford, East London.[5] Budgeted at a cost of approximately £27 million and lasting about ninety minutes, it offered a succession of extravagantly staged scenes depicting various moments in British history, each densely packed with references to significant British historical events and cultural figures: from the Industrial Revolution to the founding of the National Health Service to the creation of the World Wide Web, and from William Shakespeare to *Harry Potter* author J. K. Rowling to Mr. Bean, among others. As a theatrical event, *Isles of Wonder* was a hugely impressive undertaking, not only in terms of the inventiveness and scale of its staging but also in terms of the sheer amount of organisational skill involved in bringing it off.[6] Given that the opening ceremony attracted a peak audience of 27.3 million viewers in the UK and an estimated 900 million worldwide, it also remains possibly the most-watched live theatrical performance in British history.[7] And make no mistake, *Isles of Wonder* was theatre: its staging, performances, characterisation, and dramaturgy clearly marked it out as such, both in and of itself and in relation to other parts of the opening ceremony (such as the athletes' parade). The unusual scale and location of the show did not alter this fact. Indeed, they only amplified its efficacy as theatre.

In the UK, especially, media commentators almost universally applauded *Isles of Wonder*, regardless of their own political leanings or those of the outlets in which their work appeared (with the predictable exception of conservative newspaper columnist Stephen Glover, who complained in the *Daily Mail* that Danny Boyle 'had offered us a Marxist analysis without most of us realising!').[8] This widespread approval was not entirely surprising, since *Isles of Wonder* made a brazenly populist and good-humoured appeal to British – and often specifically English – patriotism while neatly sidestepping party politics. More intriguing, though, was the language that commentators used to describe the show. One word featured more than any other: 'bonkers'. The sense that *Isles of Wonder* was 'bonkers' (or its corollaries – that it was 'insane' or 'deeply odd') was undoubtedly produced through the interplay of several elements within the show itself: an especial density of cultural self-referentiality; a repeated interpolation of elite and mass cultural artefacts and practices; a mixing of historical periods and artistic genres; and a deployment of a very broad tonal spectrum, from the reverential to the silly to the fantastic. Taken together, these qualities somehow seemed almost quintessentially British. Weaving all of these elements into a ninety-minute narrative also meant that, dramaturgically, *Isles of Wonder* was a great deal more experimental than its populism implied, with the result that watching it was a more disorienting – if pleasurable – experience than might usually be expected of an Olympics opening ceremony (given how dull and worthy these have tended to be).

The language used to describe the performance was, however, prompted by something rather more than the show's eccentricity or eclecticism. Watching *Isles of Wonder* in the UK in 2012, it was notable how the performance, and the Olympics more broadly, played out against the programme of economic austerity imposed by the Conservative-Liberal Democrat coalition government of the time. The oddness that commentators identified in the performance was undeniably present, but it was not produced through the most obviously theatrical elements of the event alone. Instead, it resulted from the performance's ability to sustain a queasy interplay between those theatrical elements and the Olympic infrastructure on which the performance itself depended. This was most evident in the scene that so exercised Aidan Burley, and which garnered the most attention from commentators: 'Second to the Right, and Straight on

Till Morning', a celebration of Great Ormond Street Hospital, the National Health Service, and children's literature (given the title of the scene was taken from J. M. Barrie's *Peter Pan*, the royalties from which Barrie bequeathed to the hospital in 1929).[9] This scene, more than any other, threw into relief the sharply divergent political-economic scripts that the performance as a whole attempted to interpolate: a theatrically Keynesian one and an infrastructurally rentier one.

The delirium associated with the performance – what made it seem bonkers – resulted from watching the show pull off this trick. *Isles of Wonder* was an astonishingly confident performance but, more importantly, it was an exhilarating *show of confidence*. This is a distinction with an economic as well as a theatrical difference. In the social psychology of market economies, confidence plays an outsized role. We are familiar with politicians of different stripes proclaiming their desire to sustain business confidence (or restore it, or improve it, or whatever framing suits the political moment, as if business suffered from chronically low self-esteem). But in recent decades, promoting business confidence has frequently entailed governments across the political spectrum pushing through some combination of preferential tax treatment for corporations and higher earners, market deregulation, privatisation, and public spending constraint. And if capital has a complete breakdown anyway – having been made overconfident by all this care and attention – states have often responded by socialising private losses and imposing austerity, whether on their own citizens or the citizens of other countries (for example, the Eurozone's treatment of Greece after the financial crisis). This is the political-economic script that the UK government followed after 2010, but it was hardly alone in doing so.

But confidence is important in a market economy not simply as cover for state-led austerity, or for state patronage of favoured sectors like finance, but because of the central part it plays in the investment cycle. Confidence is what encourages investment when concrete knowledge about future political and economic circumstances are uncertain, at best. As Keynes puts it:

> The state of long-term expectation, upon which our [investment] decisions are based, does not solely depend, therefore, on the most probable forecast we can make. It also depends on the *confidence* with which we make this forecast – on how highly we rate the likelihood of our best forecast turning out quite wrong. If we expect large changes but are very uncertain as to what precise form these changes will take, then our confidence will be weak. The *state of confidence*, as they term it, is a matter to which practical men always pay the closest and most anxious attention.[10]

Public spending is key to instilling this state of confidence during times of economic turbulence, since it suggests an optimism about future conditions and is a down-payment on the improved productivity of the economy as a whole (since these investments are, ideally, intended to benefit producers and citizens generally, rather than reward a select few).

Of course, this has not always worked out so neatly in practice. But during the past decade, in the UK and elsewhere, the political commitment to austerity economics and the promotion of rent-seeking has hugely undermined this form of confidence-building. Here, though, is where theatre can intervene. On the one hand, *Isles of Wonder* contained, at its heart, a stirring theatrical tribute to social welfare and, through its coordination of a huge cast of performers drawn from a wide spectrum of British society, appeared to be a theatrical metonym of Keynesian forms of public investment and productivity. This was all the more appealing since that Keynesianism had largely been abandoned in the coalition government's embrace of austerity and rentier economics. On the other hand, *Isles of Wonder* successfully mobilised infrastructure (the Olympic Stadium, and the Olympics' building estate as a whole) that was a travesty of that Keynesianism. The Keynesian rationale for public investment in fixed assets is, at least in principle, to improve the productivity of the economy generally rather than to enrich particular producers. The London Olympics, however, entailed large amounts of public investment in fixed assets and the subsequent transfer of that infrastructure, at relatively low prices, to monopoly (or near-monopoly) control by private companies. The costs and risks of this investment were therefore largely borne by the public purse, but the profits (or rents) were ultimately intended to accrue to select interests in the private sector.

If in political economy these different approaches to economic governance are usually considered anathema to each other, *Isles of Wonder* demonstrated that in cultural economy this is not necessarily the case. Indeed, *Isles of Wonder* demonstrated the remarkable ability of performance to refigure what might otherwise be political-economic antagonisms into a theatrically and economically productive dialectic, if only for a short – but nonetheless spectacular – while. *Isles of Wonder* was a remarkable show of confidence, not only because it sought to instil a state of confidence that austerity suggested was no longer possible, but also because it suggested that live performance was now the best way to achieve it. Given this, it is not entirely surprising that the experience of watching it happen was so queasily wondrous.

The Age of Austerity

Owing to its heavy reliance on finance industries, the UK was hit hard by the 2008 economic crisis, which decimated the country's banking system and required massive state intervention to prop up the country's key economic institutions. The Labour Chancellor of the Exchequer at the time, Alistair Darling, subsequently observed that the cash machines of Britain had been hours away from running out of money.[11] The 2010 national election produced a hung parliament that led to a coalition government comprised of Conservatives and Liberal Democrats, and in its first budget, the new government took a hard turn towards austerity, with Chancellor George Osborne introducing measures that sharply constrained public spending and projected huge further cuts for years to come.

Austerity was a choice, and not an unexpected one. Osborne and Cameron had both made their intentions clear in advance of the 2010 election. Although they had in the past promised to match the then Labour government's spending plans, after the financial crisis both heralded the new 'age of austerity'.[12] 'The days of easy money are over', Osborne told the spring conference of the Conservative party in 2009. 'The public finances are out of control and that presents a clear and present danger to the prosperity of an entire generation. We must act and act fast. We need a government of thrift in this age of austerity.'[13] Even if it had been a mistake to strap 'the fortunes of the entire British economy on the back of the tiger of finance', it was also necessary for the government to 'fight to keep London the centre of global finance'.[14] Osborne clearly delineated the austerity logic that would subsequently underpin the economic programme of the coalition government, and he applied it especially strictly in the early years of the coalition's tenure: make deep cuts to public spending, while protecting favoured sectors of the economy like finance (even though, as he acknowledged, finance was hugely culpable for the recent crisis in the first place).

Over the course of the coalition government, Osborne would cut spending by nearly £50 billion, with the majority of these cuts occurring in the first half of the government's term.[15] The effect of the cuts was to slow economic growth at a point when the economy had finally been starting to improve. Huge parts of the public sector were also subjected to wholesale restructuring, most notably the NHS, which was put through a vast array of market-oriented reforms (after the Tories had promised no 'top-down reorganisation of the NHS').[16] The consequences of these decisions are still being felt. As the Institute for Fiscal Studies commented in 2019, the UK's economic recovery from the financial crisis 'has been extraordinarily weak', and the country 'experienced its slowest-ever post-recession recovery'. Government forecasts 'suggest that GDP per person in 2023 will be 24% lower than it would have been had it grown by 2.3% per year since 2008 (its long-run trend rate)'. (Of course, these estimates were formulated before the spread of the COVID-19 pandemic, which is likely to make them even worse.[17]) The *Financial Times* observed in 2020 that even though headline unemployment rates were historically low, 'sluggish economic expansion in the 2010s was largely the result of more people being in work, rather than greater efficiency, resulting in the slowest productivity growth [and greatest increase in number of hours worked] of any decade since the second world war'.[18]

Isles of Wonder played out against the first two, especially austere, years of the coalition (though its show of confidence has become even more peculiarly impressive with the passage of time, given the longer-term effects of the government's austerity agenda). At the time of the Olympics, the economy was slowing, and there was concern that Osborne's cuts had pushed the economy back into recession – this turned out not to be the case, but only marginally so.[19] The political desire for the Games to provide an economic boost was intense, and the Olympics stood out as one of the few examples of infrastructure spending that had not already been reduced. But this aspiration was undercut by the unique economic characteristics of the Olympic infrastructure. Since the Barcelona Olympics in 1992, the dominant rationale advanced for hosting the Olympic Games has been an infrastructural one. The massive public spending that the Olympics usually involve can be used, the argument goes, to generate significant improvements to the urban infrastructure of the host city, whether to its transportation systems, its housing stock, its urban environment, and more. This argument has the advantage of being palatable to both the political Left and Right, though for different reasons. For the Left, the Olympics can be a way to leverage public investment in infrastructure to a degree that might otherwise be politically difficult to accomplish (this was the basis on which former London mayor Ken Livingstone, previously a sceptic of London's Olympic ambitions, supported the bid to host the Games in the first place). For the Right, the prestige of the Olympics can provide political cover for types of public spending that its supporters might otherwise be reluctant to accept (indeed, the Olympics are arguably one of the few remaining areas in political discourse where conservative politicians actively support public spending on the apparently old-fashioned basis of its benefit to the wider economy).

The economic benefits of the Games, though, are thought by many economists to be negligible at best, and negative at worst.[20] Robert A. Baade and Victor A. Matheson sum up the existing research bluntly: 'the overwhelming conclusion is that in most cases the Olympics are a money-losing proposition for host cities'.[21] There are any number of reasons why the economic benefits that Olympics advocates espouse rarely arise: the bidding process often encourages winning cities to make costly and unwise infrastructural promises (the fact that Paris already possessed most of the infrastructure to host the 2012 Games was, ironically, seen as undermining its bid rather advantaging it); what seems like 'new' spending on the Games is often money reallocated from elsewhere (as happened in London when cost over-runs inevitably occurred and National Lottery revenues earmarked for the arts were redirected to the Olympics' budget); although the headline investment figure is large, it is usually spread over too long a period to have much effect on overall economic growth; if there is a post-Games contraction in spending to compensate for earlier costs incurred, as often happens, this can diminish the longer-term effects of that previous investment; and it arguably involves a less-than-ideal allocation of public resources – in order to construct needed infrastructure that they should have built anyway, governments wind up spending a lot of money on other things they otherwise would not, while paying top price for them (an Olympic Games may result in improvements to, say, a city's transport system, but this is usually bought at the expense of a number of very costly white elephants). The argument that the Olympics produce economic benefits should be treated warily, as it often effaces significant fiscal and social costs that the Olympics inevitably entail, and most economists agree that hosting the Olympics should not be justified to any significant degree on an economic basis.

Confidence

However doubtful the macroeconomic rationale for the investment, the Olympics nonetheless commonly create a large stock of built infrastructure, and London was no different in this regard. Investment for the Olympics resulted in a new stadium, thousands of units of housing, improvements to the transportation network of East London, amenities such as the Olympic Park, and a whole host of sporting facilities. Many of these are what economists call 'fixed assets', which are most commonly property, buildings, and equipment (fixed assets are distinguished from 'liquid' assets, such as cash). The construction of fixed assets is key to ensuring the long-term viability of economic production and, in a market economy, is an important show of confidence in that economy's future prospects. As Keynes observes, it is through these assets' creation that 'the economic future is linked with the present'.[22]

In his landmark *General Theory of Employment, Interest and Money* (1936), Keynes asks why investments in fixed assets are made and what the construction of fixed assets signifies more broadly. He explains the first part of this question through his theory of the *marginal efficiency of capital.*[23] Keynes argues that the marginal efficiency of capital is determined by *yield* (the value of goods produced less input costs and maintenance costs of the asset producing those goods) minus *supply cost* (the prospective cost of creating another, say, machine or factory to produce those goods instead of the assets the producer already possesses). Producers will invest in fixed assets if they expect that the marginal efficiency of capital will be greater in the future than it is today (and the reverse is also true – if producers anticipate that yields will be lower in the future then they are likely to hoard capital, use up any spare capacity, and wait until they perceive conditions are improving). Thus deciding whether or not to invest in fixed assets is a calculation based not on existing conditions but *confidence* in future, anticipated conditions. The problem, though, is that the former are much more reliably assessed than the latter – current conditions actually exist, whereas future conditions have to be projected, often disproportionately on what is already known. As Keynes observes, 'The outstanding fact is the extreme precariousness of the basis of knowledge on which our estimates of prospective yield have to be made', something that encourages investors to adopt short-term and risk-displacing approaches.[24] Public investment in fixed assets is therefore a hugely important corrective to this problem, since the state can employ a calculus of yield that is both temporally and socially more expansive than the market is likely to entertain. London's Olympic facilities, as fixed assets built through public investment, appeared to demonstrate exactly the sort of confidence in the future that was publicly needed at a time of profound economic uncertainty. Literally and figuratively, London's Olympic infrastructure purported to make the link between an uncertain today and a better tomorrow concrete.

The difficulty, though, is that this economic promise was not entirely convincing in market or social terms, due to the particularly Olympian character of the infrastructure involved. Realising any market-determined yield through Olympic facilities themselves is hugely challenging, since many of these assets cannot be monetised to any significant degree – it is hard to imagine a velodrome turning a profit. The anxious question which Olympics facilities prompt is less 'Will there be white elephants?' and more 'How many white elephants will there be?'[25] The long history of Olympic facilities is, to a significant degree, a history of trying – and often failing – to overcome the white elephant problem. Montreal's Olympic Stadium is perhaps the best known, and most extreme, example of an Olympic white elephant, but Beijing's iconic 'Bird's Nest' stadium is now idle much of the year, and Athens' Olympic Stadium sits empty (along with many of the city's other Olympic facilities, which were largely abandoned after the collapse of Greece's economy during the 2008 financial crisis). Tokyo, the host of the 2020 Olympics, scrambled to cut costs and cancelled plans for a Zaha Hadid–designed stadium after its budget spiralled (leading to a public apology from the government).

Even if it were possible to realise a market-based yield on investment in Olympic assets, this often only happens after additional public investment, on top of already substantial expenditure, and the subsequent transfer of use or ownership of the asset to the private sector at little or no cost to it. The Olympic Stadium, and the redeveloped Olympic Village, are perhaps the clearest illustration of this rentier logic. The Stadium's future life, as the home of West Ham United Football Club, would entail a further, publicly financed, and very expensive remodelling on the club's behalf (and it is not surprising that the post-Games tenancy of the Olympic Stadium was subject to much litigation by competing football clubs, given how rare it is that such an asset becomes available at so little cost). In keeping with the cost over-runs that marked the London Olympics (and which mark Olympic Games generally), the Olympic Stadium was originally budgeted at £280 million while its final cost came in at £429 million. At least some of these additional costs were due to changes to the stadium's design, from its original conception as a temporary athletics venue to its final configuration as a multi-purpose sports arena that could have a 'legacy use' once the Games were over (which, in practice, meant primarily as a football stadium). The resulting stadium was still unsuitable for football, however, and soon after the Games finished, large sections of it were removed and it was effectively rebuilt within the original shell, at a cost of an additional £272 million, for use by West Ham United. The vast majority of these conversion costs came from public funds, with the largest subventions coming from the national Treasury (a grant of approximately £150 million) and Newham Borough Council, in which the stadium is located (a £40 million loan). Newham, it should be noted, is one of the poorest local authorities, not only in London but in the United Kingdom. West

Ham United paid only £15 million towards the refurbishment, but, as with many agreements between public bodies and private enterprises in recent years, most of the details of the contract between the London Legacy Development Corporation and West Ham United were not disclosed because of strict commercial confidentiality clauses. The terms of the deal, which included West Ham paying a low rent with most of the running costs covered by public bodies, were only revealed in 2015 after the Information Commissioner ordered the London Legacy Development Corporation, which owns the stadium, to publish its contract with West Ham.[26] In a bitter irony, the London Stadium, as West Ham's home is now called, is widely considered to have among the worst atmospheres for watching football at the top end of the English leagues.

The Olympic Village, in turn, has been rebranded as the 'East Village', a new neighbourhood in Stratford, one of the poorest parts of London. East Village was promoted as a response to London's housing shortage, but it is a very particular type of response: housing built at public expense (the private investors initially sought to underwrite it never materialised) that, after a substantial write-down, was turned over to a joint venture between British real estate advisors, Delancey, and a property investment arm of the Qatari sovereign wealth fund, Qatari Diar. The vast majority of the housing units are in the private sector, with market-determined (and therefore high) calculations of 'affordability'. East Village creates housing, no doubt, but the development has been as much about creating a new private property market in East London, at public expense, as it has been about providing affordable places for people to live. One does not actually need to create a market in order to build homes but doing otherwise has become almost unimaginable in London today, politically and economically.

Isles of Wonder

The sheer exuberance that characterised *Isles of Wonder* stood in stark contrast to the rather gloomy economic environment in which the show took place. The performance was organised into seven main scenes, many of which elaborated the show's central thesis that British history has been driven by a unique interplay of industry and culture. The first scene, 'Green and Pleasant Land', was titled after a line from William Blake's poem, 'Jerusalem', and depicted an agrarian, pre-modern Britain prior to the arrival of the Industrial Revolution. The second, called 'Pandemonium' after the name John Milton gave to the capital of Hell in *Paradise Lost*, portrayed the onset of industrialisation, opening with famed engineer Isambard Kingdom Brunel (played by Kenneth Branagh) speaking Caliban's 'Be not afeard' speech from Shakespeare's *The Tempest*. This scene depicted Britain's socio-economic development from the Industrial Revolution to the 1960s. At the end of 'Pandemonium', workers 'forged' the five Olympic rings and these were lifted into place above the stadium. (A picture of the fiery rings was the most commonly used image on the front pages of the following day's newspapers in Britain.) The next scene, 'Happy and Glorious', introduced the Queen, as Head of State, through a combination of film and live performance.[27] This involved one of the key jokes in the ceremony, where James Bond (played by the then Bond actor Daniel Craig) and the Queen (played by Elizabeth II herself) ostensibly parachuted into the Olympic stadium, after which the Queen was then revealed, with the rest of her party, in her royal box. Following a rendition of *God Save the Queen* by a choir of deaf children, 'Second to the Right, and Straight on Till Morning' celebrated the founding of the NHS in 1948 as well as children's literature in Britain. (The title of the scene was taken from the directions to Neverland that Peter gives to Wendy in *Peter Pan*.) This was followed by 'Interlude', which honoured British cinema (and included a jokey appearance by Rowan Atkinson as Mr. Bean), and 'Frankie and June Say . . . Thanks Tim', which celebrated British popular music and culture (and featured Tim Berners Lee, the British inventor of the World Wide Web). The show closed with 'Abide with Me', a tribute to those who could not be present in the stadium that night, including those who died in the London bombings of 7 July 2005.[28]

The show's determination to appeal to as broad a political spectrum as possible was signalled from the outset. It opened with a scene whose title, 'Green and Pleasant Land', was taken from 'Jerusalem', and accompanied by the familiar music to which Sir Hubert Parry later set Blake's verse. Blake's poem (and his longer, separate work that goes by the same name) is one of the best-known examples of English radical romanticism: 'I will not cease from Mental Fight,/Nor shall my Sword sleep in my hand:/Till we have built Jerusalem,/In England's green & pleasant Land'.[29] Parry's popular musical adaptation, though, has served a wide variety of British political projects and institutions since its creation over a century ago. Parry originally set the poem to music during the First World War in the hope of boosting national morale; it quickly became associated with the suffragist movement, and the Women's Institute soon after adopted the song as its official anthem. It has often been characterised as England's unofficial national anthem and has commonly been sung as a hymn in religious services, especially in the Church of England. Although Clement Atlee used Blake's final verse as a slogan during Labour's successful election campaign in 1945, and Parry's anthem is still sung regularly at Labour Party conferences, the song has also been sung at Conservative Party conferences. Every year, the Last Night of The Proms, which features a programme of patriotic orchestral music, concludes with the singing of 'Jerusalem', and it was sung at the wedding of Prince William and Kate Middleton in 2011. The show's invocation of the self-evidently English 'Jerusalem' in what was ostensibly a performance of Britishness also chimed with the current moment. In theatre, as in politics and economics, 'Britishness' often has a distinctly English inflection.

In the UK, the scene that attracted the most attention was 'Second to the Right, and Straight on Till Morning'. This scene, more than any other, realised the value of the Olympic investment. The historical link between Great Ormond Street Hospital – the country's oldest and best-known children's hospital – and J. M. Barrie provided a canny way to bridge the National Health Service with children's literature. As the scene's performers, many of whom worked in the NHS, entered the stadium an announcement was made: 'Please welcome Mike Oldfield [the musician played live during the scene] and the staff of the United Kingdom National Health Service, and our very special guests this evening, patients and staff of Great Ormond Street Hospital'. Hundreds of performers costumed as hospital staff arranged beds, each carrying a child 'patient', in the shape of the logo of the Great Ormond Street Hospital Charity (a line drawing of a child's smiling but also tear-streaked face), underscored by the letters 'GOSH'. As the electric pulse of a cardiac monitor raced around the seating banks of the darkened stadium, the completed GOSH image was picked out in light. Nurses then joined the children in their beds and began to read to them. Within moments, 'Tubular Bells' gave way to raucous swing music, and the children jumped up and down on their beds (their 'mattresses' were, in fact, trampolines) and the hospital staff swing-danced, with each other and en masse, around the enormous playing area, while also miming duties such as giving injections and washing their hands. Simultaneously other cast members formed a new image in the centre of the stadium: three giant letters spelling out the current logo of the NHS, lit in brilliant white. The cast continued to dance until the swing music gave way to a lullaby, whereupon the staff tucked the children into bed, hushing them to sleep. The children, however, continued to read under their sheets, flashlights in hand, while J. K. Rowling appeared and recited a passage based on *Peter Pan*:

> Of all delectable islands, the Neverland is the snuggest. It's not large and sprawly – you know, with boring distances between one adventure and the next. It's nicely crammed. When you play at it by day, with the table and chairs, it's not a bit frightening. But in the two minutes before you go to sleep it is real.[30]

Monsters swooped around the children in their beds, led by the Child Catcher from *Chitty Chitty Bang Bang*, and giant puppets of villains from children's literature, including Cruella de Vil, Lord Voldemort, Captain Hook, and the Queen of Hearts, rose over the frightened patients. An army of Mary Poppinses then 'flew' in from high in the stadium, umbrellas open, and attacked the 'baddies', cheered on by the children and hospital staff. With the monsters chased away, the Mary Poppinses joined the children and staff in a further dance, before the children were tucked safely into bed. The scene concluded with a huge image of a baby's head, an undulating bedsheet indicating its body, to celebrate Scottish physician Ian Donald's pioneering work in developing obstetrical imaging technology at the University of Glasgow in the 1950s.

Seen in its wider context, and given the currency of the government's controversial restructuring of the NHS, it is not surprising that this scene had particular resonance. As economist Simon Wren-Lewis commented after watching it:

> The NHS embodies a principle that in critical matters involving health, all members of a society should be equal. Overall the UK is not a particularly equal society, and income and wealth inequalities have been growing, but this is one area where there is a strong national consensus that while additional income should mean that you contribute more to a health service, this does not entitle you to receive better treatment.[31]

'Second to the Right, and Straight on Till Morning' celebrated a key welfare state institution and the public values that underpin it, but if this tribute seemed at odds with the coalition government's economic policies the scene's dramaturgy cleverly forestalled ideological antagonism towards the NHS. The scene explicitly referenced the fact that the NHS was established in the same year – 1948 – that London last hosted the Olympic Games. Like 2012, 1948 was a time of economic austerity, but, as *Isles of Wonder* highlighted, it was one that prompted the creation of new forms of social welfare rather than one that imposed austerity as a pretext for their weakening. The scene also diachronically posited a historical continuity between the NHS of 1948 and 2012 by incorporating signs from both eras: the hospital staff was dressed in uniforms from the 1940s, but the NHS emblem they formed was its contemporary logo. Moreover, the fact that all of the patients were children put an optimistic gloss on who investment in the NHS primarily benefits (indeed, children featured prominently throughout *Isles of Wonder*). Rather than spending much of its resources treating an ageing population (the elderly are by far the largest users of NHS hospitals and children are the smallest), the scene proposed that the NHS was all about the kids – our confident future rather than our troublesome present.[32] The choreography of 'Second to the Right, and Straight on Till Morning' also suggested a high-minded continuum between theatrical pleasure and a unifying social citizenship, both for those characters within the conflict-free NHS depicted and for the spectators whose own enjoyment of the scene signalled their membership of the broader commons in which the NHS was the preeminent social institution.

Through its social form, the scene also looked remarkably like a theatrical version of Keynesian productivity that austerity economics seeks to disavow. As a display of tightly organised theatrical production, 'Second to the Right, and Straight on Till Morning' (along with *Isles of Wonder* as a whole) looked as impressive economically as it did artistically: it coordinated a huge cast containing 'professional' and 'amateur' performers with great skill and, in doing so, successfully created both a 'good' (in an economic sense) and a 'good' (in a social sense). In short, it offered an affective hypothesis of what an economy based on both efficiency *and* mutuality might look and feel like. This was welfare economics as social democracy intended, but with theatre rather than the state as guarantor.

This theatrical celebration could not, however, supplant the infrastructure that underpinned it. The temptation is to see *Isles of Wonder*, and especially 'Second to the Right, and Straight on Till Morning' as a kind of theatrical triumph over – or at least temporary deferral of – rentier capitalism in an age of austerity: Keynesianism is back, the show implied, just not in a way we might have expected. But if the Olympic Stadium was successfully assimilated into the mimetic apparatus of the theatrical event, this does not necessarily mean that it was also completely subsumed within *Isles of Wonder*'s ideological operations. As Marvin Carlson points out, the place of performance is a 'haunted house', a kind of 'memory machine' that not only evokes broader cultural memories but, through its built form, is an especially concentrated materialisation of those historical associations.[33] These 'ghostings', however, are not only theatrical in nature. The Olympic Stadium was not only the place where *Isles of Wonder* happened; it was infrastructure imbued with the complicated economic legacies of Olympic investment, and the political arrangements sustaining these. For a Games that traded on 'legacy' more than any previous Olympic Games, London's Olympic Stadium, along with its other large legacy project, East Village, were concrete examples of what that legacy actually meant: massive public investment to create assets that were then transferred at little cost to the private sector. This cosy arrangement suggested that London's economic future was based on state-guaranteed, rentier capitalism – an unsurprising proposition given the city's continued, and arguably deepening, reliance on finance capital, and despite the 2008 economic crisis and the UK's poor economic performance since. But it would also be wilfully romantic to pretend that this rentier legacy did not still *read* in performance – its contours were well-defined at the time of the opening ceremony, even if the full picture was not entirely filled in yet – however at odds with the more high-minded theatrical event that unfolded within the Olympic Stadium it might have appeared to be. The theatrical elements of *Isles of Wonder* could counterpoint, but not overcome, the ideologies that the stadium embodied.

When the waveforms of a cardiac monitor raced around the stands of the Olympic Stadium at the opening of 'Second to the Right, and Straight on Till Morning', it condensed the contradictions staged by *Isles of Wonder* in a single, arresting image. This opening implied that the stadium itself had become the monitor of the country's heartbeat, an unnerving proposition that the theatrical components of the show could not wholly displace but, equally, would not be undermined by. (Keep in mind that most viewers of the show were watching it on television, and one of the camera angles most commonly used during the broadcast of the performance was an aerial shot of the stadium – many of the large stage images created during the show were best seen from the air, framed by the bowl of the stadium.) *Isles of Wonder*, then, demonstrated the impressive but discomfiting ability of theatrical performance to stage political-economic antagonisms without being undone by them. In fact, part of the delirious pleasure of the *Isles of Wonder* lay in the extent to which it made these antagonisms doubly productive: as theatrical material within the live performance and as an infrastructural condition of its own production. That the show could successfully do this without careening out of control only amplified the sense that, as spectators, we were watching something 'bonkers'. But if this experience was queasily wondrous – and it was – it is because it was a confidence trick decreasingly available outside the confines of the performance. In the real world, the antagonisms that *Isles of Wonder* staged may be equally, or even more, conspicuous, but there austerity and rent-seeking have the upper hand.

Conclusion

When Aidan Burley feared that *Isles of Wonder* would include a 'welfare tribute next' he missed a key point: he was already watching one. But unlike in the past, the job of making the case for welfare – of providing Keynes's 'optimistic hypothesis' of what an economy based on efficiency and mutuality might look and feel like – had fallen to the theatre rather than the state.[34] Keynes and other advocates for the welfare state have commonly seen this as a challenge for political economy, but *Isles of Wonder* suggested that it was now also a job for cultural economy. To some extent this seemed a logical extension of the performative logic that is very much apparent Keynes's thinking: 'For if we consistently act on the optimistic hypothesis, this hypothesis will tend to be realised; whilst by acting on the pessimistic hypothesis we can keep ourselves for ever in the pit of want'.[35] And in a time of austerity and rent-seeking, *Isles of Wonder* proposed that theatre might be especially suited to fulfilling this optimistic role.

But this optimism is somewhat misplaced. The role of theatre here is not, as we might hope, to make the case for welfare over austerity. Instead, *Isles of Wonder* suggests a slightly different, and decidedly more ambiguous, role for theatre: to make the tension between welfare and austerity generative, live and in public, and in the process make capital efficient again. Whereas in political economy these approaches to economic governance have usually been considered antithetical to each other, *Isles of Wonder* implied that, by deploying the distinctive mix of artistic, organisational, and spatial techniques that theatre offers, it was still possible to make a show of confidence in a better future in a time of austerity. This may be an attractive proposition, since it implies that theatre can step in where political economy has, in recent years, faltered. But it is not an entirely reassuring one either, since it suggests that theatrical economy is, politically, profoundly ambivalent. In fact, a theatrical show of confidence in the age of austerity may even depend on this ambivalence, since making it entails embracing both welfare and rentier economics, at the same time, in the same place. For spectators this might be pleasurable, but for social citizens (and we are often both at the same time) it is more than a little unsettling.

Conclusion

> Meanwhile, there will be no harm in making mild preparations for our destiny, in encouraging, and experimenting in, the arts of life as well as the activities of purpose. But chiefly, do not let us overestimate the importance of the economic problem, or sacrifice to its supposed necessities other matters of greater and more permanent significance.
>
> John Maynard Keynes, 'Economic Possibilities for Our Grandchildren' (1930), *Essays in Persuasion* (1931)[1]

Keynes wrote this at the height of the Great Depression. Demonstrating the combination of radical intellectualism and political reformism that characterised his writings and professional life, Keynes was trying to avoid the 'two opposed errors of pessimism', he thought the Depression had induced: 'the pessimism of the revolutionaries who think that things are so bad that nothing can save us but violent change, and the pessimism of the reactionaries who consider the balance of our economic and social life so precarious that we must risk no experiments'.[2] By way of countering these 'errors', he looked one hundred years into the future, towards a time when 'the *economic problem* may be solved, or be at least within sight of solution'. The economic problem, Keynes forcefully argued, was not '*the permanent problem of the human race*'.[3]

Whether or not the moderate, 'optimistic' vision that Keynes propounded is as viable today as it turned out to be in his time is open to question. His formulation looks a little too triangulating for our current economic situation (though it is ironic that much of his economic analysis seems more left-wing now than it did then, a sign that capital is even more ascendant today than it was at the time he wrote). It is clear that, nearing the end of the century Keynes imagined, we are no closer to 'solving' the economic problem than those living in his time were. Indeed, political economy – in practise if not in theory – often seems uninterested in doing so. This is despite the fact that the 'progressive countries' – as Keynes called the economic powers of Europe and the Americas – are considerably wealthier than they were in the 1930s, in much the way he anticipated.[4] As in the UK of Keynes's time, the political response to an epochal financial crisis was to choose to immiserate the country's poorest people further, consciously and aggressively. The 2008 crisis was a new chapter in an old story that would have been very familiar to the economist: when bankers screw up, other people are made to pay.[5]

So Keynes was wrong. Or, perhaps, his faith was misplaced – the economic problem persists, and it is hard to imagine that it can ever be solved, at least as Keynes postulated. And to be fair to Keynes, the point of making such a forecast was not so much for it to come true a hundred years hence, but instead to posit alternatives in his own time (and as one of the key architects of the welfare state during the 1940s, Keynes had some success here). He also knew full well that solving the economic problem would be a tough slog ('[a]varice and usury must be our gods for a little while longer still') and that even if it were solved, this would likely provoke an almost existential crisis – we would not know what to do with ourselves when it happened.[6] The arts – and the 'arts of life' – would be one way to face this challenge.[7]

For me, though, the question is not so much whether it is possible to overcome the economic problem, or what theatre's social role would be if this happened. Indeed, decades of watching and thinking about theatre have made me more than a little sceptical that the theatres I have examined could ever surmount this problem, or even stand apart from it. Instead, the more pertinent questions for me are how theatre continues to grapple with market economies as they exist today, and what role it carves out for itself in the process. Theatre remains deeply embedded with the market and with other social institutions – especially the state – that help make marketisation possible, and the cases I have discussed repeatedly illustrate theatre trying to come to terms with that fact.

As a result, it is difficult to sustain the proposition that theatre and the market could be 'worlds apart' now, at least in the theatre cultures I have explored in this book. But this does not mean that the theatres I have discussed have themselves become marketised either – in some ways they have but in a lot of ways they have not (and in other ways they used to be and could be again). Even if they are not subsumed by the market, though, these theatres' intimate relationship with it cannot be suppressed, repudiated, or even embraced – it can only be managed, sometimes onstage but just as often (perhaps more often) elsewhere. The extent to which these theatres repeatedly attempt to resolve the antagonisms of market relations is striking, and their inventiveness when trying to do so is notable. But whether the mixed economy is, in the longer run, any more viable theatrically than it was political economically is questionable. It *appears* as though it could be, though, and in the current historical moment, that appearance is tremendously appealing, if not always entirely convincing.

As I observed at the outset of this book, the theatres I have examined are not heroic. They often do not meet the market head on and, to be honest, it is difficult to imagine a theatre that could. Instead, they deflect it, flatter it, refigure it, manage it, appropriate it, and more. They mobilise theatre's own material resources – or mobilise other material resources distinctively theatrically – in ways that the market and the state often struggle to do, and to ends they cannot achieve. These theatres are often very efficient in this regard, just not in ways we usually think about efficiency, and in places we do not always look for it.

There are limits to this efficiency, though. Sometimes its benefits are only visible in the theatre – they cannot necessarily be realised elsewhere, even if we might want them to be. At other times, it is because this efficiency arises in some places but not in others – achieving it in one part of the theatrical enterprise sometimes comes at the expense of others, including what happens onstage. Theatrical efficiency may also only be of limited duration or utility. And its achievement can call into question some received wisdom about how theatre works or should be valued.

One reason that I embarked on this book was that much of the thinking about the relationship between theatre and the market seemed to me to underplay the wide variety of ways in which theatre was grappling with it, and underestimate the extent to which theatre was engaging with some quite complex political-economic questions (even if it did not always answer these satisfactorily). These encounters were not necessarily apparent onstage – sometimes they could only be seen on reflection or grasped elsewhere – but they were happening anyway, insistently and materially. There is a counter-script at work here, in which theatre is industrious; it is productive; it produces social citizens when the market and the state cannot; it resuscitates social exchange; and it holds out the hope that the future might be better than the present. This counter-script, like any other script, is full of gaps, ambiguities, and contradictions. And it is a script that I cannot help but be ambivalent about, in part because the theatre it features is itself so ambivalent. But it is nonetheless a success story of a sort.

Notes

Introduction: Show Business

1. John Maynard Keynes, *Essays in Persuasion*, vol. 9, The Collected Writings of John Maynard Keynes (Cambridge: Cambridge University Press, 2012), xviii.
2. Arts Council of Great Britain, 'First Annual Report 1945–6' (London: Arts Council of Great Britain, 1946), 1, www.artscouncil.org.uk/sites/default/files/download-file/The%20Arts%20Council%20of%20Great%20Britain%20-%201st%20Annual%20Report%201945_0.pdf.
3. 'Expansionary fiscal contraction' (also known as 'expansionary austerity') refers to the controversial economic theory that major reductions in public spending can stimulate private consumption and lead to economic growth (in part because public borrowing is no longer 'crowding out' the private sector). The term 'Very Serious People' has been used repeatedly by economist Paul Krugman to describe the politicians, academics, and pundits who advocated austerity economics in a variety of countries following the financial crisis of 2008. In Krugman's thinking, these self-styled 'serious people' advanced policies that sounded superficially like 'common sense' but were economically unsound and destructive (austerity budgeting in the UK after 2010 and the Greek 'bailouts' being among the most notable examples).
4. Jean-Christophe Agnew, *Worlds Apart: The Market and the Theater in Anglo-American Thought, 1550–1750* (Cambridge: Cambridge University Press, 1988), 9.
5. Michael Lewis, 'When Irish Eyes Are Crying', *Vanity Fair*, 1 March 2011, www.vanityfair.com/news/2011/03/michael-lewis-ireland-201103.
6. Sam Lister, 'Boris Johnson Defends London's Financial Sector', *The Independent*, 22 July 2012, www.independent.co.uk/news/uk/politics/boris-johnson-defends-londons-financial-sector-7964856.html.
7. Department for Digital, Culture, Media and Sport, 'Britain's Creative Industries Break the £100 Billion Barrier', Gov.uk, www.gov.uk/government/news/britains-creative-industries-break-the-100-billion-barrier.

8. Larry Elliott and Dan Atkinson, *Fantasy Island* (Constable, 2007), 75.
9. Elliott and Atkinson, 72.
10. Elliott and Atkinson, 92.
11. Agnew, *Worlds Apart*, 6–7.
12. Agnew, 6.
13. Ellen Meiksins Wood, *Democracy against Capitalism: Renewing Historical Materialism* (London: Verso, 2016), 19.
14. Judith Butler and Athena Athanasiou, *Dispossession: The Performative in the Political* (Malden, MA: Polity Press, 2013), 40.
15. Karl Polanyi, *The Great Transformation: The Political and Economic Origins of Our Time*, 2nd ed. (Boston: Beacon Press, 2002). There is a large body of scholarship that engages with Polanyi and some of his key concepts (especially his theories of (dis)embedded markets, fictitious commodities, and the double movement). Within this context of this book, though, Nancy Fraser's critical revisiting of Polanyi in relation to the 2008 financial crisis is especially germane. See Nancy Fraser, 'Marketization, Social Protection, Emancipation: Towards a Neo-Polanyian Conception of Capitalist Crisis', in *Business as Usual: The Roots of the Global Financial Meltdown*, ed. Craig Calhoun and Georgi Derluguian (New York: New York University Press, 2011), 137–59.
16. Agnew, *Worlds Apart*, 2.
17. Agnew, 60.
18. Despite much talk in the UK of the Conservative government's fiscal interventionism following COVID-19's impact signaling the end of austerity, the real test of whether austerity is dead and buried will be how, once the crisis has abated, the government deals with the massive pandemic-related debts that it has incurred. Who will pay for putting the public finances 'back in order', and what will putting them back in order mean, in practice?
19. Polanyi argues that market society became entrenched in western Europe over the course of the nineteenth century. While this argument appears at multiple points in *The Great Transformation*, for a key part of it (including Polanyi's influential thesis on 'fictitious commodities'), see Polanyi, *The Great Transformation*, 71–89.
20. For a sample of this, see Michael McKinnie, *City Stages : Theatre and Urban Space in a Global City* (Toronto: University of Toronto Press, 2007); Michael McKinnie, 'Institutional Frameworks: Theatre, State, and Market in Modern Urban Performance', in *A Cultural History of Theatre in the Modern Age*, ed. Kim Solga, vol. 6 (London: Bloomsbury, 2017), 17–33; Michael McKinnie, 'Rethinking Site-Specificity: Monopoly, Urban Space, and the Cultural Economics of Site-Specific Performance', in *Performing Site-Specific Theatre: Politics, Place, Practice*, ed. Anna Birch and Joanne Tompkins

(Basingstoke: Palgrave Macmillan, 2012), 21–33; Michael McKinnie, 'Performing the Civic Transnational: Cultural Production, Governance, and Citizenship in Contemporary London', in *Performance and the City* (Basingstoke: Palgrave Macmillan, 2009), 110–27.

21. Dan Rebellato, *Theatre and Globalization* (Basingstoke: Palgrave Macmillan, 2009); Dan Rebellato, 'Playwriting and Globalisation: Towards a Site-Unspecific Theatre', *Contemporary Theatre Review* 16, no. 1 (1 February 2006): 97–113, https://doi.org/10.1080/10486800500451047; Jonathan Burston, 'Recombinant Broadway', *Continuum* 23, no. 2 (1 April 2009): 159–69, https://doi.org/10.1080/10304310802710504.
22. Not surprisingly, this was the title that the *Guardian* newspaper's longstanding reviewer, Michael Billington, gave his book on the politics of British theatre. See Michael Billington, *State of the Nation: British Theatre since 1945* (London: Faber and Faber, 2009).
23. Jen Harvie, *Theatre and the City* (Basingstoke: Palgrave Macmillan, 2009), 43.
24. David Harvey, *The Condition of Postmodernity* (Oxford: Blackwell, 1989), 207.
25. Federico Neiburg and Jane I. Guyer, 'The Real in the Real Economy', *HAU: Journal of Ethnographic Theory* 7, no. 3 (2017): 263, https://doi.org/10.14318/hau7.3.015.
26. See, for example, a British culture minister: 'Our creative industries not only fly the flag for the best of British creativity at home and abroad but they are also at the heart of our economy. Today they have broken the £100 billion mark and continue on a hugely positive upward trajectory, outperforming the wider UK economy and bringing joy and entertainment to millions. We're doing all we can to support the sector's talent and entrepreneurship as we build a Britain that is fit for future [*sic*].' Department for Digital, Culture, Media and Sport, 'Britain's Creative Industries Break the £100 Billion Barrier'.
27. Jamie Peck, 'Struggling with the Creative Class', *International Journal of Urban and Regional Research* 29, no. 4 (2005): 763.
28. Angela McRobbie, *Be Creative: Making a Living in the New Culture Industries* (Cambridge: Polity Press, 2015).
29. David Harvey, 'The Spatial Fix – Hegel, von Thunen, and Marx', *Antipode* 13, no. 3 (1981): 1–12, https://doi.org/10.1111/j.1467–8330.1981.tb00312.x. He has also returned to the theory several times since this initial articulation.
30. Bob Jessop, 'Spatial Fixes, Temporal Fixes and Spatio-Temporal Fixes', in *David Harvey: A Critical Reader*, ed. Noel Castree and Derek Gregory (Oxford: Blackwell, 2006), 162.
31. William J. Baumol and William G. Bowen, *Performing Arts: The Economic Dilemma; A Study of Problems Common to Theater, Opera, Music and Dance* (New York: Twentieth Century Fund, 1966), 161–80.

32. Karl Marx, *Capital: A Critique of Political Economy*, trans. Ben Fowkes, new ed. , vol. 1 (London: Penguin Classics, 1990), 709.
33. David Harvey, *Limits to Capital* (London: Verso, 1999), 426–31.
34. It is of course true that not every instance of overaccumulation entails a recession or a full-blown crisis. Indeed, most do not, and part of capitalism's extraordinary durability lies in the extent to which it can accommodate instances of overaccumulation without an entire regime of accumulation being undermined (this is related to what Neil Smith, echoing Harvey, calls 'the uneven geography of development'). Nonetheless, there are clearly moments where such accommodation becomes impossible, whether because of the scale or the particular configuration of the economic forces involved. This does not mean that the Great Depression or the 2008 financial crisis can be wholly explained through the spatial fix, let alone the economic fallout of a global pandemic such as COVID-19 – the causes and effects here are far more complex. But it is nonetheless a useful way to understand the spatial logic of some of the broader economic forces at work in moments of profound economic crisis. See also Neil Smith, *Uneven Development: Nature, Capital and the Production of Space*, 3rd ed. (London: Verso, 2010).
35. Jessop, 'Spatial Fixes, Temporal Fixes and Spatio-Temporal Fixes', 163.
36. Jessop, 161. To be clear, Jessop acknowledges that these concerns often emerge in Harvey's analysis of particular historical cases.
37. See, for example, Bob Jessop, 'Cultural Political Economy and Critical Policy Studies', *Critical Policy Studies* 3, no. 3–4 (2010): 336–56, https://doi.org/10.1080/19460171003619741; Bob Jessop and Stijn Oosterlynck, 'Cultural Political Economy: On Making the Cultural Turn without Falling into Soft Economic Sociology', *Geoforum* 39, no. 3 (May 2008): 1155–69, https://doi.org/10.1016/j.geoforum.2006.12.008; Jacqueline Best, ed., *Cultural Political Economy* (London: Routledge, 2009); Ngai-Ling Sum and Bob Jessop, *Towards a Cultural Political Economy: Putting Culture in Its Place in Political Economy* (Cheltenham: Edward Elgar, 2015); Andrew Sayer, 'For a Critical Cultural Political Economy', *Antipode* 33, no. 4 (2001): 687–708, https://doi.org/10.1111/1467–8330.00206.
38. This can be seen clearly in Richard Schechner's '6 Axioms for Environmental Theatre', which is one of the earliest attempts to lay out a theory of what today might be called site-specific or site-responsive performance (though in some ways Schechner's original term better accommodates the diverse spatial forms that such performances can entail). See Richard Schechner, '6 Axioms for Environmental Theatre', *The Drama Review: TDR* 12, no. 3 (1968): 41–64, h ttps://doi.org/10.2307/1144353.
39. Marvin Carlson, *Places of Performance: The Semiotics of Theatre Architecture* (Ithaca: Cornell University Press, 1989), 94–7.

40. Jenny Hughes, 'The Theatre and Its Poor: Neoliberal Economies of Waste and Gold in Les Misérables (1985) and Road (1986)', *Theatre Journal* 67, no. 1 (30 March 2015): 1–19, https://doi.org/10.1353/tj.2015.0017; Derek Miller, 'Average Broadway', *Theatre Journal* 68, no. 4 (2016): 529–53, https://doi.org/10.1353/tj.2016.0105; Hillary Miller, *Drop Dead: Performance in Crisis, 1970s New York* (Evanston: Northwestern University Press, 2016), 61–62, 67–68, 71–73. Hughes and Hillary Miller both largely accept Baumol and Bowen's cost disease theory, but Derek Miller is more circumspect about it. I discuss this more extensively in Chapter 2.
41. Agnew, *Worlds Apart*, 56.
42. Agnew, 56.
43. Joseph Stiglitz, 'After the Financial Crisis We Were All Keynesians – but Not for Long Enough', *The Guardian*, 10 October 2013, www.theguardian.com /business/economics-blog/2013/oct/10/financial-crisis-keynesians-eurozone-recession.
44. Chris Rhodes, 'Financial Services: Contribution to the UK *Economy*', Briefing Paper (London: House of Commons Library, 31 July 2019), 5, http://research briefings.files.parliament.uk/documents/SN06193/SN06193.pdf.
45. Rhodes, 7.
46. These are 2018 figures. See Rhodes, 8.

1 Industry

1. Michael Frayn, *Noises Off* (London: Bloomsbury, 2011), 162–3.
2. Frayn, 134.
3. Frayn, 164.
4. Ric Knowles, *How Theatre Means* (Basingstoke: Palgrave Macmillan, 2014), 59.
5. Karl Marx, *Early Writings*, trans. Rodney Livingstone and Gregor Benton (Harmondsworth: Penguin, 1992), 254–355.
6. Marx, 355; italics appear in the original.
7. Marx, 354.
8. Marx, *Capital*, 1:711; Isabella Bakker, 'Social Reproduction and the Constitution of a Gendered Political Economy', *New Political Economy* 12, no. 4 (1 December 2007): 541–56, https://doi.org/10.1080/13563460701661561; Stephen Gill and Isabella Bakker, eds., *Power, Production and Social Reproduction: Human In/Security in the Global Political Economy* (Basingstoke: Palgrave Macmillan, 2003); Isabella Bakker and Rachel Silvey, eds., *Beyond States and Markets: The Challenges of Social Reproduction* (Abingdon: Routledge, 2008); Silvia Federici, *Revolution at Point Zero* (Oakland: PM Press, 2012).

9. Throsby observes, '[M]any creative artists resent the thought that their activities form part of an industry.' He attributes this resentment to an anxiety about the impact of commercialism on the artistic sphere, since it purportedly 'subjugates the pure creative impulse to the demands of the marketplace'. David Throsby, *Economics and Culture* (Cambridge: Cambridge University Press, 2000), 110. One might also argue that this sentiment is symptomatic of the ideological ascendancy of the self-regulating market since the nineteenth century, as discussed by Karl Polanyi in *The Great Transformation*. The attempt to 'disembed' the market from society involved the subordination of social relations to the market rather than the reverse. Seen through this lens, then, the equation of art with industry signifies the former's submission to the latter. See Polanyi, *The Great Transformation*. See also Raymond Williams, *Keywords: A Vocabulary of Culture and Society*, rev. ed. (Oxford: Oxford University Press, 1985), 40–3.
10. Mike Alfreds, *Different Every Night: Freeing the Actor* (London: Nick Hern Books, 2007).
11. Mike Leigh, *Topsy-Turvy*, DVD (Twentieth-Century Fox, 2000).
12. Denis Diderot, *Selected Writings on Art and Literature*, trans. Geoffrey Bremner (London: Penguin, 1994), 12.
13. Marvin Carlson, *Theories of the Theatre: A Historical and Critical Survey, from the Greeks to the Present*, exp. ed. (Ithaca: Cornell University Press, 1993), 154.
14. Anne Bogart, *A Director Prepares: Seven Essays on Art and Theatre*, rev. ed. (London: Routledge, 2001); Anne Bogart, *And Then, You Act: Making Art in an Unpredictable World*, new ed. (New York: Routledge, 2007); William Ball, *A Sense of Direction: Some Observations on the Art of Directing* (New York: Quite Specific Media Group, 1984), 96.
15. Katie Mitchell, *The Director's Craft: A Handbook for the Theatre* (New York: Routledge, 2008), 179–80.
16. See also Stephen Unwin, *So You Want to Be a Theatre Director?* (London: Nick Hern Books, 2004), 164–89.
17. Harold Clurman, *On Directing*, new ed. (New York: Simon & Schuster Ltd, 1997), 104.
18. I am indebted to Rose Whyman on this point. The evolution in Stanislavsky's approach to planning can be seen by comparing his production scores. See Konstantin Sergeevich Stanislavsky, *The Seagull Produced by Stanislavsky*, ed. S. D. Balukhaty, trans. David Magarshack (London: Dennis Dobson, 1952); Konstantin Sergeevich Stanislavsky, *Stanislavsky Produces Othello*, trans. Helen Nowak (London: Geoffrey Bles, 1948).
19. Alfreds, *Different Every Night*, 348.
20. One should also be wary of accounts of the history of stage management that are sometimes given in stage management manuals. Maccoy, most notably,

offers a 'brief history' of stage management in his guidebook, but provides no sources for his claims. In support of his case for the importance of stage management (a legitimate case to make, in my view) he misconstrues Edward Gordon Craig's valorisation of the 'stage-manager' in *On the Art of the Theatre*. Maccoy takes Craig's frequent invocation of the 'stage manager' to refer to the occupation of stage manager as it is commonly understood today. Craig, though, is referring to what would now be understood as the director (a role which he wished to conceive more expansively than was commonly the case in the British theatre of his time, hence his recourse to managerial terminology). Peter Maccoy, *Essentials of Stage Management* (London: Methuen Drama, 2004), 11; Edward Gordon Craig, *On the Art of the Theatre* (London; New York: Routledge, 2009).

21. Tracy Catherine Cattell, 'The Living Language of Stage Management: An Interpretative Study of the History and Development of Professional Stage Management in the United Kingdom, 1567–*1968*' (PhD, Coventry, University of Warwick, 2015), 4–7, 60–120, 190–295.
22. Cattell, 1–120.
23. Cattell, 42.
24. Cattell argues that during the nineteenth century, the promptbook 'develop[ed] in importance as a manual for co-ordinating increasingly sophisticated and technically complex productions'. Cattell, 191.
25. Henry Fothergill Chorley, 'A New Stage Stride', *All the Year Round*, 31 October 1863, 233. I am indebted to Martin Young for bringing this to my attention.
26. Cattell, 'The Living Language of Stage Management', 190–295.
27. Edward A. Langhans, *Eighteenth Century British and Irish Promptbooks: A Descriptive Bibliography* (New York: Greenwood, 1988), xx.
28. Langhans, xx.
29. 'The Mikado Prompt Book' (Victoria and Albert Museum, ca. 1885), D'Oyly Carte Archive, Theatre and Performance Collection, www.vam.ac.uk/archives/unit/ARC17236. A complete, digitized copy of this prompt book can be seen at www.vam.ac.uk/__data/assets/pdf_file/0003/177942/53070_file.pdf.
30. Larry Fazio, *Stage Manager: The Professional Experience* (Burlington, MA: Focal Press, 2013), 145–6.
31. Lawrence Stern and Alice R. O'Grady, *Stage Management*, 10th ed. (New York: Routledge, 2013), 20.
32. Gail Pallin, *Stage Management: The Essential Handbook*, 3rd ed. (London: Nick Hern Books, 2010), 37.
33. Maccoy, *Essentials of Stage Management*, 117.
34. Soozie Copley and Philippa Killner, *Stage Management: A Practical Guide* (Marlborough, Wiltshire: Crowood Press, 2001), 69–70.

35. 'Noises Off' (Prompt Script, London, 2000), Box 1, National Theatre Archive.
36. I am indebted to O'Dair for clarifying this point for me. O'Dair joined the cast of the musical *Once* in London's West End part-way through the run of the show. Loren O'Dair, Interview with Author, 29 May 2015.
37. Nicholas Ridout, *Stage Fright, Animals, and Other Theatrical Problems* (Cambridge: Cambridge University Press, 2006).
38. Rehearsal Notes, 7 Dec. 2010. National Theatre, 'Frankenstein' (Prompt Script, London, 2011), 1, National Theatre Archive.
39. Nick Dear, 'Frankenstein' (Production Script, London, 2011), National Theatre Archive.
40. In the archived video recordings of the NT Live broadcasts of the two versions of the production, Cumberbatch puts his head in his hands slightly later than indicated in the blocking notation, and Miller does not put his head in his hands at all. Of course, the archived videos were recordings of single performances. It is possible that on other nights both actors executed the actions more closely in line with the notation, but the differences are minor (and in the context of the scene such variation would mean very little). See Danny Boyle, *Frankenstein (Benedict Cumberbatch as the Creature)*, NT Live Broadcast Recordings (National Theatre, 2011); Danny Boyle, *Frankenstein (Jonny Lee Miller as the Creature)*, NT Live Broadcast Recordings (National Theatre, 2011).

2 Productivity

1. Paul Krugman, *The Age of Diminished Expectations: U.S. Economic Policy in the 1990s*, 3rd ed. (Cambridge, MA: MIT Press, 1997), 11.
2. HM Treasury, 'Cuts by the Score', *O and M Bulletin: The Journal of Government Management Services* 7, no. 4 (1952): 21.
3. Baumol and Bowen, *Performing Arts: The Economic Dilemma; A Study of Problems Common to Theater, Opera, Music and Dance*, 165–6.
4. Arguably, both sides were ultimately defeated by the introduction of New Public Management techniques in the 1980s and 1990s. NPM, as it became known, adopted the technocratic language of experts while dispensing with the specialist expertise underpinning it.
5. At the risk of being reductive, conservatives have often sought to improve productivity in order to avoid hiring additional workers, progressives have seen productivity gains as ways to stave off wage or workforce reductions, and governments of all stripes have seen improved productivity as a way to avoid wage increases resulting in higher inflation. Krugman's use of the phrase 'in the long run' echoes Keynes's famous response to worries about inflation among

neo-classical economists: 'In the long run, we are all dead.' It is important to note, however, that Keynes has often been misrepresented here. He was not suggesting that inflation should be ignored; rather, he was arguing against misplaced faith in the business cycle to return to equilibrium, given enough time. Keynes's point was that equilibrium may indeed be achieved in the long run, but this was not much good to those suffering in the meantime. See John Maynard Keynes, *A Tract on Monetary Reform*, new ed., vol. 4, The Collected Writings of John Maynard Keynes (Cambridge: Cambridge University Press, 2013), 65.

6. Office for National Statistics, 'UK Productivity Introduction: July to September 2017' (London: Office for National Statistics, January 5, 2018), 5–6, www.ons.gov.uk/employmentandlabourmarket/peopleinwork/labourproductivity/articles/ukproductivityintroduction/julytoseptember2017.
7. Stephen Clarke, 'London Stalling: Half a Century of Living Standards in *London*' (London: Resolution Foundation, June 2018), 16, www.resolutionfoundation.org/app/uploads/2018/06/London-Stalling.pdf.
8. Clarke offers a useful analysis of London's productivity growth, based on Office of National Statistics data, in Clarke, 12–21.
9. Adam Smith, *An Inquiry into the Nature and Causes of the Wealth of Nations*, ed. Kathryn Sutherland (Oxford: Oxford University Press, 1993), 191–212.
10. Baumol and Bowen, *Performing Arts: The Economic Dilemma; A Study of Problems Common to Theater, Opera, Music and Dance*, 161–80.
11. 'Best Theatre of 2008', Time Out London, www.timeout.com/london/theatre/best-theatre-of-2008. Although this quote is unattributed in the *Time Out* article (the piece's authorship is credited to the magazine's theatre reviewers collectively), Andrew Haydon subsequently claimed credit for it in his personal blog, 'Postcards from the Gods'. See Andrew Haydon, 'Unaccustomed Provinces', *Postcards from the Gods* (blog), 11 January 2009, https://postcardsgods.blogspot.com/2009/01/unaccustomed-provinces.html.
12. For the purposes of this chapter, I use the 'tunnels' rather than 'vaults' nomenclature, since this is what they were called at the time of their opening as a performance venue, and what they are still called in railway parlance. I also want to resist the way that referring to them as 'vaults' puts a rather romantic, even ecclesiastical, spin on what very much remain scruffy tunnels under a working train station.
13. Smith, *An Inquiry into the Nature and Causes of the Wealth of Nations*, 191.
14. Smith, 192.
15. Smith, 192.
16. Byrne, Liam, '2012 Speech to the Labour Party Conference' (Labour Party Conference, Manchester, 1 October 2012), www.ukpol.co.uk/liam-byrne-2012-speech-to-labour-party-conference/.

17. Baumol and Bowen, *Performing Arts: The Economic Dilemma; A Study of Problems Common to Theater, Opera, Music and Dance*, 161–80.
18. Baumol and Bowen, 162.
19. One might point to the notable amount of unwaged labour in 'passion industries' like theatre and suggest that simply replacing waged labour with its unwaged counterpart would be the logical way to lower costs further (after all, many theatrical occupations do not require formal qualifications or certification in order to enter them and there is an oversupply of labour in many areas of the industry). This might seem especially plausible in English language theatre industries (e.g., the United States, the United Kingdom, Canada, Australia) in which short-term, freelance contracts predominate and more possible in industries, like theatre, where a worker's affective commitment to pursuing an artistic occupation mitigates poor wages and working conditions. While a shift to a universally unwaged labour force might seem superficially desirable from the perspective of the firm (however exploitative it might be to the worker), it is unlikely to occur for several reasons: it is likely to be impractical, since large sectors of the theatre industry can purchase the desirable predictability and skill that a waged workforce is more likely to provide at a relatively low cost (while 'passion' for the arts and various forms of self-subsidy can keep an unwaged, or intermittently waged, theatre worker in the labour market for a time, it is also the case that this pool of labour, while fairly constant, is characterised by enormous 'churn' – large numbers of workers leave and enter the labour market at any moment); this 'reserve army' of unwaged labour almost certainly helps hold down wages within the waged workforce anyway, since its existence means that waged labour is very likely priced lower than would otherwise be the case (there are exceptions to this – such as high-priced 'stars', where a labour monopoly can be used to extract a higher price for labour – but the exceptionality of such cases has historically resulted in little spillover into higher wages for the rest of the labour market); and, finally, it would be illegal in many jurisdictions, even if enforcement of labour law in cultural industries is often uneven (to put it mildly).
20. Baumol and Bowen, *Performing Arts: The Economic Dilemma; A Study of Problems Common to Theater, Opera, Music and Dance*, 164.
21. Baumol and Bowen, 165.
22. Baumol and Bowen, 165.
23. Hughes, 'The Theatre and Its Poor'; Miller, *Drop Dead: Performance in Crisis, 1970s New York*, 61–2, 67–8, 71–3.
24. Miller, 'Average Broadway', 537–41.
25. I distinguish here between the South Bank as a cultural district and the Southbank Centre, which is the umbrella institution that brings together

the Royal Festival Hall, the Hayward Gallery, the Queen Elizabeth Hall, and the Purcell Room.

26. For an analysis of the different types of cultural production in the South Bank, see Peter Newman and Ian Smith, 'Cultural Production, Place and Politics on the South Bank of the Thames', *International Journal of Urban and Regional Research* 24 (March 2000): 9–24, https://doi.org/10.1111/1468–2427.00233.
27. J. H. Forshaw and Patrick Abercrombie, *County of London Plan 1943* (London: Macmillan and Co., 1943), plate 48.1; Forshaw and Abercrombie, fig. 24.
28. Patrick Abercrombie, *Greater London Plan 1944* (London: HMSO, 1945).
29. Forshaw and Abercrombie, *County of London Plan 1943*, iii–iv.
30. Forshaw and Abercrombie, 131.
31. Forshaw and Abercrombie, 135.
32. Forshaw and Abercrombie, plate L. 1–3.
33. For a good account of how the 'Surreyside' theatres south of the Thames developed in concert with south London, see Jim Davis and Victor Emeljanow, *Reflecting the Audience: London Theatregoing, 1840–1880* (Iowa City: University of Iowa Press, 2001). For a comprehensive study of nineteenth-century theatre and music hall audiences in London (including south London), see Dagmar Kift, *The Victorian Music Hall: Culture, Class, and Conflict* (Cambridge: Cambridge University Press, 1996).
34. See Nick Draper, '"Across the Bridges": Representations of Victorian South London', *London Journal* 29, no. 1 (2004): 25–43, https://doi.org/10.1179/ldn.2004.29.1.25.
35. William Henry Beveridge, *Full Employment in a Free Society: A Report* (London: G. Allen & Unwin, 1944).
36. T. H. Marshall, *Citizenship and Social Class* (London: Pluto Press, 1992), 8.
37. Clive Gray, *The Politics of the Arts in Britain* (Basingstoke: Macmillan, 2000), 40.
38. While the area immediately south of the Thames was hardly held in great esteem by politicians and planners, I would caution against any nostalgia about the South Bank before the plan. Bombing of the area was extensive, many of the historical industries in the area had been either damaged or were in decline, and the housing stock in the area was often of poor quality.
39. London County Council, 'Objections to the 1951 Plan-Detailed Schedule of Objections, South Bank Area' (London, 1951), LCC/AR/TP/04/040, London Metropolitan Archives. This response was to objection 424A. The area between County Hall and Waterloo Bridge is where the Royal Festival Hall had been built.
40. Newman and Smith, 'Cultural Production, Place and Politics on the South Bank of the Thames', 17.

41. Nicholas Rossiter, 'HRH The Prince of Wales: A Vision of Britain', *Omnibus* (BBC1, 28 October 1988).
42. Carlson, *Places of Performance*, 94.
43. Bennett comments on recent political accommodation to the South Bank's current form. See Susan Bennett, 'Universal Experience: The City as Tourist Stage', in *The Cambridge Companion to Performance Studies*, ed. Tracy C. Davis (Cambridge: Cambridge University Press, 2008), 81–2. Baeten provides an in-depth analysis of political conflicts related to the area during the 1980s and 1990s. See Guy Baeten, 'Regenerating the South Bank: Reworking Community and the Emergence of Post-Political Regeneration', in *Regenerating London: Governance, Sustainability and Community in a Global City*, ed. Robert Imrie, Loretta Lees, and Mike Raco (London: Routledge, 2009), 237–53.
44. See, for example, Baeten, 'Regenerating the South Bank: Reworking Community and the Emergence of Post-Political Regeneration'; Susan Bennett, 'Theatre/Tourism', *Theatre Journal* 57, no. 3 (2005): 407–28, https://doi.org/10.1353/tj.2005.0087; Franco Bianchini and Michael Parkinson, *Cultural Policy and Urban Regeneration: The West European Experience* (Manchester: Manchester University Press, 1993); Graeme Evans, *Cultural Planning: An Urban Renaissance?* (London: Routledge, 2001); Graeme Evans, 'Creative Cities, Creative Spaces and Urban Policy', *Urban Studies* 46, no. 5–6 (1 May 2009): 1003–40, https://doi.org/10.1177/0042098009103853; Richard L. Florida, *Cities and the Creative Class* (London: Routledge, 2005); Charles Landry, *The Creative City* (London: Demos, 1995); Newman and Smith, 'Cultural Production, Place and Politics on the South Bank of the Thames'; Allen J. Scott, 'Creative Cities: Conceptual Issues and Policy Questions', *Journal of Urban Affairs* 28, no. 1 (January 2006): 1–17, https://doi.org/10.1111/j.0735-2166.2006.00256.x; F. J. Monclús and Manuel Guàrdia, eds., *Culture, Urbanism and Planning* (Aldershot: Ashgate, 2006).
45. Allen J. Scott, *Social Economy of the Metropolis* (Oxford: Oxford University Press, 2008).
46. Bennett, 'Universal Experience: The City as Tourist Stage', 78.
47. Bennett, 83.
48. In the lead-up to the 2012 Olympic Games, which London hosted, the London Organising Committee of the Olympic and Paralympic Games 2012 was an especially important body for arts organisations (via the Cultural Olympiad).
49. For an analysis of how cultural institutions have been conscripted into securing London's status as a global city – and cultivating the forms of subjectivity on which this globality depends – see McKinnie, 'Performing

the Civic Transnational: Cultural Production, Governance, and Citizenship in Contemporary London'.

50. Valverde is particularly concerned with the ways that objective, rule-driven urban planning continues to manage urban disorder through the premodern legal category of nuisance, in spite of the fact that nuisance is a 'subjective, aesthetic, [and] relational' civil law tort that contemporary land use governance aims to displace. See Mariana Valverde, 'Seeing Like a City: The Dialectic of Modern and Premodern Ways of Seeing in Urban Governance', *Law & Society Review* 45, no. 2 (1 June 2011): 280, https://doi .org/10.1111/j.1540–5893.2011.00441.x. She attempts to formulate a more diachronic understanding of urban governance than has commonly been employed within literatures on governance and governmentality. Valverde contends that James Scott's influential 'seeing like a state' model of urban governance is excessively dirigiste and tends to 'regard legal and governance inventions . . . as tools chosen to implement a fixed political project' rather than as contingent techniques whose current function may be substantially removed from their origin. Instead, she proposes the more flexible model of 'seeing like a city': a 'pragmatic approach that uses both old and new gazes, premodern and modern knowledge formats, in a nonzero-sum manner and in unpredictable and shifting combinations'. See Valverde, 280–1; James C Scott, *Seeing Like a State : How Certain Schemes to Improve the Human Condition Have Failed* (New Haven: Yale University Press, 1998). See also Marina Valverde, *Everyday Law on the Street: City Governance In An Age Of Diversity* (Chicago: University of Chicago Press, 2012).
51. Jack Kroll, 'Britain Onstage', *Newsweek*, 22 March 1976, 74.
52. I take the framing of 'absolute, relative, and relational' from David Harvey, *Cosmopolitanism and the Geographies of Freedom* (New York: Columbia University Press, 2009), 191.
53. Haworth Tompkins Ltd., 'Conservation Management Plan for the National *Theatre*' (London: Hayworth Tompkins Ltd., 2008), 52, www.nationaltheatre .org.uk/sites/default/files/nt_conservation_plans_dec_08.pdf.
54. Haworth Tompkins, 'National Theatre', 4 January 2018, www.haworthtomp kins.com/work/national-theatre.
55. 'The Vaults | ABOUT', The Vaults, www.thevaults.london/about.
56. 'House of Vans | ABOUT', House of Vans London, www.houseofvanslondon .com/about.
57. 'Commercial Estate Sale', Network Rail Property, https://property .networkrail.co.uk/commercial-estate-sale/; Rob Davies, 'Network Rail Sells Railway Arches to Investors for £1.5bn', *The Guardian*, 10 September 2018, www.theguardian.com/business/2018/sep/10/network-rail-sells-railway-arches-real-estate-investors-telereal-trillium-blackstone-property-partners;

GwynTopham, 'Private Equity Firms among Bidders for Network Rail Property Business', *The Guardian*, 1 March 2018, www.theguardian.com/business/2018/mar/01/guy-hands-emerges-as-bidder-in-national-rails-property-sell-off.

58. *Ditch* was not the first performance in the Waterloo tunnels; Punchdrunk had staged a series of installations there the previous year. The London International Festival of Theatre staged *Aftermath* in the Waterloo tunnels in July 2010, and other events have taken place there since. The Waterloo tunnels are also not the only site of their kind – performance collective Shunt produced events in its Vaults under London Bridge Station a little further east along the River Thames for several years and, before that, under a rail viaduct in Bethnal Green in the city's east end. See 'The Vaults | ABOUT'.
59. Beth Steel, *Ditch* (London: Methuen, 2010), 85–6.
60. Scott, *Social Economy of the Metropolis*, 84.
61. Scott, 84–5.
62. For the founding economic analyses of monopolistic or imperfect competition, see E. H. Chamberlin, *The Theory of Monopolistic Competition: A Re-Orientation of the Theory of Value*, 8th ed. (Cambridge, MA: Harvard University Press, 1962); Joan Robinson, *The Economics of Imperfect Competition*, 2nd ed. (London: Macmillan, 1969).
63. The classic theory of agglomeration economies is Alfred J. Marshall's (1890), which he developed in relation to the cutlery producers of Sheffield. See Alfred J. Marshall, *Principles of Economics* (Basingstoke: Palgrave Macmillan, 2013).
64. Michael Ball and David Sunderland, *An Economic History of London, 1800–1914* (London: Routledge, 2001), 14–37.
65. One might argue that live music performance functions the same way, but theatrical performance only intermittently has a recorded artifact that circulates independently of the live event (and when it does this is usually seen as a poor relation to the live event and is often consumed for documentary or pedagogical purposes).
66. This is not confined to the Waterloo *Ditch*. One can find similar qualities in Shunt's *Money* (2009–10), which ran for more than a year in a former tobacco warehouse in nearby Bermondsey. *Money* involved the construction of a self-contained theatre space (of a self-consciously mechanical sort) within the main hall of the warehouse that almost completely internalised – and rigorously disciplined – the act of spectatorship. The warehouse became rather like a container for a very carefully designed theatrical machine.

67. Karl Marx, *Capital: A Critique of Political Economy*, trans. David Fernbach, vol. 3, 3 vols. (London: Penguin, 1981); David Ricardo, *On the Principles of Political Economy and Taxation* (Harmondsworth: Penguin, 1971).
68. Robert J. Shiller, 'The Best, Brightest, and Least Productive?', Project Syndicate, 20 September 2013, www.project-syndicate.org/commentary/the-rent-seeking-problem-in-contemporary-finance-by-robert-j–shiller.
69. David Harvey, 'The Art of Rent: Globalization and the Commodification of Culture', in *Spaces of Capital: Towards a Critical Geography* (Edinburgh: Edinburgh University Press, 2001), 395.
70. Even though there was an initial decline in residential property prices in London and the UK after the financial crisis, it was not long before prices had risen above their pre-crisis levels (especially in London), and they kept rising after that. Incomes, however, did not increase along with this, so an already-existing affordability problem became even worse.
71. For a perceptive analysis of how this process plays out in material but politically ambiguous ways, see Levin and Solga, 2009.
72. Harvey Molotch, 'Place in Product', *International Journal of Urban and Regional Research* 26, no. 4 (2002): 666, https://doi.org/10.1111/1468–2427.00410. The role of the arts in securing London's superior position vis-à-vis other 'global cities' within transnational capitalism has been explicitly proclaimed in a series of public policy documents. See, for example, Mayor of London, 'Cultural Metropolis: The Mayor's Cultural Strategy–2012 and *Beyond*' (London: Greater London Authority, 2010); Mayor of London, 'Cultural Metropolis: The Mayor's Culture Strategy – Achievements and Next *Steps*' (London: Greater London Authority, 2014). For a discussion of the role of theatre and the arts in reproducing London's globality, see McKinnie, 'Performing the Civic Transnational: Cultural Production, Governance, and Citizenship in Contemporary London'.

3 Citizenship

1. Sunday Times of London Insight Team, *Ulster* (London: Deutsch, 1972), 213.
2. Kevin Schofield and Sebastian Whale, 'Karen Bradley: I Did Not Know People in Northern Ireland Voted on Constitutional Lines', *PoliticsHome.Com*, 6 September 2018, www.politicshome.com/news/uk/uk-regions/northern-ireland/news/98027/karen-bradley-i-did-not-know-people-northern-ireland.
3. Marina Hyde, 'Karen Bradley Routs Her Rival Imbeciles with Ladybird Guide to Northern Ireland', *The Guardian*, 7 September 2018, www.theguardian.com/commentisfree/2018/sep/07/karen-bradley-northern-ireland-secretary-tories.

4. Alan McGuinness and Greg Heffer, 'Northern Ireland Secretary Karen Bradley Admits There Are "No Excuses" for Her Troubles Comments', *Sky News*, 14 March 2019, https://news.sky.com/story/northern-ireland-secretary-karen-bradley-profoundly-sorry-for-troubles-comments-11657601.
5. Susan McKay, 'Tories Have Abandoned Pretence of Impartiality on North', *The Irish Times*, 9 March 2019, www.irishtimes.com/opinion/tories-have-abandoned-pretence-of-impartiality-on-north-1.3819276.
6. One sees both the Good Friday Agreement and Belfast Agreement in popular and interchangeable use.
7. For a longer history of attempting to construct forms of political identification and agency that do not conform to historical binaries and that attempt to compensate for Northern Ireland's status as a contested state, see Catherine Nash, 'Equity, Diversity and Interdependence: Cultural Policy in Northern Ireland', *Antipode* 37, no. 2 (2005): 272–300, https://doi.org/10.1111/j.0066–4812.2005.00493.x. For an analysis of the difficult challenges faced by the Northern Ireland Civic Forum – a deliberative, civil society body created out of the Good Friday Agreement but which has lain dormant since 2002 – see Vikki Bell, 'In Pursuit of Civic Participation: The Early Experiences of the Northern Ireland Civic Forum, 2000–2002', *Political Studies* 52, no. 3 (2004): 565–84, https://doi.org/10.1111/j.1467–9248.2004.00496.x; Vikki Bell, 'Spectres of Peace: Civic Participation in Northern Ireland', *Social & Legal Studies* 13, no. 3 (2004): 403–28, https://doi.org/10.1177/0964663904045001.
8. Philip Boland, Brendan Murtagh, and Peter Shirlow, 'Fashioning a City of Culture: "Life and Place Changing" or "12 Month Party"?', *International Journal of Cultural Policy* 25, no. 2 (2019): 246–65, https://doi.org/10.1080/10286632.2016.1231181.
9. Colin Coulter, 'Under Which Constitutional Arrangement Would You Still Prefer to Be Unemployed? Neoliberalism, the Peace Process, and the Politics of Class in Northern Ireland', *Studies in Conflict & Terrorism* 37, no. 9 (2 September 2014): 766, https://doi.org/10.1080/1057610X.2014.931212.
10. Coulter, 766.
11. Thomas Byrne, Trends in Foreign Direct Investment from the United States, 2003–2015' (Belfast: Department for the Economy, May 2017), 4, www.economy-ni.gov.uk/sites/default/files/publications/economy/Fulbright-Report-1-Trends-in-US-FDI.pdf. At the time of writing, these are the most recently available statistics for US foreign direct investment, but there are no indicators that the situation has changed notably since.
12. Coulter, 'Under Which Constitutional Arrangement Would You Still Prefer to Be Unemployed?', 766–7.

13. Northern Ireland Statistics and Research Agency, 'Northern Ireland Labour Market Report' (Belfast: Northern Ireland Statistics and Research Agency, July 2019), 7, www.nisra.gov.uk/sites/nisra.gov.uk/files/publications/labour-market-report-july-2019.PDF.
14. The collapse in 2008 also reflected the fact that Northern Ireland's property market had attracted considerable investment from the Republic of Ireland during the 'Celtic Tiger' years, but this largely dried up when the Republic's economy crashed in 2008. Although the housing market has recovered somewhat recently, it remains well below its 2008 peak. See Land and Property Services, 'Northern Ireland House Price Index October-December 2019 (Quarter 4 2019)', Northern Ireland House Price Index (Belfast: Northern Ireland Statistics and Research Agency, 19 February 2020), 8, www.finance-ni.gov.uk/sites/default/files/publications/dfp/NI%20House%20Price%20Index%20statistics%20report%20Quarter%204%202019.pdf.
15. For a geographical analysis of Johnston's work, see Bryonie Reid, '"A Profound Edge": Performative Negotiations of Belfast', *Cultural Geographies* 12, no. 4 (1 October 2005): 485–506, https://doi.org/10.1191/1474474005eu343oa. See also Reid's analysis of visual art practices that address public and private space in Northern Ireland in Bryonie Reid, '"Rearranging the Ground": Public and Private Space in Belfast, Northern Ireland', *Gender, Place & Culture* 15, no. 5 (1 October 2008): 489–503, https://doi.org/10.1080/09663690802300837.
16. See Jen Harvie, *Staging the UK* (Manchester: Manchester University Press, 2005), 53–66; Michael McKinnie, 'The State of This Place: Convictions, the Courthouse, and the Political Geography of Performance in Belfast', *Modern Drama* 46, no. 4 (2003): 580–97, https://doi.org/10.1353/mdr.2003.0014.
17. Between deaths and injuries it was the worst result of any single attack in the modern conflict in Northern Ireland. At the time of writing, no one has been convicted securely for the bombing, in spite of numerous prosecutions. (One conviction was subsequently overturned due to fabricated evidence by the Gardaí Siochana, the Irish national police service, and improper treatment of the accused's previous convictions at trial.)
18. David Lloyd and Paul Thomas, *Culture and the State* (London: Routledge, 1998), 47.
19. Lloyd and Thomas, 2.
20. Lloyd and Thomas' argument – a Gramscian analysis that brings together cultural history and Marxist state theory – is much more complex and extensive than this very brief précis can allow. For a fuller sense of its conceptual and historical contours, including a section on Friedrich Schiller and the stage as a moral institution, see Lloyd and Thomas, 1–58.

21. David Wiles, *A Short History of Western Performance Space* (Cambridge: Cambridge University Press, 2003), 211.
22. Jill Dolan, *Utopia in Performance: Finding Hope at the Theater* (Ann Arbor: University of Michigan Press, 2006), 90.
23. Helen Freshwater, *Theatre & Audience*, Theatre (Basingstoke: Palgrave Macmillan, 2009), 3.
24. Paul Makeham, 'Performing the City', *Theatre Research International* 30, no. 2 (2005): 158, https://doi.org/10.1017/S030788330500115X.
25. Darren O'Donnell, *Social Acupuncture* (Toronto: Coach House Books, 2006), 22.
26. Friedrich von Schiller, 'The Stage Considered as a Moral Institution', in *Sources of Dramatic Theory*, ed. Michael Sidnell, trans. Jean Wilson, vol. 2 (Cambridge: Cambridge University Press, 1994); Alexis de Tocqueville, 'Some Observations on the Drama Amongst Democratic Nations', in *The Theory of the Modern Stage*, ed. Eric Bentley (London: Penguin, 1992), 479–84; Percy MacKaye, *The Civic Theatre in Relation to the Redemption of Leisure* (New York: Mitchell Kennerley, 1912); St. John Ervine, *The Organised Theatre: A Plea in Civics* (New York: Macmillan, 1924).
27. Baz Kershaw, *The Politics of Performance: Radical Theatre as Cultural Intervention* (London: Routledge, 1992), 31–3.
28. Schechner, '6 Axioms for Environmental Theatre'.
29. Kershaw, *The Politics of Performance*, 32–3.
30. For a broader discussion of the ways that performance scholars have tended to figure the politics of site-specific performance, see McKinnie, 'Rethinking Site-Specificity: Monopoly, Urban Space, and the Cultural Economics of Site-Specific Performance'. In this chapter, I argue that performance scholars have tended to represent the politics of site-specific performance as either heterotopic, dialogic, or palimpsestic. What these accounts sometimes miss (though I would exclude Tompkins here) is the extent to which the theatrical approach to place can be appropriative as much as interrogative. For heterotopic accounts, see Michel Foucault, 'Of Other Spaces', trans. Jay Miskowiec, *Diacritics* 16, no. 1 (1986): 22–7, https://doi.org/10.2307/464648; Sarah Bryant-Bertail, 'Theatre as Heterotopia: Lessing's Nathan the Wise', *Assaph: Studies in the Theatre* 16 (2000): 91–108; Yanna Meerzon, 'An Ideal City: Heterotopia or Panopticon? On Joseph Brodsky's Play Marble and Its Fictional Spaces', *Modern Drama* 50, no. 2 (2007): 184–210, https://doi.org/10.1353/mdr.2007.0045; Joanne Tompkins, 'Staging the Imagined City in Australian Theatre', in *Performance and the City*, ed. Kim Solga, D. J. Hopkins, and Shelley Orr (Basingstoke: Palgrave Macmillan, 2009), 187–203; Wiles, *A Short History of Western Performance Space*, 8; Fiona Wilkie, 'Kinds of Place at Bore Place: Site-Specific Performance and the Rules of

Spatial Behaviour', *New Theatre Quarterly* 18, no. 3 (2002): 243–60, https://doi.org/10.1017/S0266464X02000337; Joanne Tompkins, *Theatre's Heterotopias: Performance and the Cultural Politics of Space* (Basingstoke: Palgrave Macmillan, 2014); Kevin Hetherington, *The Badlands of Modernity: Heterotopia and Social Ordering* (London: Routledge, 1997). For dialogic accounts, see Genie Babb, 'Center and Edge of the World: Frontiers of Site-Specific Performance in Alaska', *TDR: The Drama Review* 52, no. 3 (2008): 61–78, https://doi.org/10.1162/dram.2008.52.3.61; Melanie Bennett, 'Legion of Memory: Performance at Branch 51', *Theatre Research in Canada* 29, no. 1 (2008): 129–35; Katrinka Somdahl-Sands, 'Citizenship, Civic Memory and Urban Performance: Mission Wall Dances', *Space and Polity* 12, no. 3 (2008): 329, https://doi.org/10.1080/13562570802515242; Jenn Stephenson, 'Portrait of the Artist as Artist: The Celebration of Autobiography', *Canadian Theatre Review*, no. 141 (January 2010): 49–53. For palimpsestic accounts, see Victoria Hunter, 'Embodying the Site: The Here and Now in Site-Specific Dance Performance', *New Theatre Quarterly* 21, no. 4 (2005): 367–81, https://doi.org/10.1017/S0266464X05000230; Nick Kaye, *Site-Specific Art: Performance, Place, and Documentation* (London: Routledge, 2000); Melanie Kloetzel, 'Site-Specific Dance in a Corporate Landscape', *New Theatre Quarterly* 26, no. 2 (2010): 133–44, https://doi.org/DOI: https://doi.org/10.1017/S0266464X10000278P; Carl Lavery, 'The Pepys of London E11: Graeme Miller and the Politics of Linked', *New Theatre Quarterly* 21, no. 2 (2005): 148–60, https://doi.org/10.1017/S0266464X05000059; William McEvoy, 'Writing, Texts and Site-Specific Performance in the Recent Work of Deborah Warner', *Textual Practice* 20, no. 4 (2006): 591, https://doi.org/10.1080/09502360601058821; Mike Pearson and Michael Shanks, *Theatre/Archaeology* (London: Routledge, 2001); Cathy Turner, 'Palimpsest or Potential Space? Finding a Vocabulary for Site-Specific Performance', *New Theatre Quarterly* 20, no. 4 (2004): 373–90, https://doi.org/10.1017/S0266464X04000259.

31. In the UK, certainly, the increase in the number of site-specific productions in the past two decades or so is directly related to the operation of real estate markets. For a detailed analysis of one high-profile example of this – Punchdrunk's production of *Faust* in Wapping, East London – see Charikleia Marini, 'Re-Defining Urban Space through Performance' (PhD, London, Queen Mary University of London, 2013). Marini thoughtfully details the relationship between the production and property developer Ballymore's transformation of 21 Wapping Lane from a warehousing site to a high-specification residential and retail complex.
32. Stewart Parker, 'Northern Star', in *Plays 2* (London: Methuen, 1989), 4.
33. Bell, 'Spectres of Peace', 403.
34. Bell, 406.
35. Bell, 406.

36. A small but, for me, illustrative example of the appeal of citizenship rhetoric occurred during the Stewart Parker conference held at Queen's University, Belfast in 2008. Although only a minority of presentations were concerned *Northern Star*, the phrase 'citizens of Belfast' was repeatedly – and affirmatively – invoked by participants.
37. Dolan, *Utopia in Performance*, 12.
38. Parker, 'Northern Star', 81.
39. Glenn Patterson, 'The Bard of Belfast', *The Guardian*, 13 June 2008, www.theguardian.com/arts/theatre/drama/story/0,2285237,00.html.
40. I. R. McBride, *Scripture Politics: Ulster Presbyterians and Irish Radicalism in the Late Eighteenth Century: Ulster Presbyterians and Irish Radicalism in Late Eighteenth-Century Ireland* (Oxford: Oxford University Press, 1998), 11.
41. McBride, 11.
42. Gerard Delanty, *Citizenship in a Global Age: Society, Culture, Politics* (Buckingham: Open University Press, 2000), 33.
43. Delanty, 34–5.
44. McKinnie, 'Institutional Frameworks: Theatre, State, and Market in Modern Urban Performance'.
45. Parker, 'Northern Star', 81–2.
46. Michael Billington, 'He Had a Dream: Stephen Rea Has Taken Time off Filming to Direct a Play about One Man's Struggle for a United Ireland – Two Centuries Ago', *The Guardian*, 18 November 1998, sec. G2 12–13.
47. In a similar vein, Chris Morash and Shaun Richards argue that the 1998 Tinderbox production 'gave spatial form to the shared history of Dissenting Presbyterianism and the Republicanism of the United Irishmen, since occluded by sectarian conflict'. Chris Morash and Shaun Richards, *Mapping Irish Theatre: Theories of Space and Place* (Cambridge: Cambridge University Press, 2013), 162.
48. The critical counterparts to this theatrical imagination are, of course, Michel de Certeau's now-classic analysis of walking in the city (itself prefigured by Walter Benjamin's discussion of the *flâneur*) and, in a different way, Guy Debord's elaboration of the *dérive*. Walking has often figured as the mode of transit through which a particularly intense urban geography might be conducted. See Guy Debord, 'Theory of the Derive', in *Situationist International Anthology*, ed. and trans. Ken Knabb, revised and expanded ed. (Berkeley: Bureau of Public Secrets, 2007), 62–6; Michel de Certeau, *The Practice of Everyday Life* (Berkeley: University of California Press, 1988), 91–110.

4 **Security**

1. 'Vivien Leigh and the Old Vic', The Old Vic, 4 November 2017, www.oldvictheatre.com/news/2017/11/vivien-leigh-and-the-old-vic.

2. Andrew Chung, 'Border Towns Struggle with Post-9/11 Security Measures', *The Toronto Star*, 2 September 2011, www.thestar.com/news/insight/article/1048571–border-towns-struggle-with-post-9–11-security-measures; 'New Border Rules Irksome for Derby Line Residents', 14 March 2010, http://digitaljournal.com/article/289068; 'Local Man Jailed for Crossing Street', wptz.com, 15 March 2010, www.wptz.com/Local-Man-Jailed-For-Crossing-Street/-/8870596/5756044/-/8vvmjnz/-/index.html.
3. The border was drawn in 1774, when both Quebec and Vermont were British colonies.
4. Recent examples include John Gendall, 'US Canada Border Building Walls', *Architectural Digest*, 30 March 2017, www.architecturaldigest.com/story/cultural-center-on-us-canada-border-teach-us-about-building-walls; Ian Austen, 'Quebec and Vermont Towns Bond over a Sleepy Border', *New York Times*, 18 July 2007, www.nytimes.com/2007/07/18/world/americas/18border.html; Phil Blampied, 'Partly in Vermont: A Borderline Case', *Time*, 13 August 1979; Dirk Van Susteren, 'Vermont Opera Houses Continue to Entertain', *Boston Globe*, 26 February 2012, www.bostonglobe.com/lifestyle/travel/2012/02/26/vermont-opera-houses-continue-entertain/3pifjLWK3C1TsigTYIhTpJ/story.html; *The Haskell Free Library and Opera House: A Cultural Gem on the Canada-U.S. Border*, 2011, www.youtube.com/watch?v=GlVBiofRdCA&feature=youtube_gdata_player; Sarah Yahm, 'The U.S.-Canada Border Runs through This Tiny Library', *Atlas Obscura*, 7 July 2016, www.atlasobscura.com/articles/the-us-canada-border-runs-through-this-tiny-library; Chris Burnett, 'The Haskell Free Library and Opera House: A Landmark with Dual Citizenship', *New England Today*, 2 August 2016, https://newengland.com/today/travel/vermont/the-haskell-free-library-and-opera-house/; Emma Prestwich, 'Haskell Free Library and Opera House Straddles the Canada-U.S. Border', *HuffPost Canada*, 12 January 2017, www.huffingtonpost.ca/2017/01/12/haskell-free-library-and-opera-house_n_14110796.html; Derek Lundy, 'Stanstead: A Town on the Border', *Canadian Geographic*, 10 July 2010, www.canadiangeographic.ca/article/stanstead-town-border; Christopher Curtis, 'Stanstead Closes Unguarded Border', *Montreal Gazette*, 30 July 2012; Eric Weiner, 'The US-Canada Border Runs through This Tiny Library', 6 November 2017, www.bbc.com/travel/story/20171105-the-us-canada-border-runs-through-this-tiny-library; 'In Praise of Limbo', *This American Life* (National Public Radio, 28 December 2018), www.thisamericanlife.org/664/the-room-of-requirement/act-one-4.
5. John Gendall, 'What a Cultural Center on the US-Canada Border Can Teach Us about Building Walls', *Architectural Digest*, 30 March 2017, www.architecturaldigest.com/story/cultural-center-on-us-canada-border-teach-us-about-building-walls.

6. These meetings were featured in an episode of National Public Radio's popular *This American Life* programme. See 'In Praise of Limbo'.
7. I take the term 'place patriotism' from John Logan and Harvey Molotch's classic *Urban Fortunes: The Political Economy of Place*. In their formulation, place patriotism involves the cultivation and mobilisation of local attachments, especially in support of capitalist-led urban development. See Harvey Molotch and John R. Logan, *Urban Fortunes: The Political Economy of Place* (Berkeley: University of California Press, 2007). I discuss place patriotism in the context of theatre-building in Toronto in Michael McKinnie, *City Stages: Theatre and Urban Space in a Global City* (Toronto: University of Toronto Press, 2007).
8. Donald J. Trump, 'The Theater Must Always Be a Safe and Special Place. The Cast of Hamilton Was Very Rude Last Night to a Very Good Man, Mike Pence. Apologize!', Tweet, @realdonaldtrump, 5 November 2016, https://twitter.com/realdonaldtrump/status/799974635274194947?lang=en.
9. Matthew B. Sparke, 'A Neoliberal Nexus: Economy, Security and the Biopolitics of Citizenship on the Border', *Political Geography* 25, no. 2 (2006): 153, https://doi.org/10.1016/j.polgeo.2005.10.002.
10. This is not to suggest that security does not arise at all in theatre but it tends to do so in rather more quotidian forms. When an Ariana Grande concert in the English city of Manchester was bombed in May 2017, killing twenty-two people, theatres across Britain (along with many other public venues) increased measures such as bag checks and heightened building surveillance. See Georgia Snow, 'Theatres Across UK Step Up Security in Wake of Manchester Bombing', *The Stage*, 30 May 2017, www.thestage.co.uk/news/2017/theatres-across-uk-step-security-wake-manchester-bombing/.
11. Bruce Schneier, *Beyond Fear: Thinking Sensibly about Security in an Uncertain World* (New York: Copernicus, 2003).
12. Guardian Staff and Agencies, 'Professor: Flight Was Delayed because My Equations Raised Terror Fears', *The Guardian*, 7 May 2016, www.theguardian.com/us-news/2016/may/07/professor-flight-delay-terrorism-equation-american-airlines.
13. Louise Amoore and Alexandra Hall, 'Border Theatre: On the Arts of Security and Resistance', *Cultural Geographies* 17, no. 3 (2010): 303, https://doi.org/10.1177/1474474010368604.
14. Amoore and Hall, 303.
15. Christopher B. Balme, *The Theatrical Public Sphere* (Cambridge: Cambridge University Press, 2014), 43.
16. Michel Foucault, *The Birth of Biopolitics: Lectures at the College de France, 1978–1979*, ed. Michel Senellart, trans. Graham Burchell (Basingstoke: Palgrave Macmillan, 2008), 2.

17. Lloyd and Thomas, *Culture and the State*, 3.
18. Lloyd and Thomas, 3.
19. Foucault, *The Birth of Biopolitics*, 319.
20. Foucault, *The Birth of Biopolitics*, 319.
21. Foucault, 319.
22. Foucault, 294.
23. Adam Ferguson, *An Essay on the History of Civil Society*, ed. Fania Oz-Salzberger, new ed. (Cambridge: Cambridge University Press, 1996); Adam Smith, *The Wealth of Nations: Books I-III*, ed. Andrew Skinner (London: Penguin Classics, 1982); Adam Smith, *The Wealth of Nations: Books IV–V*, ed. Andrew Skinner (Penguin Classics, 1999); David Hume, *David Hume: An Enquiry Concerning the Principles of Morals*, ed. Tom L. Beauchamp (Oxford: Oxford University Press, 2006).
24. Foucault, *The Birth of Biopolitics*, 291.
25. Foucault, 272.
26. Foucault, 276.
27. Foucault, 293.
28. Foucault, 293.
29. Foucault, 294.
30. Foucault, 295.
31. Foucault, 295.
32. Foucault, 296.
33. Foucault, 297.
34. Foucault, 298.
35. Foucault, 298.
36. Foucault, 299.
37. Foucault, 300.
38. Foucault, 301.
39. Foucault, 301.
40. Foucault, 305.
41. Foucault, 305.
42. Foucault, 306.
43. The theatre opened in 1904, and the library opened the following year.
44. *Haskell Opera House Grand Opening Playbill*, 7 June 1904.
45. The opera house auditorium was not heated. The installation of heating would have been necessary to use it through the cold and snowy winters that characterise this part of North America.
46. Craig Robertson, 'Locating the Border', *Social Identities: Journal for the Study of Race, Nation and Culture* 14, no. 4 (2008): 447–56, https://doi.org/10.1080/13504630802211894.
47. Robertson, 448.

48. 'About Us | International Boundary Commission', www.internationalboundary commission.org/en/about.php.
49. Matthew Farfan, *The Vermont-Quebec Border: Life on the Line* (Charleston: Arcadia Publishing, 2009), 8.
50. This remains the case even after passage of the US-Canada Free Trade Agreement in 1984 and the North American Free Trade Agreement in 1992. These agreements greatly assisted the free movement of goods and services but only in limited circumstances labour.
51. Bruno Ramirez, *Crossing the 49th Parallel: Migration from Canada to the United States, 1900–1930* (Ithaca: Cornell University Press, 2001), 51.
52. David R. Smith, 'Structuring the Permeable Border: Channeling and Regulating Cross-Border Traffic in Labor, Capital, and Goods', in *Permeable Border: The Great Lakes Basin as Transnational Region, 1650–1990*. (Pittsburgh: University of Pittsburgh Press, 2005), 122.
53. Ramirez, *Crossing the 49th Parallel: Migration from Canada to the United States, 1900–1930*, 49. Ramirez notes that Canadians waited significantly longer than other nationalities to apply for naturalisation in the US – on average, 16.4 years.
54. International Boundary Commission, 'International Boundary Commission Official Web Site', www.internationalboundarycommission.org/history.html.
55. The bulk of this distance consists of the Pacific to Atlantic border, but approximately 2500 kilometres of the border separates the American state of Alaska from the Canadian territory of Yukon and province of British Columbia.
56. Robertson, 'Locating the Border', 451.
57. Ramirez, *Crossing the 49th Parallel: Migration from Canada to the United States, 1900–1930*, 48.
58. Robertson, 'Locating the Border', 449–50.
59. Ramirez, 'Crossing the 49th Parallel: Migration from Canada to the United States, 1900–1930', 56; Robertson, 'Locating the Border', 449.
60. International Boundary Commission, 'Living Near the Boundary', www.interna tionalboundarycommission.org/en/the-boundary-and-you/living-near-boundary .php.
61. The story commonly told is that the black line was painted on the floor after a fire broke out in the library sometime during the 1970s and the Haskell's Canadian and American insurance companies squabbled over which one of them should settle the Haskell's claim: Was the fire in Canada or the United States?
62. For a related analysis of theatre as an 'embedded institution' with the state and market, see McKinnie, 'Institutional Frameworks: Theatre, State, and Market in Modern Urban Performance'. On the reticence about thinking of theatre as an institution, see Balme, *The Theatrical Public Sphere*, 41–2; McKinnie,

'Institutional Frameworks: Theatre, State, and Market in Modern Urban Performance'.

5 Confidence

1. 'Aidan Burley Says 'Leftie Multi-Cultural' Tweet Misunderstood', BBC News, www.bbc.com/news/uk-19025518.
2. 'Aidan Burley Says 'leftie Multi-Cultural' Tweet Misunderstood'. Burley had a history of controversy, having been dismissed as Parliamentary Private Secretary to the Secretary of State for Transport the year before for helping organise a Nazi-themed stag party for a friend.
3. 'Aidan Burley Says 'Leftie Multi-Cultural' Tweet Misunderstood'.
4. 'Aidan Burley Says 'Leftie Multi-Cultural' Tweet Misunderstood'. Burley did not run again in the 2015 general election and his tweets have been deleted.
5. The opening ceremony as a whole was structured in three successive parts: *Isles of Wonder*; the athletes' procession; and a concert of different British musical acts (e.g., Arctic Monkeys and Paul McCartney).
6. *Isles of Wonder* had a running time of approximately one hour and fifteen minutes within a total ceremony of about three-and-a-half hours long (including the athletes' parade and concluding musical concert). The Olympics organisation has made a video of the complete ceremony (with its own commentary) freely available. See *The Complete London 2012 Opening Ceremony; London 2012 Olympic Games* (Olympic Broadcasting Services, 2012), www.youtube.com/watch?v=4As0e4de-rI.
7. 'London 2012 Opening Ceremony Draws 900 Million Viewers', Reuters, 7 August 2012, https://uk.reuters.com/article/uk-oly-ratings-day11-idUKBRE8760V820120807; 'London 2012 Olympics Deliver Record Viewing Figures for BBC', Press Release, BBC Media Centre, August 13, 2012, www.bbc.co.uk/mediacentre/latestnews/2012/olympic-viewing-figs.html.
8. Stephen Glover, 'Yes, a Brilliant Show and Danny Boyle's a Genius. But Why Have So Many Been Taken in by His Marxist Propaganda?', *Mail Online*, 2 August 2012, www.dailymail.co.uk/debate/article-2182328/London-2012-opening-ceremony-Danny-Boyles-genius-taken-Marxist-propaganda.html. Glover's perspective was very much an outlier. For examples of approving takes on *Isles of Wonder*, see Charlotte Higgins, 'The Olympics Opening Ceremony: My Cultural Highlight of 2012', *The Guardian*, 5 December 2012, www.theguardian.com/culture/2012/dec/05/olympic-opening-ceremony-2012-highlight; Gordon Rayner, 'London 2012: Breathtaking, Brash and Bonkers … an Utterly British Olympic Opening Ceremony', *The Telegraph*, 27 July 2012, www.telegraph.co.uk/sport/olympics/news/9433818/London-2012-breathtaking-brash-and

-bonkers. . .an-utterly-British-Olympic-opening-ceremony.html; 'Media Reaction to London 2012 Olympic Opening Ceremony', *BBC News*, www.bbc.com/news/uk-19025686; Tracy McVeigh and Owen Gibson, 'London 2012: Danny Boyle Thrills Audiences with Inventive Olympics Opening Ceremony', *The Guardian*, 28 July 2012, www.theguardian .com/sport/2012/jul/28/london-2012-boyle-olympics-opening-ceremony; 'London 2012: Opening Ceremony – Reviews', *The Guardian*, 29 July 2012, www.theguardian.com/sport/2012/jul/29/london-2012-opening-ceremony-reviews; Tom Parry, 'U.K. Media Give Olympic Opening Show Glowing Reviews', *CBC News*, 28 July 2012, www.cbc.ca/1.1193902. International coverage was in a similar vein, if sometimes a bit perplexed by the degree of cultural self-referentiality in the event: Sarah Lyall, 'A 5-Ring Circus: Olympic Opening Is Oddly, Confidently British', *New York Times*, 27 July 2012, www.nytimes.com/2012/07/28/sports/olympics/in-olympic-opening-cere mony-britain-asserts-its-eccentric-identity.html; David Rooney, 'Opening Ceremony of the London Olympics: Review', *The Hollywood Reporter*, 27 July 2012, www.hollywoodreporter.com/review/olympic-games-opening-ceremony-london-danny-boyle-355545; '"Dazzling": World's Press Heaps Praise on Opening Ceremony', *Huffington Post UK*, 28 July 2012, www.huffingtonpost.co.uk/2012/07/28/london-2012-worlds-press-heaps-praise_n_1712665.html; 'London 2012: What the World Thought of the Opening Ceremony', *The Telegraph*, 28 July 2012, www.telegraph.co.uk/sport/olympics/london-2012/9434319/London-2012-What-the-world-thought-of-the-opening-ceremony.html; Lauren Collins, 'Danny Boyle Wins the Gold', *The New Yorker*, 27 July 2012, www.newyorker.com/news/sporting-scene/danny-boyle-wins-the-gold-2.

9. 'Second to the Right, and Straight on Till Morning' runs from approximately 43.52 to 55.43 in the official video.
10. John Maynard Keynes, *The General Theory of Employment, Interest and Money*, vol. 7, The Collected Writings of John Maynard Keynes (London: Macmillan, 1973), 148.
11. Andrew Grice, 'Alistair Darling: We Were Two Hours from the Cashpoints Running Dry', *The Independent*, 18 March 2011, www.independent.co.uk/ne ws/people/profiles/alistair-darling-we-were-two-hours-from-the-cashpoints-running-dry-2245350.html.
12. 'Tory Spring Conference Speeches in Full', Politics.co.uk, 27 April 2009, www.politics.co.uk/comment-analysis/2009/04/27/tory-spring-conference -speeches-in-full.
13. 'Tory Spring Conference Speeches in Full'.
14. 'Tory Spring Conference Speeches in Full'.

15. Ben Zaranko and Rowena Crawford, 'Tax Revenues and Spending on Social Security Benefits and Public Services since the Crisis' (Institute for Fiscal Studies, 17 November 2019), 6, https://doi.org/10.1920/BN.IFS.2019.BN0261.
16. George Eaton, 'The Pre-Election Pledges That the Tories Are Trying to Wipe from the Internet', *New Statesman*, www.newstatesman.com/politics/2013/11/pre-election-pledges-tories-are-trying-wipe-internet.
17. Zaranko and Crawford, 'Tax Revenues and Spending on Social Security Benefits and Public Services since the Crisis', 2.
18. Valentina Romei, 'UK Living Standards Grow at Slowest Rate since WW2 in 2010s', *Financial Times*, 3 January 2020, www.ft.com/content/44401594-2ca0-11ea-bc77-65e4aa615551.
19. 'Gross Domestic Product: Year on Year Growth: CVM SA %' (Office for National Statistics, 11 February 2020), www.ons.gov.uk/economy/grossdomesticproductgdp/timeseries/ihyp/pn2.
20. See, for example, Stefan Szymanski, 'About Winning: The Political Economy of Awarding the World Cup and the Olympic Games', *SAIS Review* 31, no. 1 (2011): 87–97, https://doi.org/10.1353/sais.2011.0003; Evangelia Kasimati, 'Economic Aspects and the Summer Olympics: A Review of Related Research', *International Journal of Tourism Research* 5, no. 6 (1 November 2003): 433–44, https://doi.org/10.1002/jtr.449; Georgios Kavetsos, 'The Impact of the London Olympics Announcement on Property Prices', *Urban Studies* 49, no. 7 (1 May 2012): 1453–70, https://doi.org/10.1177/0042098011415436; Robert A. Baade and Victor A. Matheson, 'Going for the Gold: The Economics of the Olympics', *Journal of Economic Perspectives* 30, no. 2 (Spring 2016): 201–18, https://doi.org/10.1257/jep.30.2.201.
21. Baade and Matheson, 'Going for the Gold: The Economics of the Olympics', 202.
22. Keynes, *The General Theory of Employment, Interest and Money*, 7:146.
23. Keynes, 7:135–46.
24. Keynes, 7:149.
25. To clarify, a white elephant is an asset where the costs of its creation are too great to be recuperated, or the costs of its maintenance are excessive. The term derives from a story that the King of Siam gave white elephants to courtiers who displeased him. As the gift came from the king it could not be refused, but the costs to the recipient of maintaining the animal were ruinous.
26. E20 Stadium LLP, WH Holding Limited, and West Ham United Football Club Limited, 'Concession Agreement' (Allen & Overy LLP, 22 March 2013), www.queenelizabetholympicpark.co.uk/-/media/qeop/files/public/conces

sion-agreement-2016.ashx?la=en; Owen Gibson, 'How West Ham Struck the Deal of the Century with Olympic Stadium Move', *The Guardian*, 14 April 2016, www.theguardian.com/football/2016/apr/14/west-ham-deal-century-olympic-stadium; Owen Gibson, 'West Ham's Olympic Stadium Contract: Club to Pay £2.5m per Season in Rent', *The Guardian*, 14 April 2016, www.theguardian.com/football/2016/apr/14/west-ham-olympic-stadium-club-pay-per-season-rent; 'West Ham to Pay £2.5m Olympic Stadium Rent per Year', *BBC Sport*, 14 April 2016, www.bbc.co.uk/sport/football/36043808; Information Commissioner, 'Decision Notice' (London: Information Commissioner's Office, 3 September 2015), https://ico.org.uk/media/action-weve-taken/decision-notices/2015/1432468/fs_50556618.pdf.

27. 'Happy and glorious' is, of course, a line from 'God Save the Queen', the British national anthem.
28. In the UK, 'Abide with Me' is commonly sung at Remembrance Day ceremonies as well as major sporting events (such as the FA Cup football final).
29. William Blake, *The Complete Poems*, ed. Alicia Ostriker (Harmondsworth; New York: Penguin Classics, 1977), 494.
30. This passage can be found on the official video recording from 48.44 to 49.11. *The Complete London 2012 Opening Ceremony; London 2012 Olympic Games*. I have transcribed Rowling's speech as she performed it. Her words differ slightly from those in the *Peter and Wendy* stories published in 1911 (the text is not found in the 1904 stage play): 'Of all delectable islands the Neverland is the snuggest and most compact, not large and sprawly, you know, with tedious distances between one adventure and another, but nicely crammed. When you play at it by day with the chairs and tablecloth, it is not in the least alarming, but in the two minutes before you go to sleep it becomes very nearly real'. J. M. Barrie, *Peter Pan: Peter and Wendy and Peter Pan in Kensington Gardens*, ed. Jack Zipes (New York: Penguin Classics, 2005), 9–10.
31. Simon Wren-Lewis, 'Why the National Health Service Played a Central Part in the Olympic Ceremony', *Mainly Macro* (blog), 31 July 2012, https://mainlymacro.blogspot.com/2012/07/why-national-health-service-played.html.
32. In 2018–19, the group with the largest number of 'finished admissions episodes' in NHS England was aged 70–4, followed closely by the 75–9 group. The groups with the lowest number of FAEs were all 19 years of age or under. See NHS Digital, 'Hospital Admitted Patient Care and Adult Critical Care Activity' (NHS Digital, 19 September 2019), 5, https://files.digital.nhs.uk/F2/E70669/hosp-epis-stat-admi-summ-rep-2018–19-rep.pdf.
33. Marvin Carlson, *The Haunted Stage: The Theatre as Memory Machine* (Ann Arbor: University of Michigan Press, 2001).
34. Keynes, *The Collected Writings of John Maynard Keynes*, 9:xviii.
35. Keynes, 9:xviii.

Conclusion

1. Keynes, 9:332.
2. Keynes, 9:322.
3. Keynes, 9:326, emphasis in the original.
4. Keynes, 9:325.
5. Keynes also hoped that, in the future, 'economists could manage to get themselves thought of as humble, competent people, on a level with dentists'. This has not happened. Keynes, 9:332.
6. Keynes, 9:331.
7. Keynes, 9:332.

Bibliography

Abercrombie, Patrick. *Greater London Plan 1944*. London: HMSO, 1945.

'About Us | International Boundary Commission'. www.internationalboundarycommission.org/en/about.php.

Agnew, Jean-Christophe. *Worlds Apart: The Market and the Theater in Anglo-American Thought, 1550–1750*. Cambridge: Cambridge University Press, 1988.

Alfreds, Mike. *Different Every Night: Freeing the Actor*. London: Nick Hern Books, 2007.

Amoore, Louise, and Alexandra Hall. 'Border Theatre: On the Arts of Security and Resistance'. *Cultural Geographies* 17, no. 3 (2010): 299–319. https://doi.org/10.1177/1474474010368604.

Arts Council of Great Britain. 'First Annual Report 1945–6'. London: Arts Council of Great Britain, 1946. www.artscouncil.org.uk/sites/default/files/download-file/The%20Arts%20Council%20of%20Great%20Britain%20-%201st%20Annual%20Report%201945_0.pdf.

Austen, Ian. 'Quebec and Vermont Towns Bond over a Sleepy Border'. *New York Times*, 18 July 2007. www.nytimes.com/2007/07/18/world/americas/18border.html.

Baade, Robert A., and Victor A. Matheson. 'Going for the Gold: The Economics of the Olympics'. *Journal of Economic Perspectives* 30, no. 2 (Spring 2016): 201–18. https://doi.org/10.1257/jep.30.2.201.

Babb, Genie. 'Center and Edge of the World: Frontiers of Site-Specific Performance in Alaska'. *TDR: The Drama Review* 52, no. 3 (2008): 61–78. https://doi.org/10.1162/dram.2008.52.3.61.

Baeten, Guy. 'Regenerating the South Bank: Reworking Community and the Emergence of Post-Political Regeneration'. In *Regenerating London: Governance, Sustainability and Community in a Global City*, edited by Robert Imrie, Loretta Lees, and Mike Raco, 237–53. London: Routledge, 2009.

Bakker, Isabella. 'Social Reproduction and the Constitution of a Gendered Political Economy'. *New Political Economy* 12, no. 4 (1 December 2007): 541–56. https://doi.org/10.1080/13563460701661561.

Bakker, Isabella, and Rachel Silvey, eds. *Beyond States and Markets: The Challenges of Social Reproduction*. Abingdon: Routledge, 2008.

Ball, Michael, and David Sunderland. *An Economic History of London, 1800–1914*. London: Routledge, 2001.

Ball, William. *A Sense of Direction: Some Observations on the Art of Directing*. New York: Quite Specific Media Group, 1984.

Balme, Christopher B. *The Theatrical Public Sphere*. Cambridge: Cambridge University Press, 2014.

Barrie, J. M. *Peter Pan: Peter and Wendy and Peter Pan in Kensington Gardens*. Edited by Jack Zipes. New York: Penguin Classics, 2005.

Baumol, William J., and William G. Bowen. *Performing Arts: The Economic Dilemma; A Study of Problems Common to Theater, Opera, Music and Dance*. New York: Twentieth Century Fund, 1966.

BBC News. 'Aidan Burley Says "Leftie Multi-Cultural" Tweet Misunderstood'. www.bbc.com/news/uk-19025518.

Bell, Vikki. 'In Pursuit of Civic Participation: The Early Experiences of the Northern Ireland Civic Forum, 2000–2002'. *Political Studies* 52, no. 3 (2004): 565–84. https://doi.org/10.1111/j.1467–9248.2004.00496.x.

'Spectres of Peace: Civic Participation in Northern Ireland'. *Social & Legal Studies* 13, no. 3 (2004): 403–28. https://doi.org/10.1177/0964663904045001.

Bennett, Melanie. 'Legion of Memory: Performance at Branch 51'. *Theatre Research in Canada* 29, no. 1 (2008): 129–35.

Bennett, Susan. 'Theatre/Tourism'. *Theatre Journal* 57, no. 3 (2005): 407–28. https://doi.org/10.1353/tj.2005.0087.

'Universal Experience: The City as Tourist Stage'. In *The Cambridge Companion to Performance Studies*, edited by Tracy C. Davis, 76–89. Cambridge: Cambridge University Press, 2008.

Best, Jacqueline, ed. *Cultural Political Economy*. London: Routledge, 2009.

Beveridge, William Henry. *Full Employment in a Free Society: A Report*. London: G. Allen & Unwin, 1944.

Bianchini, Franco, and Michael Parkinson. *Cultural Policy and Urban Regeneration: The West European Experience*. Manchester: Manchester University Press, 1993.

Billington, Michael. 'He Had a Dream: Stephen Rea Has Taken Time off Filming to Direct a Play about One Man's Struggle for a United Ireland – Two Centuries Ago'. *The Guardian*. 18 November 1998, sec. G2, 12–13.

State of the Nation: British Theatre since 1945. London: Faber and Faber, 2009.

Blake, William. *The Complete Poems*. Edited by Alicia Ostriker. Harmondsworth and New York: Penguin Classics, 1977.

Blampied, Phil. 'Partly in Vermont: A Borderline Case'. *Time*, 13 August 1979.

Bogart, Anne. *A Director Prepares: Seven Essays on Art and Theatre*. rep. ed. London: Routledge, 2001.

And Then, You Act: Making Art in an Unpredictable World. rev. ed. New York: Routledge, 2007.

Boland, Philip, Brendan Murtagh, and Peter Shirlow. 'Fashioning a City of Culture: "Life and Place Changing" or "12 Month Party"?' *International*

Journal of Cultural Policy 25, no. 2 (2019): 246–65. https://doi.org/10.1080/10286632.2016.1231181.
Boyle, Danny. *Frankenstein (Benedict Cumberbatch as the Creature).* NT Live Broadcast Recordings, National Theatre, 2011.
Frankenstein (Jonny Lee Miller as the Creature). NT Live Broadcast Recordings, National Theatre, 2011.
Bryant-Bertail, Sarah. 'Theatre as Heterotopia: Lessing's Nathan the Wise'. *Assaph: Studies in the Theatre* 16 (2000): 91–108.
Burnett, Chris. 'The Haskell Free Library and Opera House: A Landmark with Dual Citizenship'. *New England Today*, 2 August 2016. https://newengland.com/today/travel/vermont/the-haskell-free-library-and-opera-house/.
Burston, Jonathan. 'Recombinant Broadway'. *Continuum* 23, no. 2 (1 April 2009): 159–69. https://doi.org/10.1080/10304310802710504.
Butler, Judith, and Athena Athanasiou. *Dispossession: The Performative in the Political.* Malden, MA: Polity Press, 2013.
Byrne, Liam. '2012 Speech to the Labour Party Conference'. presented at the Labour Party Conference, Manchester, 1 October 2012. www.ukpol.co.uk/liam-byrne-2012-speech-to-labour-party-conference/.
Byrne, Thomas. 'Trends in Foreign Direct Investment from the United States, 2003–2015'. Belfast: Department for the Economy, May 2017. www.economy-ni.gov.uk/sites/default/files/publications/economy/Fulbright-Report-1-Trends-in-US-FDI.pdf.
Carlson, Marvin. *Places of Performance: The Semiotics of Theatre Architecture.* Ithaca: Cornell University Press, 1989.
The Haunted Stage: The Theatre as Memory Machine. Ann Arbor: University of Michigan Press, 2001.
Theories of the Theatre: A Historical and Critical Survey, from the Greeks to the Present. exp. ed. Ithaca: Cornell University Press, 1993.
Cattell, Tracy Catherine. 'The Living Language of Stage Management: An Interpretative Study of the History and Development of Professional Stage Management in the United Kingdom, 1567–1968'. PhD, University of Warwick, 2015.
Certeau, Michel de. *The Practice of Everyday Life.* Berkeley: University of California Press, 1988.
Chamberlin, E. H. *The Theory of Monopolistic Competition: A Re-Orientation of the Theory of Value.* 8th ed. Cambridge, MA: Harvard University Press, 1962.
Chorley, Henry Fothergill. 'A New Stage Stride'. *All the Year Round*, 31 October 1863.
Chung, Andrew. 'Border Towns Struggle with Post-9/11 Security Measures'. *The Toronto Star*, 2 September 2011. www.thestar.com/news/insight/article/1048571–border-towns-struggle-with-post-9-11-security-measures.
Clarke, Stephen. 'London Stalling: Half a Century of Living Standards in London'. London: Resolution Foundation, June 2018. www.resolutionfoundation.org/app/uploads/2018/06/London-Stalling.pdf.
Clurman, Harold. *On Directing.* new ed. New York: Simon & Schuster, 1997.

Collins, Lauren. 'Danny Boyle Wins the Gold'. *The New Yorker*, 27 July 2012. www.newyorker.com/news/sporting-scene/danny-boyle-wins-the-gold-2.

'Commercial Estate Sale'. Network Rail Property. https://property.networkrail.co.uk/commercial-estate-sale/.

Copley, Soozie, and Philippa Killner. *Stage Management: A Practical Guide*. Marlborough, Wiltshire: The Crowood Press Ltd, 2001.

Coulter, Colin. 'Under Which Constitutional Arrangement Would You Still Prefer to Be Unemployed? Neoliberalism, the Peace Process, and the Politics of Class in Northern Ireland'. *Studies in Conflict & Terrorism* 37, no. 9 (2 September 2014): 763–76. https://doi.org/10.1080/1057610X.2014.931212.

Craig, Edward Gordon. *On the Art of the Theatre*. London; New York: Routledge, 2009.

Curtis, Christopher. 'Stanstead Closes Unguarded Border'. *Montreal Gazette*, 30 July 2012.

Davies, Rob. 'Network Rail Sells Railway Arches to Investors for £1.5bn'. *The Guardian*, 10 September 2018. www.theguardian.com/business/2018/sep/10/network-rail-sells-railway-arches-real-estate-investors-telereal-trillium-blackstone-property-partners.

Davis, Jim, and Victor Emeljanow. *Reflecting the Audience: London Theatregoing, 1840–1880*. Iowa City: University of Iowa Press, 2001.

'"Dazzling": World's Press Heaps Praise on Opening Ceremony'. *The Huffington Post UK*, 28 July 2012. www.huffingtonpost.co.uk/2012/07/28/london-2012-worlds-press-heaps-praise_n_1712665.html.

Dear, Nick. 'Frankenstein'. Production Script. London, 2011. National Theatre Archive.

Debord, Guy. 'Theory of the Derive'. In *Situationist International Anthology*, edited and translated by Ken Knabb, revised and expanded ed., 62–66. Berkeley: Bureau of Public Secrets, 2007.

Delanty, Gerard. *Citizenship in a Global Age: Society, Culture, Politics*. Buckingham: Open University Press, 2000.

Department for Digital, Culture, Media and Sport. 'Britain's Creative Industries Break the £100 Billion Barrier'. Gov.uk. www.gov.uk/government/news/britains-creative-industries-break-the-100-billion-barrier.

Diderot, Denis. *Selected Writings on Art and Literature*. Translated by Geoffrey Bremner. London: Penguin, 1994.

Dolan, Jill. *Utopia in Performance: Finding Hope at the Theater*. Ann Arbor: University of Michigan Press, 2006.

Draper, Nick. '"Across the Bridges": Representations of Victorian South London'. *London Journal* 29, no. 1 (2004): 25–43. https://doi.org/10.1179/ldn.2004.29.1.25.

E20 Stadium LLP, WH Holding Limited, and West Ham United Football Club Limited. 'Concession Agreement'. Allen & Overy LLP, 22 March 2013. www.queenelizabetholympicpark.co.uk/-/media/qeop/files/public/concession-agreement-2016.ashx?la=en.

Eaton, George. 'The Pre-Election Pledges that the Tories Are Trying to Wipe from the Internet'. *New Statesman*. www.newstatesman.com/politics/2013/11/pre-election-pledges-tories-are-trying-wipe-internet.

Elliott, Larry, and Dan Atkinson. *Fantasy Island*. Constable, 2007.

Ervine, St. John. *The Organised Theatre: A Plea in Civics*. New York: Macmillan, 1924.

Evans, Graeme. 'Creative Cities, Creative Spaces and Urban Policy'. *Urban Studies* 46, no. 5–6 (1 May 2009): 1003–40. https://doi.org/10.1177/0042098009103853.

Cultural Planning: An Urban Renaissance? London: Routledge, 2001.

Farfan, Matthew. *The Vermont-Quebec Border: Life on the Line*. Charleston: Arcadia Publishing, 2009.

Fazio, Larry. *Stage Manager: The Professional Experience*. Burlington, MA: Focal Press, 2013.

Federici, Silvia. *Revolution at Point Zero*. Oakland: PM Press, 2012.

Ferguson, Adam. *An Essay on the History of Civil Society*. Edited by Fania Oz-Salzberger. new ed. Cambridge: Cambridge University Press, 1996.

Florida, Richard L. *Cities and the Creative Class*. London: Routledge, 2005.

Forshaw, J. H., and Patrick Abercrombie. *County of London Plan 1943*. London: Macmillan and Co., 1943.

Foucault, Michel. 'Of Other Spaces'. Translated by Jay Miskowiec. *Diacritics* 16, no. 1 (1986): 22–7. https://doi.org/10.2307/464648.

The Birth of Biopolitics : Lectures at the College de France, 1978–1979. Edited by Michel Senellart. Translated by Graham Burchell. Basingstoke: Palgrave Macmillan, 2008.

Fraser, Nancy. 'Marketization, Social Protection, Emancipation: Towards a Neo-Polanyian Conception of Capitalist Crisis'. In *Business as Usual: The Roots of the Global Financial Meltdown*, edited by Craig Calhoun and Georgi Derluguian, 137–59. New York: New York University Press, 2011.

Frayn, Michael. *Noises Off.* London: Bloomsbury, 2011.

Freshwater, Helen. *Theatre & Audience*. Theatre. Basingstoke: Palgrave Macmillan, 2009.

Gendall, John. 'US Canada Border Building Walls'. *Architectural Digest*, 30 March 2017. www.architecturaldigest.com/story/cultural-center-on-us-canada-border-teach-us-about-building-walls.

'What a Cultural Center on the US-Canada Border Can Teach Us about Building Walls'. *Architectural Digest*, 30 March 2017. www.architecturaldigest.com/story/cultural-center-on-us-canada-border-teach-us-about-building-walls.

Gibson, Owen. 'How West Ham Struck the Deal of the Century with Olympic Stadium Move'. *The Guardian*, 14 April 2016. www.theguardian.com/football/2016/apr/14/west-ham-deal-century-olympic-stadium.

'West Ham's Olympic Stadium Contract: Club to Pay £2.5 m per Season in Rent'. *The Guardian*, 14 April 2016. www.theguardian.com/football/2016/apr/14/west-ham-olympic-stadium-club-pay-per-season-rent.

Gill, Stephen, and Isabella Bakker, eds. *Power, Production and Social Reproduction: Human In/Security in the Global Political Economy*. Basingstoke: Palgrave Macmillan, 2003.

Glover, Stephen. 'Yes, a Brilliant Show and Danny Boyle's a Genius. But Why Have so Many Been Taken in by His Marxist Propaganda?' *Mail Online*, 2 August 2012. www.dailymail.co.uk/debate/article-2182328/London-2012-opening-ceremony-Danny-Boyles-genius-taken-Marxist-propaganda.html.

Gray, Clive. *The Politics of the Arts in Britain*. Basingstoke: Macmillan, 2000.

Grice, Andrew. 'Alistair Darling: We Were Two Hours from the Cashpoints Running Dry'. *The Independent*, 18 March 2011. www.independent.co.uk/news/people/profiles/alistair-darling-we-were-two-hours-from-the-cashpoints-running-dry-2245350.html.

'Gross Domestic Product: Year on Year Growth: CVM SA %'. Office for National Statistics, 11 February 2020. www.ons.gov.uk/economy/grossdomesticproductgdp/timeseries/ihyp/pn2.

Guardian Staff and Agencies. 'Professor: Flight Was Delayed because My Equations Raised Terror Fears'. *The Guardian*, 7 May 2016. www.theguardian.com/us-news/2016/may/07/professor-flight-delay-terrorism-equation-american-airlines.

Harvey, David. *Cosmopolitanism and the Geographies of Freedom*. New York: Columbia University Press, 2009.

Limits to Capital. London: Verso, 1999.

'The Art of Rent: Globalization and the Commodification of Culture'. In *Spaces of Capital: Towards a Critical Geography*, 394–411. Edinburgh: Edinburgh University Press, 2001.

The Condition of Postmodernity. Oxford: Blackwell, 1989.

'The Spatial Fix – Hegel, von Thunen, and Marx'. *Antipode* 13, no. 3 (1981): 1–12. https://doi.org/10.1111/j.1467–8330.1981.tb00312.x.

Harvie, Jen. *Staging the UK*. Manchester: Manchester University Press, 2005.

Theatre & the City. Basingstoke: Palgrave Macmillan, 2009.

Haskell Opera House Grand Opening Playbill. 7 June 1904.

Haworth Tompkins Ltd. 'Conservation Management Plan for the National Theatre'. London: Hayworth Tompkins Ltd., 2008. www.nationaltheatre.org.uk/sites/default/files/nt_conservation_plans_dec_08.pdf.

'National Theatre'. 4 January 2018. www.haworthtompkins.com/work/national-theatre.

Haydon, Andrew. 'Unaccustomed Provinces'. *Postcards from the Gods* (blog), 11 January 2009. https://postcardsgods.blogspot.com/2009/01/unaccustomed-provinces.html.

Hetherington, Kevin. *The Badlands of Modernity: Heterotopia and Social Ordering*. London: Routledge, 1997.

Higgins, Charlotte. 'The Olympics Opening Ceremony: My Cultural Highlight of 2012'. *The Guardian*, 5 December 2012. www.theguardian.com/culture/2012/dec/05/olympic-opening-ceremony-2012-highlight.

HM Treasury. 'Cuts by the Score'. *O and M Bulletin: The Journal of Government Management Services* 7, no. 4 (1952).

House Of Vans London. 'House of Vans | ABOUT'. www.houseofvanslondon.com/about.
Hughes, Jenny. 'The Theatre and Its Poor: Neoliberal Economies of Waste and Gold in Les Misérables (1985) and Road (1986)'. *Theatre Journal* 67, no. 1 (30 March 2015): 1–19. https://doi.org/10.1353/tj.2015.0017.
Hume, David. *David Hume: An Enquiry Concerning the Principles of Morals*. Edited by Tom L. Beauchamp. Oxford: Oxford University Press, 2006.
Hunter, Victoria. 'Embodying the Site: The Here and Now in Site-Specific Dance Performance'. *New Theatre Quarterly* 21, no. 4 (2005): 367–81. https://doi.org/10.1017/S0266464X05000230.
Hyde, Marina. 'Karen Bradley Routs Her Rival Imbeciles with Ladybird Guide to Northern Ireland'. *The Guardian*, 7 September 2018. www.theguardian.com/commentisfree/2018/sep/07/karen-bradley-northern-ireland-secretary-tories.
'In Praise of Limbo'. *This American Life*. National Public Radio, 28 December 2018. www.thisamericanlife.org/664/the-room-of-requirement/act-one-4.
Information Commissioner. 'Decision Notice'. London: Information Commissioner's Office, 3 September 2015. https://ico.org.uk/media/action-weve-taken/decision-notices/2015/1432468/fs_50556618.pdf.
International Boundary Commission. 'International Boundary Commission Official Web Site'. www.internationalboundarycommission.org/history.html.
'Living Near the Boundary'. www.internationalboundarycommission.org/en/the-boundary-and-you/living-near-boundary.php.
Jessop, Bob. 'Cultural Political Economy and Critical Policy Studies'. *Critical Policy Studies* 3, no. 3–4 (2010): 336–56. https://doi.org/10.1080/19460171003619741.
'Spatial Fixes, Temporal Fixes and Spatio-Temporal Fixes'. In *David Harvey: A Critical Reader*, edited by Noel Castree and Derek Gregory. Oxford: Blackwell, 2006.
Jessop, Bob, and Stijn Oosterlynck. 'Cultural Political Economy: On Making the Cultural Turn without Falling into Soft Economic Sociology'. *Geoforum* 39, no. 3 (May 2008): 1155–69. https://doi.org/10.1016/j.geoforum.2006.12.008.
Kasimati, Evangelia. 'Economic Aspects and the Summer Olympics: A Review of Related Research'. *International Journal of Tourism Research* 5, no. 6 (1 November 2003): 433–44. https://doi.org/10.1002/jtr.449.
Kavetsos, Georgios. 'The Impact of the London Olympics Announcement on Property Prices'. *Urban Studies* 49, no. 7 (1 May 2012): 1453–70. https://doi.org/10.1177/0042098011415436.
Kaye, Nick. *Site-Specific Art: Performance, Place, and Documentation*. London: Routledge, 2000.
Kershaw, Baz. *The Politics of Performance: Radical Theatre as Cultural Intervention*. London: Routledge, 1992.
Keynes, John Maynard. *A Tract on Monetary Reform*. new ed. Vol. 4. The Collected Writings of John Maynard Keynes. Cambridge: Cambridge University Press, 2013.
Essays in Persuasion. Vol. 9. The Collected Writings of John Maynard Keynes. Cambridge: Cambridge University Press, 2012.

The General Theory of Employment, Interest and Money. Vol. 7. The Collected Writings of John Maynard Keynes. London: Macmillan, 1973.

Kift, Dagmar. *The Victorian Music Hall: Culture, Class, and Conflict*. Cambridge: Cambridge University Press, 1996.

Kloetzel, Melanie. 'Site-Specific Dance in a Corporate Landscape'. *New Theatre Quarterly* 26, no. 2 (2010): 133–44. https://doi.org/10.1017/S0266464X10000278P.

Knowles, Ric. *How Theatre Means*. Basingstoke: Palgrave Macmillan, 2014.

Kroll, Jack. 'Britain Onstage'. *Newsweek*, 22 March 1976, 74.

Krugman, Paul. *The Age of Diminished Expectations: U.S. Economic Policy in the 1990s*. 3rd ed. Cambridge, MA: MIT Press, 1997.

Land and Property Services. 'Northern Ireland House Price Index October-December 2019 (Quarter 4 2019)'. Northern Ireland House Price Index. Belfast: Northern Ireland Statistics and Research Agency, 19 February 2020. www.finance-ni.gov.uk/sites/default/files/publications/dfp/NI%20House%20Price%20Index%20statistics%20report%20Quarter%204%202019.pdf.

Landry, Charles. *The Creative City*. London: Demos, 1995.

Langhans, Edward A. *Eighteenth Century British and Irish Promptbooks : A Descriptive Bibliography*. New York: Greenwood, 1988.

Lavery, Carl. 'The Pepys of London E11: Graeme Miller and the Politics of Linked'. *New Theatre Quarterly* 21, no. 2 (2005): 148–60. https://doi.org/10.1017/S0266464X05000059.

Leigh, Mike. *Topsy-Turvy*. DVD. Twentieth-Century Fox, 2000.

Levin, Laura, and Kim Solga. 'Building Utopia: Performance and the Fantasy of Urban Renewal in Contemporary Toronto'. *TDR: The Drama Review* 53, no. 3 (2009): 37–53.

Lewis, Michael. 'When Irish Eyes Are Crying'. *Vanity Fair*, 1 March 2011. www.vanityfair.com/news/2011/03/michael-lewis-ireland-201103.

Lister, Sam. 'Boris Johnson Defends London's Financial Sector'. *The Independent*, 22 July 2012. www.independent.co.uk/news/uk/politics/boris-johnson-defends-londons-financial-sector-7964856.html.

Lloyd, David, and Paul Thomas. *Culture and the State*. London: Routledge, 1998.

'London 2012: Olympics Deliver Record Viewing Figures for BBC'. BBC Media Centre. Press Release, 13 August 2012. www.bbc.co.uk/mediacentre/latestnews/2012/olympic-viewing-figs.html.

'London 2012: Opening Ceremony – Reviews'. *The Guardian*, 29 July 2012. www.theguardian.com/sport/2012/jul/29/london-2012-opening-ceremony-reviews.

'London 2012: Opening Ceremony Draws 900 Million Viewers'. Reuters, 7 August 2012. https://uk.reuters.com/article/uk-oly-ratings-day11-idUKBRE8760V820120807.

'London 2012: What the World Thought of the Opening Ceremony'. *The Telegraph*, 28 July 2012. www.telegraph.co.uk/sport/olympics/london-2012/9434319/London-2012-What-the-world-thought-of-the-opening-ceremony.html.

London County Council. 'Objections to the 1951 Plan-Detailed Schedule of Objections, South Bank Area'. London, 1951. LCC/AR/TP/04/040. London Metropolitan Archives.

Lundy, Derek. 'Stanstead: A Town on the Border'. *Canadian Geographic*, 10 July 2010. www.canadiangeographic.ca/article/stanstead-town-border.

Lyall, Sarah. 'A 5-Ring Circus: Olympic Opening Is Oddly, Confidently British'. *New York Times*, 27 July 2012. www.nytimes.com/2012/07/28/sports/olympics/in-olympic-opening-ceremony-britain-asserts-its-eccentric-identity.html.

Maccoy, Peter. *Essentials of Stage Management*. Methuen Drama, 2004.

MacKaye, Percy. *The Civic Theatre in Relation to the Redemption of Leisure*. New York: Mitchell Kennerley, 1912.

Makeham, Paul. 'Performing the City'. *Theatre Research International* 30, no. 2 (2005): 150–60. https://doi.org/10.1017/S030788330500115X.

Marini, Charikleia. 'Re-Defining Urban Space through Performance'. PhD, Queen Mary University of London, 2013.

Marshall, Alfred J. *Principles of Economics*. Basingstoke: Palgrave Macmillan, 2013.

Marshall, T. H. *Citizenship and Social Class*. London: Pluto Press, 1992.

Marx, Karl. *Capital: A Critique of Political Economy*. Translated by David Fernbach. Vol. 3. 3 vols. London: Penguin, 1981.

Capital: A Critique of Political Economy. Translated by Ben Fowkes. new ed. Vol. 1. London: Penguin Classics, 1990.

Early Writings. Translated by Rodney Livingstone and Gregor Benton. Harmondsworth: Penguin, 1992.

Mayor of London. 'Cultural Metropolis: The Mayor's Cultural Strategy–2012 and Beyond'. London: Greater London Authority, 2010.

'Cultural Metropolis: The Mayor's Culture Strategy–Achievements and Next Steps'. London: Greater London Authority, 2014.

McBride, I. R. *Scripture Politics: Ulster Presbyterians and Irish Radicalism in the Late Eighteenth Century: Ulster Presbyterians and Irish Radicalism in Late Eighteenth-Century Ireland*. Oxford: Oxford University Press, 1998.

McEvoy, William. 'Writing, Texts and Site-Specific Performance in the Recent Work of Deborah Warner'. *Textual Practice* 20, no. 4 (2006): 591. https://doi.org/10.1080/09502360601058821.

McGuinness, Alan, and Greg Heffer. 'Northern Ireland Secretary Karen Bradley Admits There Are 'no Excuses' for Her Troubles Comments'. *Sky News*, 14 March 2019. https://news.sky.com/story/northern-ireland-secretary-karen-bradley-profoundly-sorry-for-troubles-comments-11657601.

McKay, Susan. 'Tories Have Abandoned Pretence of Impartiality on North'. *The Irish Times*, 9 March 2019. www.irishtimes.com/opinion/tories-have-abandoned-pretence-of-impartiality-on-north-1.3819276.

McKinnie, Michael. *City Stages: Theatre and Urban Space in a Global City*. Toronto: University of Toronto Press, 2007.

City Stages: Theatre and Urban Space in a Global City. Toronto: University of Toronto Press, 2007.

'Institutional Frameworks: Theatre, State, and Market in Modern Urban Performance'. In *A Cultural History of Theatre in the Modern Age*, edited by Kim Solga, 6:17–33. Cultural History of Theatre. London: Bloomsbury, 2017.

'Performing the Civic Transnational: Cultural Production, Governance, and Citizenship in Contemporary London'. In *Performance and the City*, 110–27. Basingstoke: Palgrave Macmillan, 2009.

'Rethinking Site-Specificity: Monopoly, Urban Space, and the Cultural Economics of Site-Specific Performance'. In *Performing Site-Specific Theatre: Politics, Place, Practice*, edited by Anna Birch and Joanne Tompkins, 21–33. Performance Interventions. Basingstoke: Palgrave Macmillan, 2012.

'The State of This Place: Convictions, the Courthouse, and the Political Geography of Performance in Belfast'. *Modern Drama* 46, no. 4 (2003): 580–97. https://doi.org/10.1353/mdr.2003.0014.

McRobbie, Angela. *Be Creative: Making a Living in the New Culture Industries.* Cambridge: Polity Press, 2015.

McVeigh, Tracy, and Owen Gibson. 'London 2012: Danny Boyle Thrills Audiences with Inventive Olympics Opening Ceremony'. *The Guardian*, 28 July 2012. www.theguardian.com/sport/2012/jul/28/london-2012-boyle-olympics-opening-ceremony.

'Media Reaction to London 2012 Olympic Opening Ceremony'. *BBC News*. www.bbc.com/news/uk-19025686.

Meerzon, Yanna. 'An Ideal City: Heterotopia or Panopticon? On Joseph Brodsky's Play Marble and Its Fictional Spaces'. *Modern Drama* 50, no. 2 (2007): 184–210. https://doi.org/10.1353/mdr.2007.0045.

Meiksins Wood, Ellen. *Democracy against Capitalism: Renewing Historical Materialism*. London: Verso, 2016.

Miller, Derek. 'Average Broadway'. *Theatre Journal* 68, no. 4 (2016): 529–53. https://doi.org/10.1353/tj.2016.0105.

Miller, Hillary. *Drop Dead: Performance in Crisis, 1970s New York*. Evanston: Northwestern University Press, 2016.

Mitchell, Katie. *The Director's Craft: A Handbook for the Theatre*. New York: Routledge, 2008.

Molotch, Harvey. 'Place in Product'. *International Journal of Urban and Regional Research* 26, no. 4 (2002): 665–88. https://doi.org/10.1111/1468–2427.00410.

Molotch, Harvey, and John R. Logan. *Urban Fortunes: The Political Economy of Place*. Berkeley: University of California Press, 2007.

Monclús, F. J., and Manuel Guàrdia, eds. *Culture, Urbanism and Planning.* Aldershot: Ashgate, 2006.

Morash, Chris, and Shaun Richards. *Mapping Irish Theatre: Theories of Space and Place*. Cambridge: Cambridge University Press, 2013.

Nash, Catherine. 'Equity, Diversity and Interdependence: Cultural Policy in Northern Ireland'. *Antipode* 37, no. 2 (2005): 272–300. https://doi.org/10.1111/j.0066–4812.2005.00493.x.

National Theatre. 'Frankenstein'. Prompt Script. London, 2011. National Theatre Archive.

Neiburg, Federico, and Jane I. Guyer. 'The Real in the Real Economy'. *HAU: Journal of Ethnographic Theory* 7, no. 3 (2017): 261–79. https://doi.org/10.14318/hau7.3.015.

'New Border Rules Irksome for Derby Line Residents', 14 March 2010. http://digitaljournal.com/article/289068.

Newman, Peter, and Ian Smith. 'Cultural Production, Place and Politics on the South Bank of the Thames'. *International Journal of Urban and Regional Research* 24 (March 2000): 9–24. https://doi.org/10.1111/1468–2427.00233.

NHS Digital. 'Hospital Admitted Patient Care and Adult Critical Care Activity'. NHS Digital, 19 September 2019. https://files.digital.nhs.uk/F2/E70669/hosp-epis-stat-admi-summ-rep-2018–19-rep.pdf.

'Noises Off'. Prompt Script. London, 2000. Box 1. National Theatre Archive.

Northern Ireland Statistics and Research Agency. 'Northern Ireland Labour Market Report'. Belfast: Northern Ireland Statistics and Research Agency, July 2019. www.nisra.gov.uk/sites/nisra.gov.uk/files/publications/labour-market-report-july-2019.PDF.

O'Dair, Loren. Interview with Author, 29 May 2015.

O'Donnell, Darren. *Social Acupuncture*. Toronto: Coach House Books, 2006.

Office for National Statistics. 'UK Productivity Introduction: July to September 2017'. London: Office for National Statistics, 5 January 2018. www.ons.gov.uk/employmentandlabourmarket/peopleinwork/labourproductivity/articles/ukproductivityintroduction/julytoseptember2017.

Pallin, Gail. *Stage Management: The Essential Handbook*. 3rd ed. London: Nick Hern Books, 2010.

Parker, Stewart. 'Northern Star'. In *Plays 2*. London: Methuen, 1989.

Parry, Tom. 'U.K. Media Give Olympic Opening Show Glowing Reviews'. *CBC News*, 28 July 2012. www.cbc.ca/1.1193902.

Patterson, Glenn. 'The Bard of Belfast'. *The Guardian*, 13 June 2008. www.theguardian.com/arts/theatre/drama/story/0,2285237,00.html.

Pearson, Mike, and Michael Shanks. *Theatre/Archaeology*. London: Routledge, 2001.

Peck, Jamie. 'Struggling with the Creative Class'. *International Journal of Urban and Regional Research* 29, no. 4 (2005): 740–70.

Polanyi, Karl. *The Great Transformation: The Political and Economic Origins of Our Time*. 2nd ed. Boston: Beacon Press, 2002.

Prestwich, Emma. 'Haskell Free Library and Opera House Straddles the Canada-U.S. Border'. *HuffPost Canada*, 12 January 2017. www.huffingtonpost.ca/2017/01/12/haskell-free-library-and-opera-house_n_14110796.html.

Ramirez, Bruno. *Crossing the 49th Parallel: Migration from Canada to the United States, 1900–1930*. Ithaca: Cornell University Press, 2001.

Rayner, Gordon. 'London 2012: Breathtaking, Brash and Bonkers ... an Utterly British Olympic Opening Ceremony'. *The Telegraph*, 27 July 2012. www.telegraph.co.uk/sport/olympics/news/9433818/London-2012-

breathtaking-brash-and-bonkers...an-utterly-British-Olympic-opening-ceremony.html.

Rebellato, Dan. 'Playwriting and Globalisation: Towards a Site-Unspecific Theatre'. *Contemporary Theatre Review* 16, no. 1 (1 February 2006): 97–113. https://doi.org/10.1080/10486800500451047.

Theatre & Globalization. Basingstoke: Palgrave Macmillan, 2009.

Reid, Bryonie. '"A Profound Edge": Performative Negotiations of Belfast'. *Cultural Geographies* 12, no. 4 (1 October 2005): 485–506. https://doi.org/10.1191/1474474005eu343oa.

'"Rearranging the Ground": Public and Private Space in Belfast, Northern Ireland'. *Gender, Place & Culture* 15, no. 5 (1 October 2008): 489–503. https://doi.org/10.1080/09663690802300837.

Rhodes, Chris. 'Financial Services: Contribution to the UK Economy'. Briefing Paper. London: House of Commons Library, 31 July 2019. http://researchbriefings.files.parliament.uk/documents/SN06193/SN06193.pdf.

Ricardo, David. *On the Principles of Political Economy and Taxation*. Harmondsworth: Penguin, 1971.

Ridout, Nicholas. *Stage Fright, Animals, and Other Theatrical Problems*. Cambridge: Cambridge University Press, 2006.

Robertson, Craig. 'Locating the Border'. *Social Identities: Journal for the Study of Race, Nation and Culture* 14, no. 4 (2008): 447–56. https://doi.org/10.1080/13504630802211894.

Robinson, Joan. *The Economics of Imperfect Competition*. 2nd ed. London: Macmillan, 1969.

Romei, Valentina. 'UK Living Standards Grow at Slowest Rate since WW2 in 2010s'. *Financial Times*, 3 January 2020. www.ft.com/content/44401594-2ca0-11ea-bc77-65e4aa615551.

Rooney, David. 'Opening Ceremony of the London Olympics: Review'. *The Hollywood Reporter*, 27 July 2012. www.hollywoodreporter.com/review/olympic-games-opening-ceremony-london-danny-boyle-355545.

Rossiter, Nicholas. 'HRH The Prince of Wales: A Vision of Britain'. *Omnibus*. BBC1, 28 October 1988.

Sayer, Andrew. 'For a Critical Cultural Political Economy'. *Antipode* 33, no. 4 (2001): 687–708. https://doi.org/10.1111/1467–8330.00206.

Schechner, Richard. '6 Axioms for Environmental Theatre'. *The Drama Review: TDR* 12, no. 3 (1968): 41–64. https://doi.org/10.2307/1144353.

Schiller, Friedrich von. 'The Stage Considered as a Moral Institution'. In *Sources of Dramatic Theory*, edited by Michael Sidnell, translated by Jean Wilson, Vol. 2. Cambridge: Cambridge University Press, 1994.

Schneier, Bruce. *Beyond Fear: Thinking Sensibly about Security in an Uncertain*. New York: Copernicus, 2003.

Schofield, Kevin, and Sebastian Whale. 'Karen Bradley: I Did Not Know People in Northern Ireland Voted on Constitutional Lines'. *PoliticsHome.com*, 6 September 2018. www.politicshome.com/news/uk/uk-regions/northern-

ireland/news/98027/karen-bradley-i-did-not-know-people-northern-ireland.
Scott, Allen J. 'Creative Cities: Conceptual Issues and Policy Questions'. *Journal of Urban Affairs* 28, no. 1 (January 2006): 1–17. https://doi.org/10.1111/j.0735–2166.2006.00256.x.
Social Economy of the Metropolis. Oxford: Oxford University Press, 2008.
Scott, James C. *Seeing Like a State : How Certain Schemes to Improve the Human Condition Have Failed*. New Haven: Yale University Press, 1998.
Shiller, Robert J. 'The Best, Brightest, and Least Productive?' Project Syndicate, 20 September 2013. www.project-syndicate.org/commentary/the-rent-seeking-problem-in-contemporary-finance-by-robert-j–shiller.
Smith, Adam. *An Inquiry into the Nature and Causes of the Wealth of Nations*. Edited by Kathryn Sutherland. Oxford: Oxford University Press, 1993.
The Wealth of Nations: Books I–III. Edited by Andrew Skinner. London: Penguin Classics, 1982.
The Wealth of Nations: Books IV–V. Edited by Andrew Skinner. Penguin Classics, 1999.
Smith, David R. 'Structuring the Permeable Border: Channeling and Regulating Cross-Border Traffic in Labor, Capital, and Goods'. In *Permeable Border: The Great Lakes Basin as Transnational Region, 1650–1990*. Pittsburgh: University of Pittsburgh Press, 2005.
Smith, Neil. *Uneven Development: Nature, Capital and the Production of Space*. 3rd ed. London: Verso, 2010.
Snow, Georgia. 'Theatres Across UK Step Up Security in Wake of Manchester Bombing'. *The Stage*, 30 May 2017. www.thestage.co.uk/news/2017/theatres-across-uk-step-security-wake-manchester-bombing/.
Somdahl-Sands, Katrinka. 'Citizenship, Civic Memory and Urban Performance: Mission Wall Dances'. *Space and Polity* 12, no. 3 (2008): 329. https://doi.org/10.1080/13562570802515242.
Sparke, Matthew B. 'A Neoliberal Nexus: Economy, Security and the Biopolitics of Citizenship on the Border'. *Political Geography* 25, no. 2 (2006): 151–80. https://doi.org/10.1016/j.polgeo.2005.10.002.
Stanislavsky, Konstantin Sergeevich. *Stanislavsky Produces Othello*. Translated by Helen Nowak. London: Geoffrey Bles, 1948.
The Seagull Produced by Stanislavsky. Edited by S. D. Balukhaty. Translated by David Magarshack. London: Dennis Dobson, 1952.
Steel, Beth. *Ditch*. London: Methuen, 2010.
Stephenson, Jenn. 'Portrait of the Artist as Artist: The Celebration of Autobiography'. *Canadian Theatre Review*, no. 141 (January 2010): 49–53.
Stern, Lawrence, and Alice R. O'Grady. *Stage Management*. 10th ed. New York: Routledge, 2013.
Stiglitz, Joseph. 'After the Financial Crisis We Were All Keynesians – but Not for Long Enough'. *The Guardian*, 10 October 2013. www.theguardian.com/business/economics-blog/2013/oct/10/financial-crisis-keynesians-eurozone-recession.

Sum, Ngai-Ling, and Bob Jessop. *Towards a Cultural Political Economy: Putting Culture in Its Place in Political Economy*. Cheltenham: Edward Elgar, 2015.

Sunday Times of London Insight Team. *Ulster*. London: Deutsch, 1972.

Szymanski, Stefan. 'About Winning: The Political Economy of Awarding the World Cup and the Olympic Games'. *SAIS Review* 31, no. 1 (2011): 87–97. https://doi.org/10.1353/sais.2011.0003.

The Complete London 2012 Opening Ceremony; London 2012 Olympic Games. Olympic Broadcasting Services, 2012. www.youtube.com/watch?v=4As0e4de-rI.

The Haskell Free Library and Opera House: A Cultural Gem on the Canada-U.S. Border, 2011. www.youtube.com/watch?v=GlVBiofRdCA&feature=youtube_gdata_player.

'The Mikado Prompt Book'. Victoria and Albert Museum, ca 1885. D'Oyly Carte Archive. Theatre and Performance Collection. www.vam.ac.uk/archives/unit/ARC17236.

The Vaults. 'The Vaults | ABOUT'. www.thevaults.london/about.

Throsby, David. *Economics and Culture*. Cambridge: Cambridge University Press, 2000.

Time Out London. 'Best Theatre of 2008'. www.timeout.com/london/theatre/best-theatre-of-2008.

Tocqueville, Alexis de. 'Some Observations on the Drama amongst Democratic Nations'. In *The Theory of the Modern Stage*, edited by Eric Bentley, 479–84. London: Penguin, 1992.

Tompkins, Joanne. 'Staging the Imagined City in Australian Theatre'. In *Performance and the City*, edited by Kim Solga, D. J. Hopkins, and Shelley Orr, 187–203. Basingstoke: Palgrave Macmillan, 2009.

Theatre's Heterotopias: Performance and the Cultural Politics of Space. Basingstoke: Palgrave Macmillan, 2014.

Topham, Gwyn. 'Private Equity Firms among Bidders for Network Rail Property Business'. *The Guardian*, 1 March 2018, www.theguardian.com/business/2018/mar/01/guy-hands-emerges-as-bidder-in-national-rails-property-sell-off.

'Tory Spring Conference Speeches in Full'. Politics.co.uk, 27 April 2009. www.politics.co.uk/comment-analysis/2009/04/27/tory-spring-conference-speeches-in-full.

Trump, Donald J. 'The Theater Must Always Be a Safe and Special Place. The Cast of Hamilton Was Very Rude Last Night to a Very Good Man, Mike Pence. Apologize!' Tweet. *@realdonaldtrump*, 5 November 2016. https://twitter.com/realdonaldtrump/status/799974635274194947?lang=en.

Turner, Cathy. 'Palimpsest or Potential Space? Finding a Vocabulary for Site-Specific Performance'. *New Theatre Quarterly* 20, no. 4 (2004): 373–90. https://doi.org/10.1017/S0266464X04000259.

Unwin, Stephen. *So You Want to Be a Theatre Director?* London: Nick Hern Books, 2004.

Valverde, Mariana. *Everyday Law on the Street: City Governance in an Age of Diversity*. Chicago: University of Chicago Press, 2012.

Valverde, Mariana. 'Seeing Like a City: The Dialectic of Modern and Premodern Ways of Seeing in Urban Governance'. *Law & Society Review* 45, no. 2 (1 June 2011): 277–312. https://doi.org/10.1111/j.1540–5893.2011.00441.x.

Van Susteren, Dirk. 'Vermont Opera Houses Continue to Entertain'. *Boston Globe*. 26 February 2012. www.bostonglobe.com/lifestyle/travel/2012/02/26/vermont-opera-houses-continue-entertain/3pifjLWK3C1TsigTYIhTpJ/story.html.

The Old Vic. 'Vivien Leigh and The Old Vic', 4 November 2017. www.oldvictheatre.com/news/2017/11/vivien-leigh-and-the-old-vic.

Weiner, Eric. 'The US-Canada Border Runs through This Tiny Library', 6 November 2017. www.bbc.com/travel/story/20171105-the-us-canada-border-runs-through-this-tiny-library.

'West Ham to Pay £2.5 m Olympic Stadium Rent per Year'. *BBC Sport*, 14 April 2016. www.bbc.co.uk/sport/football/36043808.

Wiles, David. *A Short History of Western Performance Space*. Cambridge: Cambridge University Press, 2003.

Wilkie, Fiona. 'Kinds of Place at Bore Place: Site-Specific Performance and the Rules of Spatial Behaviour'. *New Theatre Quarterly* 18, no. 3 (2002): 243–60. https://doi.org/10.1017/S0266464X02000337.

Williams, Raymond. *Keywords: A Vocabulary of Culture and Society*. rev. ed. Oxford: Oxford University Press, 1985.

WPTZ.com. 'Local Man Jailed for Crossing Street', 15 March 2010. www.wptz.com/Local-Man-Jailed-For-Crossing-Street/-/8870596/5756044/-/8vvmjnz/-/index.html.

Wren-Lewis, Simon. 'Why the National Health Service Played a Central Part in the Olympic Ceremony'. *Mainly Macro* (blog), 31 July 2012. https://mainlymacro.blogspot.com/2012/07/why-national-health-service-played.html.

Yahm, Sarah. 'The U.S.-Canada Border Runs through This Tiny Library'. *Atlas Obscura*, 7 July 2016. www.atlasobscura.com/articles/the-us-canada-border-runs-through-this-tiny-library.

Zaranko, Ben, and Rowena Crawford. 'Tax Revenues and Spending on Social Security Benefits and Public Services since the Crisis'. Institute for Fiscal Studies, 17 November 2019. https://doi.org/10.1920/BN.IFS.2019.BN0261.

Index

For EU product safety concerns, contact us at Calle de José Abascal, 56–1°, 28003 Madrid, Spain or eugpsr@cambridge.org.

www.ingramcontent.com/pod-product-compliance
Ingram Content Group UK Ltd.
Pitfield, Milton Keynes, MK11 3LW, UK
UKHW020352140625
459647UK00020B/2414

* 9 7 8 1 0 0 9 3 4 6 4 2 9 *